Cry of the Invisible

Cry of the Invisible

Writings from the Homeless
and Survivors of Psychiatric Hospitals

Edited by Michael A. Susko

To the psych Dept.
Here this is of interest

Michael A Susko

msusko@mindspring.com

A HARRISON EDWARD LIVINGSTONE BOOK
by the
CONSERVATORY PRESS
Baltimore   Montréal

We hope that this book begins a new dialogue on the meaning and causes of mental illness, and that such illnesses be seen within their social, economic and political context.

Book Jacket painted by James Joyner

Bookstores may order from Baker & Taylor

*In the U.S. copies by mail for $16.95
plus $2 shipping and handling.*

*Hard Bound copies are available for $19.95
Plus $2 shipping and handling.*

All book stores and libraries 40% off.

*Send orders to The Conservatory Press,
P.O. Box 7149, Baltimore, MD 21218*

*ISBN: 0-941401-05-7
Library of Congress No. 90-082024*

What's madness but nobility of soul
At odds with circumstance? The day's on fire!
I know the purity of pure despair,
My shadow pinned against a swearing wall.
That place among the rocks—is it a cave,
Or winding path? The edge is what I have.

                              Theodore Roethke

For those who have died, especially those remembered in this book:
Hugh Rivers, Michele Dear, Jay Knighten, Linda Saks, Ethel Perez, and
Don Shack.

Table of Contents

ILLUSTRATIONS

"As long as this country continues to believe that it's all right for large numbers of people with serious mental illness to be on the streets, in jails and shelters, we will be shameful among the nations of the world."

> Dr. Sidney Wolfe,
> Director of Public Citizen Health Research Group

Much Madness is divinest Sense—
To a discerning Eye—
Much Sense—the starkest Madness—
'Tis the Majority
In this, as All, prevail—
Assent—and you are sane—
Demur—you're straightway dangerous—
And handled with a Chain—

> Emily Dickinson

Our current mental health system based on the dogma that coercion and medical treatment can be combined, and practiced by means of dangerous mind-diminishing drugs, memory-destroying electroshock, isolation cells, and four-point restraint has driven people to the streets and to prefer the streets to such treatment.

> Ron Thompson, Member of the Board of the
> National Association of Rights, Protection, and Advocacy

Preface

by Marcio V. Pinheiro. M.D.

In modern America corporations and government are forever "trimming the fat" in order to cut costs and maximize profits. Vulnerable citizens break down under the pressure and fall by the side of the road, excluded as members of this wealthy society. If this vulnerability is mental and leads to one or more episodes of severe distress that can be labeled mental illness, the situation is even worse. Nobody is willing to foot the bill of providing minimally decent treatment for the casualties of this ruthless and competitive battle ground. Both government and insurance companies are devising a thousand ways to deny proper treatment for this population.

Even some psychiatrists—the professionals who should have their client's interests as their main priority—are joining forces with government and insurance companies devising "psychiatric" explanations to justify the denial of funds. As this happens, American psychiatry is shifting towards accommodating rather than influencing these powerful institutions. The ideology surrounding the causes and treatment of mental disorder is moving fast toward simplistic biological explanations and short term pharmacological intervention.

Even worse, in this process not everyone is being heard: government, employers, insurance companies and even associations of relatives of those who are hospitalized are the main determinants of what research and treatment will be offered to these vulnerable American citizens. The two most important groups are left out of this debate: *front-line clinicians*, and their *patients*.

It is about time the people who actually receive treatment to speak out in order to be heard by all. When I was informed of the efforts to prepare this book, I was immediately sure that it will be an important, timely, and necessary publication. Maybe we clinicians should also think about doing the same, that is: bring to the open our feelings when we hear the *cries of the invisibles*—and feel impotent to do much about it. We are controlled and manipulated by government and corporations taking away from us our most cherished asset: the ability to make clinical decisions and recommend treatments that will make a difference in the person's life.

And, most important, let's start listening to the patients. This book begins a project which for one of the few times in history will allow us to hear their voices, aware that liabilities can be turned into assets, and that the American health delivery system needs to pay attention to them.

Introduction

by Michael A. Susko

Cry of the Invisible seeks to give voice to two of the most hidden groups in our society: the homeless, and those who have been in psychiatric hospitals. Usually an editor is besieged with submissions, but I had to seek out writers. As they are wounded people who are not used to being heard, it was at times a difficult matter to gain their trust. I would say hello to a homeless person in my neighborhood for days before risking a conversation. Ten years of involvement in a halfway house put me in touch with many psychiatric survivors. Some were wary that this project was part of the "system" and wouldn't understand them. Indeed some stories were lost. But many were willing to share their stories—often with the belief that it would help others.

The stories speak for themselves. But patterns emerge: first, there is the *invisibility*. The homeless are painfully seen, but with averted gaze—by those who would prefer not to see. And if the homeless are "seen," more rarely does someone listen to them. The hospitalized are even more invisible; not only are they removed from sight, but they report that once within the hospital their true feelings and needs are not taken as real. This frightening invisibility and invalidation thrust on them is the source for the title of this book.

Another pattern that relates to invisibility is the failure of the system to know a person's true story. Modern psychiatry thinks it no longer needs to know a person's past: the doctor can simply observe symptoms, diagnose from a manual, and give drugs. In these accounts we see the system's failure to ask the most basic questions:

1.) Why are you homeless?
2.) What was your practical situation?
3.) What happened to you before you were hospitalized?
4.) What painful experiences did you have as a child?

Indeed, one need only ask to find out that in a great number of people there are deep wounds going back to childhood. The attempted resolution of these traumas into adulthood is perhaps the leading cause of "mental illness." Many people in this book have been willing to share their past, yet often there is a reluctance out of family loyalty, social and fear of stigmas. Many stories remain anonymous.

Another pattern that invariably appears in the stories is abuse of drugs or alcohol. What originally may be a problem of abusing illegal drugs becomes transformed into "mental illness." Abuse of drugs which requires detoxification can lead to a dependence on psychiatric drugs.

The hurt and damage from abuse whether from childhood wounds or from drug abuse can be so severe that the person is not fully responsible for his actions. It is at this point that the person is entrusted to us, not to be abused, but to be protected, nurtured—placed in God's hands—and listened to as to what their struggle means.

This leads us to yet a third factor often totally neglected by the mental health system: the person's search for deeper meaning, for spirituality. This puts him or her at odds with a world that has become increasingly materialistic and devoid of symbolic meaning. The person who goes on a "quest" can get lost, and find himself in the psychiatric system—a system which often treats any spiritual phenomenon as symptomatic of a neuro-chemical imbalance.

Whether from emotional trauma, stress, drug abuse, or spiritual neglect, the real needs of the person are not met—and so the person screams.

The cry takes on startling forms. In some of the stories, the cry is silent: the person retreats into a womb of invisibility. At times, he or she runs away, across country, into homelessness. An inner world may erupt, changing the landscape into a symbolic one.

The cry is often what we see, what is labeled mental illness, and which doctors try to stop with powerful tools. Ironically, the hospitalized learn not to express their inner world, and to present a false self in order to get released.

When the psychiatric system does not recognize this cry of pain for what it is, the person is *invalidated* and the abuse continues. The real self goes into even deeper hiding. The person recedes into invisibility. Blood is coming from wounds, a blood of a different color because it is psychic—but no one pays it any mind. The real person who has real needs has become *invisible*. Symptoms of pain are not allowed to be expressed. The meaning of the cry becomes muffled, often by heavy tranquilizing drugs and increasingly by electroshock.

Electroconvulsive therapy has made a powerful comeback since the late 1970's; conservative estimates say thirty to fifty thousand Americans are "treated" with shock every year. Doctors claim it is modified and does no significant damage, yet we still read of memory loss for weeks, months, and even years.

Psychiatric drugs, heralded as a breakthrough, have a dark side. The stories reveal that they do not offer deep healing; many report their original pain continues—it is only the cry of the pain, the symptoms, that are taken away. It should be noted that there are a minority of people who report being helped by the drugs. But many report serious harm. Repeatedly we hear accounts in this book of agonizing pain due to neuroleptic drugs—especially *akathisia*, a motor disorder where the person can't stay still. For some reason, many professionals do not see this—or see it as a sign of mental illness.

With such problematic treatments, the rule of thumb should be to let patients make the choice. And when people are so disturbed that it seems they cannot make a choice, society should limit itself to protecting them—and refrain from intrusive "medical treatments."

Those who break down in our society can easily find themselves the targets of *forced treatment*. Theoretically, they may have a "right to refuse." In practice, forced druggings are routine experiences in these accounts—and in some instances there is forced shock treatment. There is tragedy in forcing treatments that have damaging "side" effects. Trust, needed in a healing relationship, breaks down. "Paranoia" may ensue, and the abuse continues.

Yet places of saftey, hospices, are needed where people are given time for their strength to emerge, where care or counseling are provided for as long as it takes to heal. There are paradoxes in this process less obvious to the public. Although a wounded person may be inactive, appearing to do nothing, there is often a hidden, inner struggle toward healing. People, even in crisis, are making choices towards the good as they see it, or towards negation. In many of these stories, it is the presence of a friend—someone who is near the person in their pain—which helps to bring about the breakthrough.

There are also double binds. Repeatedly we see people going off the psychiatrists' drugs when outside the hospital. Physiologically, they may suffer a "rebound reaction"—the brain has built extra receptors to compensate for the drug which blocks them. Like a lid taken off the steam kettle, the feelings finally break out, the cry is redoubled—and the person may end up homeless before being shunted back into the hospital to receive an even larger dosage. In some cases, the resolution is premature death. As some writers suggest, we must ask ourselves if our society is operating an invisible "Gulag."

The people of the helping profession suffer too—though we only have glimpses of it in this book. They often face impossible tasks and become targets of the anger and rage redirected at them, transferred from their original cause. Professionals are often strapped for funds to provide meaningful care. And their own feelings and questions, like that of their clients, may be buried.

Despite these limitations, it is time that the *Invisibles* be heard not only by doctors but by society—not as fitting some diagnostic category but as human beings, each with a story.

Based on the themes within the stories, this book is divided into five sections: 1. *Wandering* (often the homeless); 2. *Invisibility*; 3. *Wounded Since Childhood* 4. *Quest* and 5. *Advocacy*. The last section includes writings from professionals.

Finally, there is a lot of pain within these stories. At times it seemed too much for me to absorb. The stories themselves suffered from the incompleteness and fragmentation that reflected the wounds of their bearers. And although there was some editing, the stories have been left largely as they were written or spoken.

Yet, despite the traumas, the pain and the abuse contained in them, there is something more remarkable which stands out—the courage of people to survive, to continue. Each story uncovers a heroic effort wrestling with great internal conflict as well as the evils of society. Often the story-tellers were up against overwhelming odds. Yet some of these people found a measure of hope. They were able to draw on something deep within themselves, and claim some responsibility for their lives. Tragically, others failed and took their lives. But a few of these have now left a testament—in their words or in remembrances by their friends.

Some got well, and in time became happy, to live a more fruitful and meaningful life.

We invite you now to listen to the *Invisibles*, to hear their cry.

Acknowledgements

Many people have helped in the making of this book, but first and foremost I want to thank the writers who entrusted their work to this project. Without that trust—in which they often shared stories of a sensitive and personal nature—this book could not have been done.

I would like to thank the people who helped me edit the often difficult oral stories and did so without payment: Robin Deschenes, Bill White and Marion Jervey. Also, I wish to acknowledge Kate Hamill, George Scheper, and Dorothy Schnell who helped with special problems on the text.

Yet others, helped with the typing, John Turner, and Louise Hofmann. Denise and John helped with the transcription of poetry. I want to thank also the artists who struggled with making the theme of invisibility concrete in some fashion. Jack Gardner and Ron Thompson served as consultants on key decisions regarding the book.

Especially, I want to thank Harrison Livingstone, who not only served as a publisher and a good second editor, but had the vision to see how this project should be done, and drew it out of me.

There are many others un-named who gave encouragement along the way, who saw the project worth doing. For their moral support—and often that is what keeps one going—I would like to extend my thanks.

And lastly I thank God, who's hand was at work behind this.

We invite readers to submit their stories for a future book. In particular we would like people to include the causes leading to homelessness or psychiatric hospitalization, careful descriptions of treatment or the lack of it, including the effects of prescribed drugs, electro shock etc. and your inner experience at the time—as well as what really helped you.

Descriptions of childhood trauma where the person feels it caused emotional distress and life problems are particulary desired by the editors.

Send your story or poems to Editors, Cry of the Invisible, The Conservatory Press, P.O. Box 7149, Baltimore, Md. 21218, U.S.A.

I. Wandering

Who will give me wings like a dove,
to fly away and find rest?
How far must I wander
to find shelter in the wilderness?

I do things to get people out of their mummy stage.
If they get mad, at least they react.

by Lois Tragessor

Since this is some poor wanderer who has come to us, we must now take
care of him, since all strangers and wanderers are sacred in the sight of
Zeus, and the gift is a light and dear one.

The Odyssey, *by Homer*

1

DOROTHY'S STORY

I don't think I'll ever get over what "therapy" has done to me. For the first year at a hospital in Maryland, I was drugged up on Haldol every day. I was allergic to it. My first reaction to it was that I felt like I was dying and my soul was falling straight into hell minute by minute.

I used to call my mother in San Diego, California and beg her if I could come home. Well, she had untied her apron strings and put the apron on me. Over the phone as usual she was the best mother in the world but action wise she was a sitting duck.

Every guy that came on the hall wanted me in one way or another. They blinded me to Stan and Brian . . . the two most important men in my life. I was lonely and to comfort myself I smoked cigarette after cigarette and somehow learned how to play pool, a game that never appealed to me.

The staff on this particular hall were kind to me. They never threw me in seclusion, but they had no idea of the pain I was in because of the Haldol. I finished my last year of High School there and I didn't do too bad although I had a hard time concentrating. I was supposed to be discharged after six months but they stretched it out to one year, a month, a week and a day—I guess until my father's insurance wore out.

One day the staff made me stay in my room all day long because I had failed to get out of bed on time in the morning. My roommate, Maureen, had painted pictures of snakes and dragons on the walls around the bathtub at which I sat and stared for hours.

We used to lay in bed and listen to her Black Sabbath albums which were very fitting for the occasion. In the TV room there was graffiti on one wall. One person wrote: "If Jesus was on earth today, they'd put him in a mental institution."

Once and a while, someone would bring marijuana on the hall and I'd sneak some in my bathroom. Two years before that, I had quit smoking pot through a born again experience. All in all, West-One wasn't as bad as the experiences to come.

I was discharged in January of 1980. I went to live with my father and enrolled in school at Montgomery College. That was a fairly successful experience despite the circumstances. I had moved into an apartment in Gaithersburg and lived there for seven months. I stopped taking medication since I had been out of the hospital and came to see that whole year as a waste.

I had a boyfriend who'd take me out and eventually concluded that I was an alcoholic. Before that, I lived with my dad again and then rented a room in a man's house for a month or two. Then I went back to Dad's. One night while Dad was away, I built a fire in the fire place and had a glass of wine. Well Dad came home and was very angry. Earlier, out of fright, I took a Haldol pill because my mind felt like it was doing strange things. When my dad saw I built a fire without his permission and was drinking wine, he grabbed the bottle and my arm, then threw me toward the stairs and said, "Go upstairs to bed."

That night I must have taken about ten baths trying to revive myself of what the Haldol was doing to me. I thought I was dying and began to hear voices. The voices were frightening and confusing. I heard the devil and a choir of angels telling me not to talk to him. I heard my old boy-friend, Brian. I became very delusional.

When I woke up in the morning, I felt like a fetus in my mother's womb . . . like she actually had me in her stomach. I heard a loud gun-shot and heard my step-father, Russell's voice say that Mom killed herself. Then I thought maybe Dad killed himself and ran downstairs to his bed-room but no one was there. A voice told me that I was pregnant which since then has been a common theme among my voices.

After that I stayed home another couple of weeks and went to see a counselor in Rockville. I missed one appointment and my dad decided I needed to be in the hospital because I was still hearing voices. He had two policemen come in my room one morning, wake me up and cart me away to Suburban Hospital. There I stayed tied to a bed by my ankles and wrists for at least eight hours.

Every single day, I struggled to change. The sad thing is that I tried too hard. In Suburban Hospital, a famous doctor, my father's therapist, came to see me. He asked, "What should we do with you?" I said, "Do what you want." So the papers were signed and off I was carted back to the other hospital again.

THE STREETS

Satin sheets and walking along the street; the opposites
Walking inside the air-conditioned house
Knee-deep in snow trying to find food
Anger, carousal of peril, and the sense of discombobulation
Where is the sense of sense?
No one knows where to go in dangerous times
One drives to the fixture of safety and if there is none—
Simply put, the end is in sight and life goes on
Life goes on and there is no hope
Satin sheets in an air-conditioned home
Pure comfort brings back memories of the womb
Years of searching for the ultimate home to live in
Now walking through the snow looking for food
Love is the answer for it gives one life
Something to have and something to live in
Searching for the correct life
I live in desperation but there is love and there is life
However there is no moral decency
What to do with walking the streets for my soul?
Life goes on simply, painfully and purely

Mark Miller

The Bathing Suit Tribe lives in California and Florida. They like
to lay on the beach half-naked where it's warm in the sun.
There are people who wear wool in the summer. It hurts to be
rejected, spit upon. We aren't of the Bathing Suit Tribe.

by Lois Tragessor

To woods—finding tree
My own age—sharing hard times
I imagine counting
tree rings and wrinkles around
my eyes holding back the tide.

by Michael O.

TIM'S STORY

When you're on the street, nobody pays much attention to you. They sort of see you, but don't really want to. They think you're a loser, that you don't want to work. They act like you're a nuisance, bothering someone, a menace to society. They look at you like they wish you'd take a trip to Florida and not come back. You feel no one likes you, no one cares. Some people help you.

I've stayed in the shelter at the Baltimore Rescue Mission. They feed you soup, bread and tea at night. That's the basic menu. Then you have to go for one hour of church service every night. They make you stand up and read a verse from the Bible before you eat. It's a nuisance, an inconvenience, to read the Bible just to get something to eat.

You have metal racks you sleep on, like bunk beds in the Army. There are no mattresses, only thin gymnastic mats. They're always dusty and sprayed with disinfectant. One time, I got bugs from sleeping there. They sprayed chemicals all over my body and threw my clothes away.

In the shelter we talk about being poor, not having any money, eating in a soup kitchen. Some people might come up to you, saying you owe them money, or get racial with you because you're white. Some people just want to bother you.

I was evicted from an apartment because I had a D.W.I. (Driving While Intoxicated) charge against me. There were two other charges: trespassing and destroying private property. We had busted up a picnic table to put boards under a car that was stuck in some sand. I had to pay a lawyer a thousand dollars. I was saving money to pay him so I didn't pay my rent. I didn't want to go to jail for two or three years.

I've always had a psychiatric problem, an emotional problem since I was about six or seven years old. It just got worse when I got older and had to work. As a child I read hundreds of books and would be out playing in the sun. I was shy, kept to myself, the kind of wimp who wouldn't fight. I looked at things differently. I stayed in a fantasy world with TV, and didn't have any girlfriends. I felt I didn't fit in, that I was an outcast.

My mother used to feed the birds, and the neighborhood boys would throw rocks at my house, calling me Bird Boy. They'd call me a wimp, too. They thought my mom was nuts because of the birds and her ten cats and two dogs. She was preoccupied with animals, more than people. They tried to blame it on me, that she fed the birds. I said, "I didn't tell her to do it." I even told her to stop.

Things started to change when I was about sixteen. I was the first in my family to smoke Marlboros and marijuana, and to drink whiskey. Nobody did that before—they were still playing with G.I. Joe dolls. I got high a lot to make friends. I was insecure, and the high made me feel good. Everyone used to say I was a "trip" because I was the person to be around, the life of the party. But it got out of hand and I became addicted to alcohol.

Before I went into the hospital, I was depressed, not having a good time. I wouldn't tie my shoestrings, I just looked around like I was crazy. I wouldn't do anything, not even comb my hair or wash myself. I started sleeping in the woods. I was in this world, but I couldn't make myself come out of this mood.

A born-again Christian took me off the street for three months. He gave me a chance. But he put me out when he caught me with a bottle of wine. The Christian stuff was starting to drive me nuts anyway, so I went back to the street.

I tried AA, but they kicked me out because I was still drinking. Then I went back to the shelter, because I was homeless again.

I was living on welfare and drinking on it. I was afraid I'd be a bum all my life. It made my psychological problems worse. So I went to the hospital—the psychiatric section of Maryland General. A psychiatrist evaluated me, and said I had a psychological problem: schizophrenia, the type where you're paranoid and think people are against you. But I didn't believe I was psychotic; I didn't have hallucinations or hear voices.

On the psych ward, you ate, watched television and played a lot of cards. The doctor was trying to figure out what medication I needed, but he didn't. He tried Haldol on me, but I got spaced out. When I drank whiskey before, I got spaced out. The psychiatrist said I was too nervous, but he couldn't figure it out. I wasn't there long enough; my medical insurance ran out in two weeks and they released me.

They tied me up with a place, a domiciliary care nursing home in Bolton Hill, because they said I had a psychological defect. I wasn't psychotic, I just needed something for my nerves. I was on Haldol for a year there. But I didn't take it all the time. I hid it under my tongue and flushed it down the toilet. I wouldn't let anyone make me sick for nothing. On Haldol I got weird thoughts, like a thought on top of a thought. There were real delusions, like: "I'm going to kill myself," or "I'm going to die." I couldn't stop them. It made me real uneasy, tense all the time. My mouth went into spasms, my tongue rolled out. It was the weirdest thing I've ever felt.

I've lost the desire to drink; I just got tired of it. My brother has tried to help me get out of the situation. He said, "You don't deserve that way of life, you're from a middle class family. You don't want to just be lazy, watch TV, chase girls, and get drunk."

It's been six months since I've been in the shelter. The friend I live with now is a bad alcoholic and drug user—he's always in detox. My brother is trying to get me out of there.

I'm trying to live in the most positive way, the right way. I try to think through my problems clearly, get the right sleep, eat the right foods, and stay calm.

April 21, 1990 [*dictated*]

My conscience tried to run away
Desperately, I tried to catch it.
My memory just slipped away.
I walked around looking wretched.
I left myself alone one day.
Didn't know if I should return.
Everything around turned to stone—
     statuesque display.
Feelings fled to where they could be seen. . .
     like every nerve on earth
     was a photograph
       staring emptily from magazines
     or wholly like a craft
stone in one shade
  and only one
like the background of a cave
    life was all done; but,
      one person was left
    to sweep the remains
and keep it for their worldly gains.

by Barbara Bleakley 1990

REALIZATION OF SELF
or Self Reconstruction

A Survival Manual for the Homeless

1. *HOME*: Where are you? Brown's church. The home environment here gives the comfort, the relaxation to figure out these things. If you don't have stability where can you go?

2. *WORK:* Check your skills. What are your resources for getting out of here. What are you capable of doing, whatever it takes to create a job?

3. *GOALS*: Goals are up to the individual. What do you *really* want?—within the goal pattern. How do you maintain it, walking up the steps of your goals.

4. *PAST*: Things you would like to correct or eliminate, things that usually distract you from your goals, reasons you were put out from before. Did you mismanage your money because you bought drugs? Or by association—did you give money to someone else to pay rent who didn't? There are problems: family, alcohol, and drugs—how to put these in perspective. What are your weak links in your chain that may cause you to fall?

This is a resume of your life, realizing your life, finding where you are.

Alvin Bennet

Creativity cares about everything.
This world is but a piece of paper to God.

by James Brown

[*Editor's Note:* James Brown used to be seen walking continually up and down Charles Street in Baltimore. He rarely spoke, except to ask for change, or make an unusual comment. Mercy Hospital was kind enough, one day, to look at his infected feet. "I feel like I'm from another world," he said.]

A city street

by Sois

LOIS'S STORY

PART ONE

John Kennedy had just been shot. I went into the room to watch the TV, people were screaming and hollering. I got down on my knees, I don't know why. They started to play the funeral march, and that's all we heard day after day.

They gave me shock treatments at Springfield State Hospital and at Sibly Memorial. They were having a peace march in Washington D. C. when Dr. Sam P. gave me shock treatment. He was teaching at the Kennedy Center at the time. They took all our clothes off and wrapped us in sheets. Then they put iron things over our heads, like ear muffs—a wire led down to a box. They pressed a lever and we went into an epileptic seizure. We were knocked out for about an hour and when we came to, we were kind of vague as to where we were, who we were.

We were put on beds. When we could manipulate our minds right, we were allowed to get up and put our cotton dresses on—ugly state dresses. I had three of them. When I was at Sibly I was knocked out, but when I was at Springfield they didn't give me any medication. It hurt, like being electrocuted.

They gave me psychiatric drugs and they were terrible. They made you sleepy. The staff made you sit up in a chair and not lay down. You sat in chairs until it was time to eat. One time, I fell down on the floor, knocked my head and passed out. I just lay there, came to, my pocketbook laying there. Nobody helped me out. I tried to tell them it was the medicine that was doing it. They were busy. Sometimes I was so dizzy, I couldn't go down to the dining room and eat. I just lay there on the floor. I tried to tell them, but they didn't do anything. I still had to take the medicine.

My first breakdown was after the birth of my last baby, Madeline. I was weak and run down; I just lay down on the couch and couldn't do anything. I had to go to my six-month check-up and this doctor said, "This woman is sick. We have to send her to a hospital." I don't know how long I was there. I must have weighed 70 pounds, and my husband had to bottle feed the baby. When I next saw the doctor, he said, take her to Springfield.

I came home from Springfield when the doctor said I was well enough. It seemed like every time I went home, the situation got worse. My sister and brother came down from Pennsylvania, and they started getting mad at me because I wasn't doing anything. My husband took me to Paul Clinic, a general hospital, and I did just fine. I was there a couple weeks.

Then he took me to Harrisburg State Hospital, and that was hell. The nurse came over and wanted us to clean trays and beds where women lay in bed. They had bowel movements over everything, food on the trays that was hard. I wasn't there too long. My father and brother came up and brought me back home.

I'm still in that spell the doctors put me in from the shock treatment. They didn't really want to help me; they used me and destroyed my brain. No one helped me much there, no more so than in jail. I was in many hospitals, but the worst one was in Crownsville. They said it was a *punishment hospital* at the time. If you didn't go down into the bushes with the men patients and have sex, you were afraid they might beat you up and get away with it.

The doctors and nurses didn't really seem to care. If we had group therapy, no matter what you said, the doctors would more or less contradict you. It's like when a lawyer is trying to prove a person is guilty. Maybe this person is not guilty for a murder, let's say, and the lawyer manipulates words. That's the way they did. You would say something in your own way, which was the truth probably, and it felt like they were calling you a liar.

I was in seclusion many times. I was always on medicine—some of it was very rough. It made you dizzy, weak; you couldn't walk right like you were going to fall down. They were torture chambers; I think you get put in those places to be tortured for your sins.

PART TWO

In the beginning I went back to my husband. It never worked. I don't know if it was me or him. When I got back out of the hospital at St. Elizabeth's, I lived on the street. It was pretty bad on the streets, bad as concentration camps—not during hot weather but during cold weather. I ended up on the street willingly. The landlord and my friend Ronnie started fighting with a Fredie, a tenant, and I got nervous about it. I walked out of the house not knowing what to do, went down North Avenue, and down Maryland Avenue. I got on a Greyhound bus, went to D.C. and stayed there on the streets almost a year.

I tried to get a place to live downtown, but they didn't have any vacancies. "Try the Salvation Army," they said. But that was only temporary and they had a lot of strict rules there. The girl who answered the door and was living there gave me a list of rules. You couldn't come and go; you were in and had to stay in.

The police let me sit in their lobby one night, across from the Roosevelt hotel. Another time I was taken to the state trooper's office. They were testing me, seeing what I'd do. But I didn't say a word. Finally they said, "It's time to leave." "Leave?" I said, "I don't know where I am." You should have seen my shoes, not fit to walk in. They pointed me in a direction.

You can see when a person lives on the street, it shows. Michael O. is getting that look now, and he's not that old.

When I came back, Ronnie said they were wondering where I was. I said, "Well, I didn't know what to do after you started picking on Fredie, and the Landlord was dead."

We helped each other out by giving each other a cigarette, buying a cup of coffee. You can't get real friendly with people, You say "Hi, how you doing," something like that. You see, the medicine does something to your thinking capacity up here. Normally you can read books and all, but a mental person on pills—you're not the same.

Once you become mentally ill, you're "mental" the rest of your life. That's why most families want to have nothing to do with you. I don't care who you are, even if you come from a good family. You've changed, and probably it's been someone in your family that caused you to be that way.

My husband caused me to be that way. I always looked on him as being very intelligent. I'd always ask, "Why did you marry me?"—I was a drop out. He used to play a lot of chess with his brother, and he used to buy hundred dollar electronic books. Naturally, when I bought groceries, I had to think of those $100 books.

He only hit me once. There was snow on the ground, an electrical storm came up and I told him it was the end of the world. He kept on sleeping. "Walter, Walter wake up!" I said. "I think it's the end of the world." He wouldn't wake up and so I ran over to Michael, who was five years old. I said, "Michael, run next door and tell the neighbors, I think your father's going to kill himself." That's when Walter woke up and hit me. He didn't hit me hard, then he went over and hit the wall.

When Madeline was born at home, he was sleeping. I lay in the bathroom and there were sheets thrown on the floor, and she came out. He went to call the ambulance and I cleaned her up.

They said it was a post-partum psychosis. I believe I was tortured because I was breast fed by my mother and because I breast-fed my babies. I think I spoiled my system doing that, nine months each. I was reading in a book that when you have your breasts you have strength. You see, I don't have any strength because I don't have hardly anything up here.

PART THREE

I always had a fear of lying down in the day. It might date back to my childhood, when my father didn't have a job, and my mother didn't work either. My sister and I came back from school and they might be laying down. It seemed like they were asleep. My father was a construction worker during the depression and he couldn't get work till '41. A sign in front of the treasury department said, "War is Business."

Between sixteen and twenty-six I was working. I saw a movie with Olivia D. Havelin, called the *Snakepit,* and I never thought I would be in one. She fell in love with the psychiatrist, walked around the grounds with him. She claimed she saw snakes going up the wall. Her condition is like the medication—it can make you see psychedelic things. I don't know if the doctors know what it's doing to you. I wondered if I were the only one going through it; everyone else was acting normal. With me, they were using anything they could dig out of the medicine chest.

For twenty-four years I was on the wrong medicine. It would make you feel funny, feel terrible. It made your eyes blurry, you could hardly see. I would look at your face, and it would be distorted. You wouldn't know where to look because everything was distorted.

My daughter was on Thorazine when she was eight years old. I went over to Woodbridge, Virginia in a white bus to see her. She was thin, her legs and arms were like my wrists. They told her to either sit down or lay down. They said she was hyperactive and they wanted her on Thorazine. But she wasn't any different than any other child, running around. Then they put her on something else for her heart murmur.

You take children and put them under a different parent, but they know they're missing something. You're going to have a reaction from children. A child may go along with a man in car, simply because she doesn't have a father anymore. The mother is working, hiring a baby sitter. Something has to replace the mother or father that's missing.

You don't know how many people there are that are mental, but just in this country alone, there are millions of them. Where I live is run by Catholic Charities, Section Eight and Methodist Church. There is a lot of space going to waste in that place. I mention it—not in a demanding way—because they should change it and let more people live there. But you know those kind of people. They don't want to spoil the looks inside; it was built in the 18th century and all that.

One person can not do what has to be done. I would do away with mental hospitals, and put them in homes in society.

February 27, 1990 [dictated]

When you got out to visit people in the state hospital you are God to them. Coffee, cigarettes and donuts: that's Godsend. That's what the people think out there. The therapists and Reverends keep people alive. With a little bit of religion they see a cross. They see a cross and the raging bull in them becomes a lamb.

by Lois Tragessor
From Street Images, 1987

MY LITTLE SPOT

[Editor's Note: In the winter of 1983, Clem was hospitalized for frostbite, and lost all his toes. While laying in the hospital bed, he wrote this fantasy.]

My little spot weaves and bobs, walks and runs and changes colors, hues and dimensions. For example, it can become San Francisco, Philadelphia, Milwaukee, or Chicago; it may be either autumn in Denver, with all its varying shades, or Valle after a heavy snowfall; a child walking or running across a playground; or a cork weaving and bobbing above the water as some trout swims beneath the surface.

As I awake in the morning, my little spot appears as a small speck on the wall. While I attempt to tune-in the world, it becomes clear one minute and blurry the next, until all sleep has gone from my eyes. Later it becomes a television screen, showing the faces I must meet during the day and places where we must meet.

During breakfast, lunch and dinner, my little spot goes over each and every item, asking that this be added and that be deleted. It demands hot food in comparison to cold and must have coffee and milk with each meal. It even blurs my vision when it thinks I have had enough or when it thinks I am eating the wrong foods.

As I leave home for work, it seems to sit next to me as I turn on the ignition, telling me when to start my automobile, when to back out of the driveway, and which route to take to work. It even tells me where to part in the company's parking lot.

As I walk from the parking lot, my little spot seems to meet and greet all the people I pass. When I get into the office, it seems to meet and greet every employee. It generates a warm feeling even on mornings when my moods are rapidly changing.

When I answer the phone, my spot seems to go out in an attempt to view the caller and his surroundings. It usually returns with a face and the entire environment from which it comes.

As I write letters and memos during the day, it changes to varying shades. When it thinks I have chosen the wrong word, it colors the entire word lightly. When it wants a word or passage deleted, it places a dark spot above that portion.

As I leave work, my little spot leaves with me, telling me which route to take, what speed to drive at, and which lane to drive in. In this Los Angeles traffic it takes some people an hour and half to get home. It only takes me forty-five minutes.

by Clem Batiste

I know I'm not making waves. Waves
make people uneasy. I make a ripple from
time to time. A ripple you can cope with.
A ripple can make you aware.

by Earnest Hawkins

No gurus arise
in cold weather. We share priests
Bag men and poets.

Michael O.

SAM WILLIS'S STORY

[*Editor's Note:* Sam, who can be seen roaming the streets of Baltimore, makes his own exotic hats. The hat he's wearing now has a black band with a white netting on top. A small mirror stands up in the back. In front there's a match book, its inside showing an automobile accident, an advertisement for insurance. To its left is a picture of a lady.]

I was born May 3, 1932, right here in Baltimore. I worked thirty-one years, washing dishes, janitor work, anything I could find. I've been homeless before. I have a place now, but I sleep outside as long as I can during the year, by the bridge where the birds are. I go out to exercise, get fresh air and get quiet.

When I was a kid I used to sleep in the vestibule. My parents were nice to me at times. That's where feelings are: they covered me up at night.

I had a heart attack when I was kid. My parents smacked me, threw books at me. I got hit by stones in New York one time by some kids. My parents sat around, talked about themselves. My father drank a lot when he came out of the Army; he was alcoholic. Once when my step mother hit me, I smacked her down.

I was in a boy's village training school since I was six or seven. I hated it, so many punks were there. The police worker put me there; I had been hooking school. But I liked the training school. The kids there couldn't understand it. They used to worry me to death; I almost think they're out looking for me now.

In 1962-3 I was in Springfield and Crownsville for a few weeks. It's all right, except for the needles in my arm. I didn't like that. I left; in fact I stopped doing everything.

Once, I was up in New York, sitting on Union Avenue and studying dictionaries. I hate to talk about it; it causes so much pain. I was hit by a car, and my legs felt like they were broken. One ankle and one arm was sprained. I do a lot of walking now to keep the muscles and bones in place.

I make hats to make stories. People can't stand people with wisdom and knowledge. The story of this hat is when I got hit by that car. That's why the match box has a car accident on it. It was dark that night: that's why the band is dark. The bureau mirror is like the Bureau of Investigation. It was very cold that night. . . . A lady is on there too, because one day a lady picked me up out of the snow.

June 8, 1990 [*dictated*]

AMONG HORATIAN FREEMAN
(To the tune of "Oh God Our Help in Ages Past")

Since first the hills in order stood,
Mattheans' sympathetic blast,
Has born down good-named sons.

And we who decidedly care,
Know of the callousness
Of pietistic libertines
Of their Matthean biddies roosts.

Wanting life without illusion
Sentiment as of Horace
Among the reasoning freemen
Is different than the "Dualists."

With intemperate kindnesses,
Since euphemism was begun
We have the prating clergyman,
Of academic righteousness.

They've breath such breed with souls so dead
Who to themselves have not said,
"This our own community,"
So that no fellows are they.

Such parochially true biddies,
Walk their sentimental strand,
As they walk on so, mark ye well,
Of them there is no glad-tale.

High though their status, proud,
Boundless their influence, their names, they claim,
Despite their status, pride and chaff,
Such biddies lack mindful self.

by Bob Page

[*Editor's Note:* This poem was written by a homeless man who spoke eloquently, as if from the 1800's. His writings were often a polemic against a type of religious hypocrisy which he characterized as "Matthean" or as "Pietistic Biddies."]

RICK MELVIN'S STORY

PART ONE

I was born in 1957 and lived in Edmonson Village with my parents and my older sister. We stayed there until I was ten years old, and I was basically "trouble free." Although I was a hyper kid, I didn't have any real serious fights, or scrapes with the law—that all came later.

Once, when I was seven, I got hit by a car. I ran out in front of the traffic thinking I would cross the street. The car knocked me down—it was only going about five miles per hour—and I blacked out. I woke up on the sidewalk and told everyone I wanted to get a haircut, I was fine. The police took me to a hospital, and found out I was all right.

We moved to Baltimore County in a section called Woodmoor; we had a nice home out in the suburbs. I had a lot of expectations from the family to be a normal son.

By ninth grade I was smoking cigarettes and drinking beer; soon after, I was smoking marijuana and dropping acid. It all happened so fast. By the time I was eighteen I was in a mental institution. I looked back on my past and I couldn't figure out what I had done wrong. I didn't think at that time that drugs could be that bad; there wasn't that much awareness of drugs. I didn't know I had been damaging my brain.

One hot night in the summer of 1976, I was driving my father's Volkswagen, and I had a psychotic episode behind the wheel. I ended up in Dundalk, going down a one-way street, when a policeman pulled me over. He questioned me about my actions. I was together externally at first: I gave him my license and waited to get my ticket. But I was scared, like a paranoid schizophrenic. While the cop looked at the license, I pulled off down the one-way street, driving like mad.

Six police cars chased me. They finally got me on a field and pulled me out of the car. They hit me with a stick; I got beat up. I had a gash in my forehead and I was taken to a special police hospital to have stitches put in. Using substances led to some weird things.

This incident led to my first hospitalization at Provident Medical Center. A counselor I was seeing and my parents decided I needed hospitalization. I remember how alienated and alone I felt, and how the patients were abusive. One fellow there was court committed. He had stolen some furs, and he was acting like he was king of the place and we were his servants.

I lied and told the staff I wasn't on any drugs, but they must have found out—they did blood tests. For treatment they put me on medication: Haldol, then Thorazine. It was pretty strange—Haldol is a very powerful anti-psychotic. It was a different kind of feeling; I don't want to say a different high—by no means are these medications a high. I felt bad but they stabilized me for a period of time, till I could go out and get more drugs.

In the hospital I thought I was an extra-terrestrial. I had read a lot about extra-terrestrials from occult scientists. We were here to usher in a new age and help mankind. Since I was from another planet, I thought I had special powers. Sometimes, I could pick up universal vibrations that would help me to play music. I would see trees move and when I'd see a certain flight pattern of birds I would think a certain way. You start putting that together day after day, week after week, and you begin to think that you have control over nature and man.

I became telepathic; I could listen to anything, even plants and trees. The birds in the trees would have a voice. With me musing in my thoughts, I would have a conversation. "Hi, how are you doing, a sunny day isn't it?" The birds would say, "Fine, it's a nice day." They would reflect my thoughts. I would talk to my plants too. It's a fine line between reality perception and fantasy because a lot of people talk to their plants and they do grow better. I still talk to my plants, and they grow pretty good.

The therapists dealt with it by restricting me on the ward, making it hard for me to obtain status. That's when I really learned I was just as normal as the next guy—when I couldn't get a grounds pass just because I wanted one. I had to show some merit to get the pass.

I got a lot of jealously because I thought there was something about me that was innately better. Once, at Spring Grove, some patients invited me to smoke marijuana. "I don't want to smoke," I told them, because I didn't want to end up on the street. They laughed at me, calling me a sissy and a punk. They were going to use me as an outlet for their stress, knocking me all day. I said I wasn't going to take it. I went to the staff. I told them was who doing it and when. Then all I got was hatred. "Wow, you finked on us!" they said. "You rat fink!"

I kept being rehospitalized, a dozen times at Taylor Manor, Spring Grove, and Liberty Medical Center. It was a matter of using drugs on top of having manic-depressive symptoms. Being manic is like being allergic to drugs. When I took the drugs, I would go into a "Dr. Jekyll and Mr. Hyde."

Once I tried to jump out of a window. It was rough living with my dad. We weren't getting along, arguing a lot, and I took an overdose of Thorazine. We got into a fight, and he said he was going to call the police. I said, "If you call the police, I'm going to jump out the window!" He called the police, and I jumped. As I went out the third-story window, I managed to twist myself around and hang onto the rail. I finally climbed back in, talked to my dad and the police, and things worked out.

A lot of times I didn't stay on the medication. It's one thing for them to be giving you the drugs and another to self medicate. I would stop using the drugs because of paranoia. They were trying to give me something that wasn't agreeable to my system. I experienced side effects like jitters, dry mouth, and blurred vision. I have some kind of dyskinesia; I'm being treated for that by being given another medication. I didn't know what they were trying to do, but I didn't think they were trying to help me.

Sometimes, pleasant things would happen. Once I was hitching across country. When I got to Lincoln Nebraska, I met this guy who said he had a hot car from New Jersey. He wanted to go to L.A., ditch the car, and catch a jet back. This sounded good because I didn't have any money, and he didn't have any money. But I was mad when I found out the car was stolen. "You got to let me out," I said. "I'm just going to L.A," he said. "Why don't you go with me?" We were in Washington State. Like the dummy, I said, "Yeah, I'll go ahead."

We arrived at L.A. and dumped the car. "What are we going to do now," I asked. He said, "Let's stow away on a jet and go back east." "Stow away!" I said. "How are you going to stow away on a jet? You can't just walk on a jet." He said, "Sure you can. Let's go." So we walked on this jet and told the stewardess that we left our tickets past the metal detectors. She bought that and let us on a flight to New York. We sat in some open seats in the back. I often wondered why she let us on, if she was from the same planet as I.

Once I went to jail because of a musician friend of mine. He invited me over to jam. We were raided by the State Police, who were looking for some cocaine he had. And he did have it. Because I was on the premises I went to jail. In the cell I was sitting, doing my meditation, taking it through to God. After four hours of holding me in the cell, they let me go. That's a work of God. I could have faced fifteen right there.

I'm not religious but I am spiritual. I really do think somebody intercedes from a higher plane if I get into something serious. I would get out with the least problematic thing happening. I still do this meditation every day, a *Hu* chant, an ancient word for God in Sanskrit. You can feel it vibrating; it starts to build up energy, you can see light.

PART TWO

It got to a point where through hospitalization after hospitalization, coming back on the streets, doing more drugs, going back to the hospital, that I finally decided I was going to end the cycle at twenty-five. This was after a stay at a halfway house, and a boarding home on the west side.

My family had untied me from their breast; they didn't want to take care of me any longer. In fact, they wanted to keep as much distance from me as possible, because they figured I was bad news. They didn't understand my illness.

Mental illness affects so many people. Sometimes their families become afraid of them; sometimes they get over-sympathetic and fuel the fire. Sometimes it's hard to interpret the two when you're ill. You can sort of see your way through it, manipulate—but you don't want to manipulate—you just get caught up in that bag of manipulating. My family was mostly in anger. They didn't understand where I went ill. They're more sympathetic now that I've accepted therapy and treatment.

At the age of twenty-five when I stopped using drugs, my doctor at Spring Grove said I had a manic depressive illness, inherited from birth. He said I might have to take medications all of my life. I was saddened about that, but there is a chance I could come off them, especially if I don't abuse substances.

There was a time when I thought it was all fixed, under control, when I was living at the halfway house. I thought I could use a little bit of marijuana, get away with it, that nobody would know. I could be drunk and stay in my room, be unsocialable. But I don't want to live my life that way. And I'm not.

I have a production company now; I'm working with musicians on a jazz band project. It's hard with this handicap, because I know there are so many temptations in the music business. We're winding down, we're out at a bar, and someone wants to buy me a beer. But I can't drink, I have to tell them that. I really can't handle that, I never could. Even when I thought I could handle it, I would get into trouble with the law.

I'm thirty-two now, a professional musician, and I play free lance at places. In a lot of ways it's like being fifteen all over again; I feel so young compared to the regular crowd. They grew up and matured right away. It's scary sometimes because I don't fit in with that crowd. It's scary because I know I ran myself into this position and it's only me—it's not the doctors, not the therapists, not the counselors—it's only me who's going to pull me out of this position.

April 25, 1990 [*dictated*]

JOHN HUBBERT'S STORY

[*Editor's Note:* John spends hours writing on newspapers in front of churches. The writing is indecipherable. Eventually, John shared about his life and the meaning of his writing.]

I'm just a doodler to while away my time while I'm on the street. My writing's about the dawn of creation, about Adam and Eve. I think about how I got here, and when I kick the bucket I don't know where I'm going—heaven or hell.

When I was a kid I used to draw pictures from nature, like still lifes of trees or animals. Then it developed into people, something from mankind when God first developed the earth. I used to draw my German Shepherd dog all the time.

I was born in Baltimore in University Hospital on March 11, 1936. I was poor like I'm poor now. After I finished the ninth grade my mother and father told me to get work—that was during the war. My first job was a stock clerk in a clothing store but I've been mostly a janitor.

I've been in the mission for eight years. I haven't made much attempt to find work. I never married, I can hardly take care of myself. My philosophy is to each his own. I don't bother them, they don't bother me. Strife and war comes from people meddling in other peoples affairs.

I'm still trying for a world of luck, playing the lottery. I keep on hoping I'll win something, like a fantasy. If I won the lottery I'd get four walls and shelter, a blanket—like the day I was born. I get myself straightened up locally first. I'd pay up for the whole year. Then I'd take a nice long trip. New York would be my first stop and then California. I'd jump over to Puerto Rico. I like the music, the drums of the Hispanics; they teach me some of the language at the mission.

I've been all my life in Baltimore. I'd take off; I have no reason to stay here.

May 18, 1990 [*dicated*]

He washes away last night's mess
To put on the new hope of morning.

by Gary

[*Editor's Note:* When Michael is out of the hospital he resorts to alcohol for self-medication. He writes poetry in Japanese forms called Haikus and Tankas.]

MICHAEL O'S STORY

from Walter P. Carter Center

Before I was committed here, I was ninety days in the rain—homeless. I got kicked out of both missions. I couldn't go anywhere. I stayed around in restaurants, like the York Steak House. I tried to get in the hospital, but no one would let me. I would fall asleep at bus stops. I'd sit there and wait for buses, go to Towson and back.

My father came down to a bank I was in. He said, "Get out of my bank." I was on the bottom floor of the building, trying to get hold of my brother. I was arrested for trespassing, when I went to my father's office. I don't call him father anymore.

I can't remember the past, it's not there. It feels like part of my brain is gone, like I've had a lobotomy. I've been raped of my rights, violated. Everyone here lives in a TV world, watching sit-coms. I feel like I'm not a human being anymore. I'm on so many medications, seven of them—I don't know what they are. Someone says they've done something in the past. I say it could have been me.

There's no one to communicate to. You wonder how long it will last. The doctor comes and talks to you, and you know all he wants to do is give you medicine. I used to take the medicines and play the game. I feel like a coffee cup laying around.

It's like T.S Eliot's *Wasteland*: it leads nowhere with maybe a surprise ending. Somebody just turns off the TV set and goes to bed. It's a constant grunt, ad nauseam. We're like monkeys on trees—we have feeding trays.

The doctors Med-paneled me, forcing me to take medicines. Call me Michael O. They wear little badges, often inverted. They know they're killing you, little by little. They can't stand their jobs anymore. It feels like a "professional death." It's like they come in and ask, "Which coffin did you chose? We don't have any record. . . . Copper did you say? What did you say your name was. . . ." Then they just use plastic, burying you alive.

I've been in the Quiet Room a lot. I take the rights book with me. Usually I get sent there because I keep talking at the meetings. I refer to

Nazi Germany. I'm always reading the rights in the pamphlet to people because they don't know them.

I get up early each morning, looking for life. Everyone's dead. There's one plant in the corner here that's still alive. Another plant that had blood red leaves, broad with elephant-like ears, was taken away. It's just how it goes.

Oct 28, 1990

Constitutionally, I have found you have a right to refuse medication, but not practically. They've got you hostage. I've been on a locked ward for five months now. Last week, I got my head knocked by two orderlies in the Quiet Room. It's a hostage situation.

Recently a nurse told me, "We're on the honor system here." I thought to myself, "Honor system! They strip off your pants and shoot you up with a needle and talk about an honor system!"

The streets are better than the hospital. You have a change of scene. You don't have needles shot into you. If you run into a tangle on the streets you can move away from it. Here, you can't.

November 7, 1990

I escaped from the Carter Center. They took me next door to the Dentist office. My teeth hurt, grinding them so much from the medication. They had a big, athletic attendant watching me. When I saw the reception room was crowded, I knew I had a chance. There was one seat by the door. Nonchalantly, I sat down, looking relaxed. Earlier I spent time talking with the attendant, loosening him up, making him think I was a good guy.

I waited awhile and said to myself, when the door opens again I'm going out. I could never do it in the hospital because the exit was next to the Quiet Room—that was a stopping point for me, too much pain.

The door opened and I slipped out. I went to the elevator and hit G level. At first I felt the elevator was moving up, that I would never get out. But I entered on the ground level. When I hit the street, I started to run. For three blocks I ran, till I started to walk, realizing I was free.

June 13, 1990 [*dictated*]

[*Editor's Note:* The author of this letter is the late Ethel Perez, a woman who was homeless—diagnosed as retarded and psychotic. She died at the age of forty-four, killed by a car while crossing Liberty Heights Avenue. The following letter refers to an appearance Ethel made testifying to the plight of the homeless in a hearing at City Hall.]

Dear Sister Patty Ann,

I know you really care about the homeless men and women and also children. But Sister Patty Ann, you care about me. I was homeless myself. Pattie Ann I love you, and I know you love me and care about me. I was so unhappy that I did not have shelter over my head, and I was in the cold sitting at City hall.

So I was brought into city hall, out of the cold, and I was the first to speak. After the hearing you all took me to the Viva House to stay there for seven days and shave all of my hair off my head. Then you took me to Walter P. Carter Center. So I stayed there a real long time, and then I was put into Springrove and they could not handle me. They put me back in Walter P. Carter Center and I stayed there.

I went back to Springrove and I stayed in the locked ward for a little time. I was doing OK there and the head supervisor there let me go to My Sister's Place and everywhere I wanted to go.

So I go to a home. I live with Mrs. Mattie May. And I was so long living with her, I got a shelter, staying at the Salvation Army. And when I stay at the Salvation Army for about a month, Jane Rowly starts being my social worker. So she talks to me and I talk to her, and she got me a white home. I only stay for three months and that's all. So I have a little bit of money in my pocket and I got right in front of the center, not the one I go now. So I went down at My Sister's Place, it's about closing time. I went to the pay phone across the street and I buy myself a pack of cigarettes and a can of colt 45 and Jane came and took me to the Carter Center.

Then I went to University Hospital. So I stay there about three weeks. Now Jane took me to two houses, first it was a West Indian house. I did not like it there, so Jane Rowly took me to Regnia. I love it there. Now I am here and I am going to stay here for the rest of my life. I am not going anywhere at all, so I am to stay. I am happy here, so this is my story that I got to say.

So God bless you Pattie Ann and merry Christmas to you from

Your girl,

Ethel May Maria Perez

BLEEDING EYES OBLIVIOUS TO THE WIND

Bleeding eyes oblivious to the wind
increase lines surrounding our smiles
Satiny bites of this fragrant night
spring slowly surrendering to our miles
Winding,
rolling,
churning,   and
turning
dirt roads,
highways, and
city streets
leave an unfortellable burning
beneath
our somewhat cement feet.
We're implanted in any wind
be us afoot,
abike,
ahoy, or
whatever.
Lent nothing, as we are one
to find
and find
and continue to endeavor.
Goose bumps only lend some solace
as we pass by city trollies.
Wherever we go—-everyone's happy,
dancing,
shopping, or
being snappy.
Swift minded,
swift footed
out to get the kids some goodies.
Even when our bones are broken
We just sit around joking!
No matter what swing we fall from,
we will overcome!

by Barbara Bleakley
1990

ADVENTURES OF A MISERABLE PROPHET
(Anonymous)

PART ONE

I was on the street for three weeks. I lost thirty to forty pounds; my weight reached 80 pounds. I had been living at this church, then I left because I was preaching the gospel. I started hitchhiking. I met this guy—he was gay and wanted me. I tried to convert him. For an hour and a half I rode with him, way out in northern Maryland.

Next, I got picked up by a famous 92 Star radio announcer. She thought I was very intelligent. I told her I was preaching the gospel. She said, "Good luck. . . . You'll never know who'll you'll meet in this world." I said, "Take me anywhere, far away from here. I'm sick of Baltimore."

After that, I walked around for a few days. I came to a big town. It might have been Philadelphia, maybe it was Wilmington. It was the oddest thing. I asked someone, "What town is this?" He wouldn't tell me, but we started walking and went to a bar. I asked him if he wanted to go across country. He was 90% sure he wanted to do it, then backed out. He had too many responsibilities.

I started preaching at the top of my lungs in the neighborhood. I rang someone's doorbell, thinking I was an apostle and that I could stay at people's houses by saying I'm a Christian.

I ended up in Springfield from March to May 1983. They wouldn't let me out of the yellow day room for months. But hope kept me alive. It was like a little blip on a computer screen. It was faint, like a little cool wind that stayed with me. Meditating in Indian style, I asked God for one gift: *hope* to keep me going. It was all I had. I was taught that hope was one of the seven spirits of God.

Soon I started to run the place, like an aggressive jackass, a punk. It was the only way to survive. This motorcycle punk said he would keep me cool, protect me, that he would beat them up if they bothered me. But he turned on me too and kicked me with his steel-toed boot.

I was converting people to the gospel, singing and preaching. A song would come on the radio and I would sing my own words with gospel meaning. *I converted a Vegetable hall to a Christian hall.* Everyone was preaching the gospel by the time I got through.

At times, I thought I was Jesus. I wanted Reagan to come and crown me king. By mind power, I tried to force him to come but he went to a parade in a southern town instead. Because I had to stay in Springfield I decided to punish the world by creating these Giant Ants and Moths.

I shaved my head because I wanted to prove to this guy that I didn't have 666 on my head. I had a scar where my Great Dane bit me—on the same spot where Damian, a character from the movie *Omen*, had the mark. It was a tense moment because, to me, the whole world was wondering if I was the Anti-Christ.

The medication was bad; I was on Mellaril and Loxitane. It took ten minutes to have one thought. All my thinking was confused. I was "just a daze;" I personified myself as "just a daze."

I was so hungry that I would eat anything on my tray including the rotten beets. I ate weeds in the gardens and scallions. I snorted salt to get high. I tried to poke my eyes and ears to become deaf, dumb and blind. It didn't work. I was doing it to meditate better, to have healing power. In the hospital I would practice electrifying my body. I wanted people to touch me and be healed. I laid hands on people.

One day, when I was at the Mennonite church, my whole head was electrified. It was like a force coming down from heaven, then my head felt like stone—the presence of God healing my brain. I healed some people on the ward; I could tell because they got discharged sooner.

They wanted to give me ECT. They were going to give it to me at five o'clock. We had volleyball that day. I hid in the bathroom and forced my way out of the main building, past this lady. "Mark, come back!" they yelled. "You have to stay!"

I hid in the woods and made a blanket of twigs and leaves, near the Sykesville Prison. I was hallucinating that German shepherds were coming after me. I got up and went by row after row of fences, trying to find a way out. Finally, there was an opening, a farm. I climbed through barbed wire. There were cows, wheat in the field. I got as far away as I could and went up some railway tracks. I drank from a spring and saw a large wolf-like animal pass nearby.

I found a road, but it was bad luck. It led to Rosewood, an institution for the mentally retarded. At the entrance I saw one of the doctors from my treatment team come out. I ran back into the woods and went up a highway. While I was waiting at a gas station to reach a friend, the police picked me up. I gave a fight; it took them a long time to put me in shackles.

They still planned to give me ECT. I signed an appeal with a lawyer and asked for a couple days to prove myself. After that, they said I was healthy enough not to have it. I just needed more time off the hall. I went out to Highs, and out to pizza with my social worker. I got better. I wasn't sick when I got to the hospital. I just needed a place to stay.

I stayed for a while in a supervised living arrangement. I had been cooking on the stove—they didn't allow that—and I kept the place messy. I got kicked out, and they put me in Sinai Hospital.

At first, I had a good time there playing softball, hitting home runs, beating people at volleyball. I lost my virginity with a patient. But they started keeping me on the hall all the time because I was throwing up in the dining room. They saw I couldn't control myself; the tension was too much.

Soon they said my time was up, and they sent me to Sheppard Pratt. After a couple of days there, I decided to split. I went to the bottom of a fifteen-step staircase, doing a roll without breaking my ankle. I had set three fires: in my bedroom, in the girls' bathroom, and in the living room trash can. The diversion worked: I got out as the staff came in with fire extinguishers.

I was walking around Towson, crying out, screaming out for help because it was so dark. Every step was hard, with each step I thought I would fall into hell. I saw a light in someone's backyard and ended up in a creek. I went toward some big houses. I went into someone's car and took a hat—a clown hat made of plastic and a music tape. I thought I was in an imaginary land.

I went into the house and saw a teenage couple sitting on pillows watching TV. I asked for juice. "Who are you?" they asked. "I escaped from Sheppard Pratt," I said. "Can you help me get back?" The boy gave me some cranberry juice. He was going to grab me because he thought I was crazy. "I'm going to leave now," I said. "No, you're going to the hospital," he said. I agreed and went out to the car. He tried to grab me; he wanted his tape back. I did my Kung-fu feints on him. He tried to wrestle me to the ground. I just ran.

I found an abandoned car near a gas station. I kept trying to start it for a half hour, but it didn't have any gas. I found some white caulk and put it all over the car. I lit it. I was thinking of committing suicide by staying inside.

A policeman came by and I stopped him. "I'm the one who escaped from Sheppard Pratt and set the fires," I said. "I need help. I'm a danger to others." At first, he didn't want to help. Then he said, "Wait there." I waited for a half hour and then walked down the road. Three or four police cars surrounded me. I said, "Hey I'm not crazy." I shook the officer's hand. I thought I was on Mars, and that I was overloaded with tremors—a "tremor psychosis."

They took me to the police station somewhere north of Towson. I didn't know where the hell I was. They were very friendly. "I'm trying to cope with this illness," I said. "There are several charges against you," they said. I told them I was just trying to find some cigarette butts in the car. They handcuffed me to a post.

An ambulance came. They brought me back to Sheppard and put me on another hall. For four days and nights, I was in seclusion. I slept. When they came in, they would surround me with eight or ten staff members at a time. I thought I was in hell or purgatory—-a catacomb where people are punished. Then they strapped me down and took me in an ambulance to Springfield State Hospital.

At Springfield, my mind was totally out of shape. People were pushing me. My friend Ginger was with me on the hall. I felt the other patients were all having sex, being so cool, so I seduced a woman to show them they weren't so hot.

This guy named Tony was picking on me. Once, he stuck his finger in my cheek and I grabbed his arm. We almost fought. A week later he beat me up. I wouldn't fight, I turned my cheek. He was kicking me in the face. I yelled, but the staff let it happen for a few seconds before they stopped me. My nose was broken. My head was quaking; my body felt electrified. Getting hit, beating your head gets your blood going. The staff wanted to put me in seclusion, but I had punched him only once. I had to defend myself.

PART TWO

I started having these episodes because I smoked pot—perhaps PCP was laced in it. I heard voices. If you ask me, I don't have an illness. I smoked too much pot and had a bad trip. After five days in the hospital I was well. But they made me stay three weeks. I got nervous and sick again.

It started with a sudden explosion in my head. Mostly, I felt pain. The voices were a response to the pain. They would seduce me, tell me I'm intelligent. The voices hurt me; I couldn't concentrate on reality. The doctors told me I had a disease. They said it was a chemical imbalance, nothing to do with the marijuana.

That was in 1979 when I was in tenth grade and at the top of my class. I had been smoking for two years before that. I thought my intelligence would be strong enough to fight any problems caused by the pot, but it didn't work. I'd turn on a radio in Driver's Ed class and think they were talking about me. The voices would comment on my thoughts. "Oh, do you really think that?" I even used to practice it, fall into my psychosis, allow it to happen.

I used to wonder if I was a "psychotic child." I was abused by my parents and by my sisters. My sisters wouldn't let me sleep; they'd poke me and tickle me mercilessly. One time my sister and her friend glued my eyes shut.

Once, I threw a light bulb down the stairs and it exploded. My mother hit me and my hand started bleeding. Then I hit the floor real hard. My mother would have her bad days. . . .I would try to leave her alone. Because of the abuse, I didn't start talking until I was three years old.

I was sexually precocious as a child. Once, when I was three, I was fondling a young girl. Her mother came and slapped me hard on the head. I had an early sexual experience when I was four with my sister's older friend.

I watched Hercules, my favorite cartoon. After my father gave me a birthstone ring, I thought I was Hercules with a ring of power. I went down the stairs to zap someone, a friend of my parents. She hit me hard, and I went upstairs crying. I've told this to the psychiatrist, but they don't say anything. They just like to hear me talk.

I found out from my parents that I had got very ill from Penicillin when I was six months old. I was allergic to it. I asked because I was trying to understand why I was always thin.

The doctors said I wasn't abused. I had delusions I was raped by my father, but he was just giving me a hard back rub. He abused me, yelling in the car everywhere we went, in shopping centers. He'd be drinking and get off on it. He was an alcoholic and so was my mother. She used to scold me; she held grudges and was proud to hold a grudge.

My room was a mess even after my mother died. My father wanted me to learn to keep my room clean on my own, without teaching me. Six months after my first breakdown, my mother died from cancer.

I have a lot of anger because I couldn't talk till three, because my sisters controlled my life, because my parents were alcoholic. I didn't get mother's and father's care when I needed it. I was a third child. I didn't get love, never got touched. I was supposed to be independent. I had no one to care for me—the typical genius-neurotic problem. When I was fourteen, my mother tried to make it up to me.

Only my first doctor suggested my parents were abusive. He treated me by putting me on Mellaril and shots of Prolixin. My sexual energy was lowered by the Mellaril; it makes you impotent. The doctor taught me it was OK to dislike my father, and tried to get me off pot.

A week ago I went in to Maryland General and was able to relax. I had seen the pills on my desk and thought I would take them. I went to the Emergency Room and told this nurse.

They changed my diagnosis from schizo-affective manic disorder to undifferentiated schizophrenia. I'm glad because it sounds less complicated. I don't need a fancy place with a lot of professional people, just an inexpensive hospital where I can relax, have a meeting once a day.

June 1990 [*dictated*]

Travel to the distant
Realms of the imagination
I have embarked upon; led
me this once to a frame
of the mind's eye, still
Enchanted with the primal
Squall hushing a Canadian
Meadow where I stood
Thinking equally silent,
About the mornings I spent
Alone and those I
spent with you.
I travel again there
And the place lurks
Like it's overgrown with
Glaciers, but you know
How adventuresome
A spirit can be.

by Bruce L. Whitcomb

BRUCE WHITCOMB'S STORY

I was homeless for about seven years. When I first came to Baltimore, I lived well. I had a nice apartment on St. Paul Street and supported myself, working for my step-father. But I couldn't afford the rent. I had to work too many hours a day, and it was a crazy schedule. I couldn't stay there without my step-father lending me money constantly. I became a street person not because of that, but in spite of that. I moved out, took to the streets.

When I became homeless I learned to like it, staying at the missions, staying at friend's houses, at churches—I got more experience. I became attached to the life.

I had some hard times; there were people who would have something against me. You know how people can be when they're out of work and don't have much money—they feel like robbing somebody twenty-four hours a day. They ask for money, they ask for this and that. They may become "pal and pal," and "buddy, buddy." Pretty soon you're having a disagreement. At first, I kept my distance by trying to be devout and law abiding. Eventually I found out that was a mistake.

I got better and better at living out on the street. You'd know the best place to go during the day, in any city. I got more calm going to a church, learning how to break into a church and sleep there, or sleep there when it was open. I found out how to spend my time, who not to associate with, who not to ask for a cigarette.

I used to travel to different cities. In terms of the business aspect, the institutions and establishment, there's no difference at all between them— the same thing is happening. But for each city there was a particular mood, atmosphere, rhythm I got into. I like Baltimore—I've been here the longest. It has a changing rhythm.

In between towns, I often had a hard time getting any female company whatsoever. Most of it consisted of flirting, sparse encounters. If a woman offers me a ride—I usually wait for what comes around to come around. Most of my female friends I've found in town.

One time, I was down and out near the border of Pennsylvania. I was losing a girlfriend in the city at the time, and trying to get my mind off things by hitchhiking. I saw a car in a gas station and something about it attracted me—a 1979 Gremlin. It was cold and I wanted some sleep, so I got in the car and saw the keys in the ignition and that the gas tank was full. I took a chance and headed west, a natural instinct for me.

After a while, I got bleary eyed. I got a mental block that I was a bad person for having done this. The Bible talks about removing motes from your eye. I felt like I had a million motes in my eye. They were white, like white stars. I felt guilty and shameful. My driving was terrible. They finally caught me after I took a tank of gas without paying for it. I didn't hear any sirens so I thought I was safe. God had told me to stop the car and start hitchhiking before they found me, or run through the woods and hide. But the cops pulled me over and asked for my driver's license. It was a sinking feeling after all that fun I had.

For weeks, I was in jail in Garrett County, Maryland. The only time I enjoyed myself there was with a fellow who had a guitar and played Grand Funk Railroad. I got beaten up a couple of times. I'm not going to steal a car anymore, even though I've seen a lot of cars on the side of the road since then that I could have stolen.

One time, I stole shoes from a store in the county. The shoes I had were uncomfortable, wet from sloshing through puddles and mud. They arrested me right away, but dismissed the charges. They let me keep the shoes. I only take the things I need on the road.

The first time I was in a psychiatric hospital goes back to the 1970's when I was working, before I was homeless. I had a nervous breakdown from overwork at a lumber yard. I had had thirteen jobs in two years; I worked for Manpower repeatedly, getting temporary jobs. I kept going to job after job, and it got to me. My mind became disturbed. I couldn't think right, feel right. I started to hear voices in my head.

In the hospital they put me on drugs that are "reductive-reactive," a phrase I've coined. I had reactions to them, and they reduced my ability to cope, by causing so much reactions. I got used to the medication after a while. It's about the same when I'm not on the medication, but I'm more tempted to do something stupid without it—such as hiding when someone's knocking at the door, instead of answering. The medicine does take away the voices sufficiently, although I still hear them at times.

The doctors would give me different diagnoses. One said I had schizoid tendencies, another said I was a paranoid schizophrenic. They need their money, they have their operation. The doctors no longer ask me questions about how I'm feeling. They look me up on a file and just write the order for medication.

People just don't like to look at me because I look too conflicted. Nobody wants to deal with a hampered person. I don't think I'm crazy; I'm just nonconformist and sometimes anti-social. Without medication I can get mildly self-destructive at times. It doesn't last that long, about an hour.

I don't know why it happens. I think it has something to do with my environment as a kid, growing up in different environments, leading me to look for something that wasn't there. I've lived in Illinois, California and Maryland. I remember only four things in Illinois. One of them was going through a corn field, seeing a tractor and being terrified of being run over. I was a well-behaved kid until I was eighteen years old. The tantrums may have been an offshoot of learning how to smoke pot and drink beer.

If pressed to reflect, I would say a combination of factors led to my breakdown: too much drugs and too much work. I took drugs because I could afford them, and they were prevalent at the time. I liked to get high; I was a "California kid." But the real cause, I believe, was trouble with the opposite sex. I had an "obsessive compulsive syndrome" with females, even while I was still a virgin. I was very troubled why they didn't pay any attention to me.

I didn't have a nervous breakdown, I just started to hear voices. They were obnoxious, insulting, like "You're no good" and allusions to my sex life. They said things that would make anyone's anger flare up. The voice itself was a "translucent acoustical sound within a sound." I would hear the whining of wheels on a forklift, and sub-sounds would occur at points within the whine. The voices were high pitched, but frustratingly complacent and calm. The provoked me to anger. At first, I controlled my anger and did the natural thing, which was to escape. Sometimes I would yell and destroy my things.

When I discovered that the voices were a negative occurrence, making me unhappy, I quit my job. I think the voices came from sexual frustration—my lack of experience with the opposite sex—and evil spirits. The voices sounded evil. I start talking with them sometimes because there's nobody to keep company with. Loneliness is a function of it.

I'm a Sagittarius, a born wanderer. We have to travel or die. When I get tired of seeing the same street corners, I get up and about and leave. Usually it's in the spring, but sometimes it's the dead of winter. Once in 1986, I hopped on a train, and like a fool I didn't notice that the boxcar had a closed door. I was weary and getting bleary eyed that cold February night. I became heartbroken because I knew it would be trouble; it would be hard to hang onto that ladder. Twenty five or thirty minutes later I became tired. I had a black-out of some kind, and my foot slipped underneath the ledge of the boxcar to one of the couplings underneath the chassis. My foot got scrunched for what seemed like a good amount of time—I was screaming.

When I came to, I was out of there and still holding on. It was miraculous I didn't fall. I held on tighter to the edge of the train, hopping around to the ladder, praying for the train to slow down. It did. I got off, hobbled to a gas station and was rushed to a hospital.

I had three operations on the foot. It took a long while to heal as I kept tearing off the cast. I wanted to be normal again. It got infected and my step-father tried to have me committed. But the doctor said I wasn't crazy, just irresponsible.

I can walk OK now. The only time it gives me pain is when I hit it against something. I tried to hop a train once when I went out west this last time, but I couldn't catch up with it.

In 1987 I tried to go out west to the Pacific Northwest. But I petered out. I got more and more uneasy the closer I got to the coast. I started to have flashbacks of my life, real clear and crystallized.

When I'm on the road, I read the Bible constantly. Sometimes I'd read it to cars in a mock gesture for not picking me up. I felt like a spiritual vagabond, or a recluse, but I knew that God was taking care of me. Supposedly, God lives in a blue room in heaven, but I don't think he's up or down or any direction. I don't attach any name ideas to him; it's an intangible, unfathomable spirit that I believe in. I think God wants to be liked.

I'm a man, but sometimes I believe I'm a spirit, possibly belonging to another universe. If I lost all the weight I have on me, I would see what I actually look like as a spirit. I've never experienced the other world, but only the idea of it.

I argue with God a lot about material things. I'd rather eat in a Deli or a gourmet shop than have a crust of cheese sandwich picked off the road. Life on the road is hard enough, but the food is vicious. Often, I'd look up in the sky; God would see me and know what was on my mind. If I get mad at God, I don't bother to look straight up until I get to the next town. For miles and miles I'd look around at low hills and tall trees; sometimes it would get dull.

At times I stare up at the sun, or if I'm inside, at lights. Everyone says something different about it, but it has the same effect: it bothers people. It's a fidgety, nervous habit; my eyes are constantly darting about.

I stopped becoming homeless when a person named Mark took me in. It was almost by force; he wanted a chess partner.

I used to ask, "Are you happy or you're married?" Now I've got my own apartment with my wife. I never thought I would ever get married. When I did, I was mad at myself for saying I do. She had proposed to me, and I wanted to see what it was like. We were together for several months, before she left me for an old boyfriend. Now she's back with me again.

My profession is art. I'm working on a bird picture right now: two sandpipers on a beach—they're short-billed dowhichers. I started drawing birds when I first moved to Maryland. My dad had gotten me interested in bird life; he was a bird watcher from a long time ago. Once we were working on a scientific project at the Patuxent Research Center, conducting a census of birds in tracts of wooded areas where there were considered to be fluctuating populations. We took a census of the last of the virgin forests in Maryland—100 acres of really tall trees.

Years ago, with my father I took a trip to the Bahamas to watch birds. I saw a Mangrove Coo-coo, like a yellow-bellied Coo-coo, but bigger and more slouched looking—it had a very retiring way about it. I had to listen to it for a long time before I finally found it. I was deep in the woods, and stared out at it through binoculars. It almost floored me, how beautiful it was. I took a picture of it.

It feels good being off medicines now; it's a much lighter feeling in the solar plexus, the origin of my good feelings. I feel like I'm more myself now. I don't have to worry about the drowsiness in my head, the motor reactions in my mouth—basically feeling under the weather. And I don't have to worry about buying it, listening to a doctor tell me to come in at a certain time. I think that any changes in my body's chemistry should could from internal changes, not external ones. I feel cheap when I'm taking it; I feel sick that I would have to be propagated by a man-made chemical to feel natural.

Expressing myself by writing is helping me, making me feel part of the community rather than like a vagabond, hanging around in ditches, the byways of America. Art is an outlet for emotions, for energy, to do one's own thing. It's better than pursuing the wind—that's what I've been doing all my life. I've been searching for Utopia, whatever Plato wanted.

May 7, 1990 [*dictated*]

KNOWLEDGE

Joy's light for my
Bosom, yet flickering
And billowing much
As the spring
Bulrushes taunt forever
The sad, papery wind.
Know not the season,

Or her uninvited Majesty
Be rather keen
To the sea, from which
Not one wave that
Goeth forth, lingers
Unto the voyage back.

by Bruce Whitcomb

I long to see a hillside
    To see the sun glint through the dirt
       by a stream

To walk out of the gray wooden walls
    stand alone,
    with hillsides and mountains
       all around me

cold air
    in my nose
in total darkness

by Jean Levinthal

THE RAFT

Truly a vacumned feeling about
Little pebbles of disarray: The unarmed man
Slow winter of regret
No niceties. Just cold.

I cannot live this way in the drone of the low morn.
I cannot spare the blood, the draining of the vein.
True life is toasty and on its heels.
It is brushed and swept and clean.
Suddenly the mountain ranges and we have peaked again.
We then smile.

Oh, how we feel the glad and with the spoil all gone
But the raft, the raft,
Does it come in again?

by John Travis

II. Invisibility

Medical Civilization tends to turn pain into a technical matter and thereby deprives suffering of its inherent personal meaning. The new experience that has replaced dignified suffering is artificially prolonged, opaque, depersonalized maintenance. Increasingly, pain-killing turns people into unfeeling spectators of their own decaying selves.

Medical Nemesis, *by Ivan Illich*

"You mean you don't want to see me, is that it?"

"Oh, it's not that. While you're in here I get a feeling that it isn't really you at all. And it isn't, is it? It's you sick. It's you sort of suspended—you know what I mean, suspended animation.

The Doctor is Sick, *by Anthony Burgess*

Due to the drug, I was completely invisible.

by Jack

41

MICHAEL P.'S STORY

PART ONE

My story is crying out to be told. Nobody as far as I know has experienced a dissociative state for four years. This "condition" I *suffer* from began in the Spring semester 1986 of my third year of college. After habitual drug use over a two year period, I suddenly stopped using. I went through a withdrawal—somehow my drug use had caused a dependency on T.H.C. Without the drug in my system I began to experience severe anxiety, stress and hyper-tension. I began to "dissociate" from my self; I lost sense of self—I lost touch with my consciousness. . . .

The stress was so much that I couldn't cope with it. My conscious mind retreated and I began to feel *unreal*. My environment became unreal. . . . This caused me immense pain and suffering which has continued until today, February 23, 1990.

When the condition continued unrelieved, I sought professional help, and eventually I ended up in Sheppard Pratt. Once in the hospital, my condition worsened quickly. I dissociated to the point where I became suicidal and desperate. Other symptoms appeared. I stayed for almost a year until I eloped. . . .

On one hand, the hospital was partially to blame for how sick I am—I was involuntary committed and forced to stay a year and a half. Before I went in I was at least functioning, but when I came out I was sicker. On the other hand, they've offered me treatment for four years now, even after my insurance ran out.

Once out, I began to use THC again with hopes of returning the drug to my system and "reassociating." This failed, but there was some relief from the unbearable PAIN.

More hospitalizations continued until I made a serious suicide attempt in February of '88. This sent me back to the hospital for a stay of seventeen months. More suicide attempts in and out of the hospital . . . hanging, cutting, asphyxiation, etc.

Dissociation is hard to describe. You don't feel like you exist, you don't even feel like you're sitting here. You feel like your body is here, and that your mind is gone—nowhere. Although I'm dissociated from my body, it's really the only thing I'm experiencing. Everything I experience is physical. I'm so stressed out that parts of my body hurt constantly. It's mental pain, but I feel it in my body. My mind is not there, so the pain is not in my mind.

Dissociation makes me want to end my life, because it's so painful. It cuts me off from enjoying things in life. I had clinical depression to begin with and that's a lot of pain, but dissociation is like a constant blanket of pain. It's like the pain after you've been depressed for a year, and you're sitting in the middle of the desert—it's 120 degrees—and you have no food and water, and you're going to be there for a week, with no chance of anybody coming to get you. No needs can be met: you can't have sex, you can't have friends, you can't feel close—everything's pain. You're cut off from the human experience. No matter what anyone does, they can't reach you. It's like you don't exist, you're a non-person. Sometimes I try to reach out of it.

I'm the invisible man, there's no doubt about it. When I'm alone, I don't feel like I exist, unless someone is looking directly at me, or talking to me. Either I feel intensely self-conscious, like everyone's staring at me, because I'm a freak, I'm bizarre. Or on the other hand, no one can see me—I'm invisible. At home, I feel I'm unreal, the world's unreal. The only thing that's real is the pain.

The doctors think it's a form of depression, since a lot of people complain of the same symptoms with severe depression. They complain of not being real, but I know it's a lot more than that. These symptoms as I know are not understood—the physical pain, and my vision where things in my environment appear unreal, weird, ugly.

I get a different response from the doctors, but what I'm saying is so vague. There's no way I can be sure they understand me. Some say I'm totally off base and am not dissociated, and some say I am. A big part of my ailment is the belief I have that this illness is undocumented and completely misunderstood by the professionals. There is no mention in any diagnostic manual of an illness that results from the THC use where you end up in a permanently dissociated state.

They tried all the medications on me: the antidepressants, the antipsychotics But none have helped.

When I'm in the hospital, I take the antidepressants, just to cooperate with the staff. I've been labeled before as a resistant, non-compliant patient. Now I try to do what they say whenever I can, although there have been times when I've refused medication, shock treatments, tests and talking to my doctor. I can remember being intimidated and having privileges withheld if I didn't take Prozac or whatever. I've been almost Med-Paneled before, but they weren't able to force me to take the medication or ECT's for some reason.

It's strange how the medicines seem to help some people—yet most of the schizophrenics and manics complain about the meds hurting them. But the doctors swear by the meds. Maybe it's because they are actually powerless over some illnesses, yet they think they're doing something by forcing meds on us. . . .

Psychiatry really is an inexact science, but the staff and doctors won't tell you that. They're convinced that they know everything that will ever be known on the topic of mental illness. They won't listen to me when I tell them that my illness is rare and undocumented, so their diagnoses and treatments are pretty useless.

I was recently discharged from Sheppard on July 2, 1989. Stays in Halfway Houses were unhelpful. This chaotic lifestyle of eviction and homelessness has continued until now. . . .

PART TWO

I say a "bong" killed me. My present doctor says my childhood killed me. But she's wrong. By "bong" I mean a water pipe, used for smoking pot. It took about 1,000 hits to make me sufficiently dependent on pot, so that once I withdrew, I dissociated. I used to smoke pot with my dad, my brother and my friends—everybody smoked. "Oh, I would not feel so all alone. Oh, everybody must get stoned." (Bob Dylan)

Once my dad moved out of the house, my mother treated me pretty badly. She yelled at me, she asked me if I was gay. She told me to get out of the house. So now I just hang out and try not to suffer so intensely all the time.

Everywhere I go, I feel I make people uncomfortable and make them feel I'm strange. They want to understand why I'm ruining their experience. "People are strange when you're a stranger." (Jim Morrison) It's a terrible torment just to walk down the street, just to see people living. To see girls is a special torment; I can't have them ever again. The other day a friend of mine slit her throat because her doctor refused to see her anymore. They put her back in the hospital. That's where I belong, in a hospital, so far away.

I spend a lot of time watching TV, about 80% of my waking time. TV is real, realer than life to me. I feel closer to the cast of Cheers and to David Letterman than I do to my closest friends. TV is the reality of my life. It's the only thing in my life that stayed the same before and after the dissociation. TV stayed unreal, it was always unreal. Yet weirdly, TV has become more real to me—because the rest of my life has become so unreal. The last ten days of my life, the only thing I've been concerned about is getting cable so I can get more channels. I've been more concerned about that than being around real people. I'd rather have good TV than companionship, sometimes.

Recently, I got an apartment with *At Jacob's Well*, an organization that provides supervised housing for people in need. Before, I was living one of my endless series of little rooms in the city. It was just a room, but it was cheap and crummy. I had no company and was lonely. I was forced to get out and do things when I was there.

Here I can move around because I've got more room, but I don't get out as much. I'm sitting in a room that could be an apartment in the suburbs. There's lots of food because once a month we can get $50 worth of groceries for two dollars. Everything's taken care of—the heat and electricity. All you have to do is come up with $125 a month.

My TV is hooked up to cable, about forty channels. I don't watch TV all the time because I want to—I don't feel like I have that much choice. I don't feel I can have a life outside the house. I tend to retreat in the house and stay there. I'm just killing time till one of the stray bullets in the neighborhood catches me. I'm not kidding. The other day, a truck overturned nearby and there were gun shots fired. We're living in the DMZ around here. Recently, I was assaulted during the day by three adolescents.

The dissociative illness I have encourages me to stay in my room, because the world has become a painful and unreal place for me. It is easier to retreat to my four walls and a TV screen and try to escape into a movie.

*   *   *

There are fleeting moments of hope when I think if only they would try something different, some new therapy or treatment, like hypnosis—maybe then I could reassociate. . . . Getting well feels impossible with an illness no one even knows about. The therapists were only taught the pat responses. When they hear something new, they can't come up with their own response.

My only hope is that I'll die soon and it will have some meaning to me and others. It probably won't. I have no hope of getting better . . . only suffering less.

Luckily, I finally found someone who wants to help and doesn't want to be paid. I hope what I end up writing is presented in a clear way so people will get some idea what has happened to me. . . . Maybe some record of me and my "Illness" will help give meaning to my wasted life. . . .

February 23, 1990

Do you know what it is like to go mad
Fading in and out of reality
Not remembering the memories you've had
One minute you're there, one minute you're not
It's not as if you're a fatality
You're body lingers on to rot
Do you know what it's like to be lost
The fog in your mind covers your eyes
And the tears that tear through the body are the cost
But you see I don't feel all that sad
It's a beautiful world in all those lies
Do you know what it's like to be mad?
Do you know what it's like to see yourself
    disappearing
And the labels they've stuck on you can't
    keep you around
All those who seem to help are only learning
While I build a guilty mound
That will be my burial ground
Do you know if it's better to be dead or mad?
Do you know

by Lynn

THE MADWOMAN

her art is grief
her chalk-white face
streaked with mascara
her sobs keep time
with the day-hall clock
as she crawls
from wall to wall
of solitary
shrieking
her anger never subsides
her twisted mind & body
scattered like wind-driven leaves
she wails
wrings her hands
rocks to and fro
crooning her song of pain
she makes an art of madness
wears rags to express
her spiritual poverty
paints her clown-face
with too many colours
one day she will
beat her brains out
on the concrete floor
until then she is anathema
even to the hospital priest
who blesses the
twisted crazy
in fall she sits
in a pile of leaves
and the leaves like her mind
are withered and strewn
    withered and strewn

by Theodora Snyder

JACK'S STORY

In November of 1988 I was on a trip to New Haven, Connecticut to help do a workshop at a National Conference of the Mental Health Association. One night I couldn't sleep, having forgotten to bring my medication. Thoughts from my first hospitalization, fourteen years before, started to arise. That period of over-medication, I had always regarded as a kind of a blank. I had always been concerned about how destructive the medication was to me, the discontinuity it introduced in my life, and how I had to begin things all over.

I had never before examined the thoughts that would have told me what my predicament was. So that night, I wrote them down on scrap paper. In the hospital I had been suffering on the drug and was trying to point this out to staff. I complained that I was tired, gaining weight, and having great difficulty walking. They told me it wasn't the drug, which further induced feelings of despair. Something was happening to me, and no one was noticing it. It was scary. Whatever thoughts I had about what was happening to me were invalidated by the people I tried to talk to. *I was invisible.*

That summer, before my hospitalization I had an unexpected experience which altered the course of my life. In Casteneda's work it was termed as "Stopping the World." It occurred in the presence of a few friends, one of whom was a woman named Susan, who I met the night before.

Visually, the experience was as if a strong light had been turned on in the room—which was dark. It was early evening—midsummer—and I thought that someone had opened the door in the dark room and the light had come in. Within a few minutes I was deep into a trance state. I was aware of the sound of people talking, yet my attention was drawn to this experience of incredible depth and sensuousness, of a flowing and milky type of energy. It had substance to it, transcending the ordinary boundaries of my body. I felt unbounded by my body; I was merging into this energy. It was as if something came up from beneath me—everything physical seemed to be transcended by this metaphysical substance. I was looking down at the ground and was virtually immobile for a long time. It felt very good.

Between this point and my hospitalization, I became increasingly unable to function because my attention was always being drawn inward. The intense experience began spontaneous changes in me. Initially, I spent five days trying to ignore it and to rebuild. On the fifth day, a kind of a flashback occurred in which I recalled an image, a vivid recollection of Susan, whom I met the night before. With all the intensity of the sensory experience, I saw her. Thus began a fearful and anxious period with her, the insecurities of any love relationship, magnified by my intense experience. It was the first time I was in love with anyone.

The experience began to catch up to me, and I became increasingly withdrawn. My mind was becoming filled with unfamiliar images and ideas—sometimes frightening, sometimes sublime.

The turning point that summer occurred when my mother asked me if I wanted to go into the hospital. I answered yes, and in saying this I was admitting the fact that I no longer believed I could manage my life. We were sitting on the front porch when the conversation occurred, after an embarrassing incident in which I ran out of the house with nothing but a towel on. I did this to stop some unbearable sensations of melting, which psychiatrists might call "tactile hallucinations."

Periodically, ever since I had "stopped the world," I had what I referred to as "melting." Something inside me was dissolving in a way I could not stop. To control it I usually took a cold shower, four or five times a day, or as many times as necessary. I knew I wasn't actually dissolving, but that I was being opened to energies from the outside. I was *sensitized* and unprotected from energy I would normally be protected from. The cold shower would work but only temporarily.

All that summer, the melting had gotten worse. One time, the shower didn't work, and upon coming out, I was seized by the strongest feeling of dissolving that I had yet had. I grabbed a towel and ran outside. I knew that running on concrete in the alley with barefeet would ground me and regain my solidity. It did, but I was left exhausted, realizing that this couldn't go on.

The previous week, my father had taken me to see a psychiatrist who prescribed medication for me. The day after the intense "melting," we had an appointment with the Chief of Psychiatry at Sinai Hospital. At that meeting it was discussed whether I should go into the hospital. I didn't feel anyone was pushing me in, but except for my mother's original query, no one seemed to be very interested in what I thought.

My "streaking" incident was brought up—streaking was big then—and labeled by the doctor as a "psychiatric condition." I said it had something to do with the medication I had taken the night before. At the time I tried to blame the medication and avoid the issues at hand. I still believe, however, that the medication intensified the dissolution. It was denied that the medication was any part of the problem. I was concerned that my "streaking" was going to be considered without regard for whether I had a good reason to do so. The doctor asked about the incident, but not about why I did it, or if I was, I didn't feel comfortable talking about it. Given the fact that I was being told I had a "psychiatric condition," I was alarmed enough to be guarded about what I would talk about. I knew that they were going to act on that idea and I was afraid of what they might do, given the control and power they had.

I was trapped between my own inability to manage my own life, and those whom I couldn't trust—the psychiatrists. When they told me, in the assertive fashion: "We know what it is, it's a psychiatric condition," I felt intimidated, alarmed and scared. I was a lot more scared of that, than of the original problem—*that* I understood, although I couldn't help myself with it.

After the "stopping the world," I felt a loosening up of tension. The body armor that had made me distant and afraid was breaking down. Usually my body and muscles were tensed, keeping my feelings guarded and protecting me from painful feelings. The "melting," as I understood it, was not only a result of the release of subconscious feelings but a breakdown of my usual means of protecting myself from awareness outside my normal range of consciousness. I used the word "connection" at the time: I was making connections between formerly repressed feelings and my place in the outer world.

At the meeting with the Chief of Psychiatry, it was decided that I should be hospitalized. I was in agreement. The first three weeks were beneficial and helpful, and I have to this day good memories of it. I had no more of the "melting," and no more "voices" which had occurred some weeks prior. I also began to regain a sense of ease and trust with people, and made good friends among the patients.

One afternoon I was sitting on my bed in my room. In my consciousness came a clear intrusion that said to me, *He will make one mistake that he will regret the rest of his life.* I hesitate to call it a voice, but it was clearly worded. The question I have asked since then was: was it an entity distinct from me—which I tend to believe now—or was it my subconscious talking to me? It caused me some alarm, a lot of anxiety. Was it a mistake that I was there, or was I doing something wrong in the hospital? The voice highlighted my fear, which I had learned to suppress, that some tragedy would befall me. I was always a perfectionist. I didn't like to make mistakes, and that trait was intensified in this period.

There was one thing I knew, without question, however: whatever had happened that summer was something very valuable to me, and which I knew I had wanted my entire life. I must protect it above all else.

Three weeks into the hospitalization, I was in my room when the psychiatrist walked in and explained he was prescribing medication. The first thing I said was, "They are very powerful drugs." He said, "Yes, they are." I said, "What do they do for you?" He said, "They're like a *thought-straightener.*" Not knowing what a thought-straightener was, I went to a nurse. She said, "It helps calm the inner turmoil." Not feeling I needed that, I went to a second nurse. With an angry look on her face she said, "Come over here." She quickly read a description of the drug from a medical book whose jargon I had no hope of understanding and snapped the book shut. "Now, do you understand?" she asked. At that point I knew whether it was good or bad, I was going to have to decide on my own.

After I took the drug the first time, I began to realize as the clock ticked by, that I was loosing my ability to think. I tried to sit down and decide whether I should really take this. I said, "This stuff feels like hell," but then I said, "This is the stuff that's supposed to help me." It really alarmed me that it was taking away my ability to think independently and critically for myself. As it grew stronger in my body, I felt I was being overwhelmed by something, that I was losing control.

I decided not to take it and spit it out. Unfortunately, this decision that was forced upon me placed me in a position where I could no longer *trust.* I was back to square one. I didn't think people were deliberately persecuting me. They believed that this drug was supposed to be helping me. I was also aware that they were not open minded, particularly about the value I placed on my own prior experiences. I was fearful of having something taken away from me, based on someone else's thinking. I questioned their right to determine what was real.

Not taking the drug and having to hide gave me back the sense of isolation, insecurity and fear that I came into the hospital with. It reached a point where I felt I had to have a reliable and authoritative answer to my dilemma. I looked for the answer in myself and I found one: to give in. It was at least the answer to the anxiety I had. Whether the voice I had that told me I was making a mistake was "psychotic" or not, I now consider it to be right. It was, in fact, the authoritative answer I had been looking for.

On Friday, after four weeks in the hospital, and after spitting out the meds for a week, I finally got in touch with the lady I loved. I had not yet made any attempt to contact her since I entered the hospital. With the encouragement of another patient, I mustered the courage to call her.

When she answered the phone I was struck with fear and shock. The conversation—which I repeated for many years in my mind—went like this: She said, "Hello." "Susan, how are you?" She said, "Fine, how are you?" "Fine." She said, "By the way, who is this?" I said, "It's me, Jack." "Oh . . . it's you," she said, "It doesn't sound like you're very happy to hear from me." She said, "Can you think of a good reason why I should be?" "It doesn't sound like you want to see me." "Can you think of a good reason why I should?" After some hesitation, she added, "Why don't you just come and see me?" I said, "I'm in a hospital." She said, "What did you do to yourself?" "I'm in a psychiatric ward." "What did they put you in there for?" I told her, "I went a little crazy with my parents." (Which was true; I even took as swing at my father.) She said, "Ahhh. . ." in mock sympathy. Then she said, "What do you want me to do?" "You could come and visit me," I said. "No, I don't think I could do that," she said. At that point I was ready to crawl away from there. She ended by saying, "When you get out, give me a call."

When I finally took the Haldol later that night, it must have been a "suicidal gesture." I knew it was destructive. It was like jumping off a bridge, after being rejected by a woman.

After a week of spitting out this drug and having the fear that the staff would discover it, I admitted to Dr. L., who was actually a third year medical student, that I wasn't taking it. He had been planning to double my medicine. I finally agreed to take it. The bottom had fallen out and I felt I needed something. They were confidant this would help me; there was no doubt in their mind whatsoever. I was unrealistically hopeful that this pig in a poke—buying something you couldn't see—was going to work for me.

The doctor left the room to go to the medicine closet, and for the second time, this intrusion on my consciousness told me, *You are making a big mistake*. I was too afraid and anxious to change my mind about the drug, because I would have to put up with his pressure. I didn't realize that I was strong enough to say no.

I don't remember much about what happened after that night because I was so drugged. For years and years until this past February, I had no real feelings associated with those experiences. When I was on the medication, what I thought were real feelings were in fact panic, alarm and confusion created by the drug. I also felt a sense of disorientation about myself and my life. I was very intimidated by all those around me and no longer talked with my friends. I moved very slow because the drug slowed down all my neurological and motor skills. I had great difficulty with coordination, and had anxiety that felt like an itch under my skin. I couldn't sit still; I had to constantly keep moving because if I stayed still I would become too aware of this discomfort. It occupied my thoughts all the time.

I consistently appealed to Doctor B., the resident psychiatrist who replaced the medical student, by telling him that something was wrong.

He denied that the drug was doing it. Once, I approached him in the hallway and asked, "Why am I always so tired?" Smiling, he pointed to his head and said, "It's all up here." Another time I said, "The side effects of this drug are killing me." "Blurry Vision?" he asked. *Blurry vision*, I thought. *Is this guy real?* The doctor murmured, "There are a lot of possibilities for how slow you are moving, but the medication is way down the list."

That statement in itself was a shock to me. It made me despair even more, and I had difficulty getting out of my mind for years. After all my encounters with psychiatrists since this time, they still don't recognize many effects these drugs have. They don't understand that the person they are dealing with is a drugged one.

The most painful part of the entire experience was not the drug itself, but the complete aloneness I had amidst a hospital full of patients and staff. It was as if something happened to me that absorbed all of my energy, mind, body and spirit, as if some tremendous disaster was happening around me, and those around me did not recognize it at all. Due to the drug, *I was completely invisible.*

In the hospital I would try to convince people to let me out. Once a week I would call my father and ask, "Can I leave the hospital and come home?" He would say, "Ask the doctor what he thinks." When I asked the doctor, he said I had to have a social life, a family life and a job. "That's the criteria for being released," he said. It was astonishing to me that he would say this—some patients did get jobs while still in the hospital. But I knew that was impossible for me. I had a job and social life before I went in, but now I didn't. I think he was saying it to pressure me.

There was however one small act of defiance: it was one evening—movie night—and without any idea why, I began to practice sitting still, something that was impossible without great discipline. I was succeeding for perhaps ten or fifteen minutes, when my former doctor happened to visit. He explained that he had come up to see how I was doing. Silence. I remained immobile. Then I muttered without looking at him, "Fine." I remember feeling sadness, something unusual for those weeks. It was unusual to have felt anything at all.

In early December, after a long two months of stunned confusion and immobilization, Dr. B. said, "We can sit here until February." This got a reaction from me so intense with dread that I was capable of spontaneous animation very rare in the drugged state. "You would do that?" I said.

Finally, with no more consistency or rationality than had occurred with anything else, I was told I would be going home for Christmas. They thought it would be "good for me."

Although I was relieved, I knew my real problems would begin again at home. And there I felt, waiting for me was nothing. I had lost the girl, and I was so drugged that I was changed for life. Whatever symptoms or confusion I had, whatever was "wrong" with me that people were trying to change was gone, I guess, but so was what I loved and longed for most in my life. But I would be able to attempt to continue what I had sought that summer, to build a new life.

It took me over three years to find the meaning that summer and fall had for me. My "symptoms" were actually the result of the profound but authentic change of personhood that I was undergoing. My apparent disintegration was primarily a result of my increasing preoccupation with these changes, and my inabilities to deal with the fears and anxieties I had surrounding them. The change of personhood I was undergoing was hardly complete and was the result of the need to reorder myself both within and without.

One Sunday morning in February 1990 when I woke up thinking about this hospitalization, I uncovered feelings of sadness that I had never felt before. I understood these feelings to have been present at the time of my hospitalization and that I hadn't been able to feel because of the drug. The sadness had to do with letting myself be intimidated and not choosing what I really wanted. Several times, remembering the formerly unconscious thought, I repeated with tears, "Oh, Lord, what have I done?"

For a while, all of it was put completely behind me. Then suddenly similar changes took place: a heightened self-awareness, acute perceptual improvement, "flight of ideas." Medication was once again prescribed. I rebelled, the melting began to return, and so I consented. Much of the subsequent time has been spent balancing my need for the open awareness of my mind and the need to use the medication to help control it.

In the intervening sixteen years, I have needed to enlist the professional help that would secure for me that foundation. Those who helped in professional capacities, although indispensible, have been very consistent with perpetuating the original problem—being unable or unwilling to recognize the validity of my need to build something new on that summer's experiences. After sixteen years, vis-à-vis every professional I've been to, some very capable, I have essentially the same fears and feelings of threat, and discordant notions of my health, my life, and rights as I had then. I am much stronger in part because of their help, but I am aware of how easily what I have worked for could be taken away. Those who have suffered the same or similar condition have picked up where professionals left off.

August 7, 1990 [*dictated*]

ARRIVAL

The dream fades
For a few seconds . . . or minutes . . . or hours. . . .
I hover in the unemotional limbo that fills
    the void
Between unconsciousness and reality.
Slowly I slide further and further away
Until I can no longer touch the peaceful world that
    cradled me for an eternity
Or maybe only an instant.
I reach out to grasp for it,
To try to bring it back,

But it is gone.

I am vaguely aware of waiting
    Waiting for what?
I wonder.
It is my first thought of the day.

Before I can open my eyes, the answer to my
    question comes washing over me, like an angry
    wave, forcing me to sink down. . .
                down. . .

Until the mighty force has settled,
And all that remains is the lonely stillness

Of despair.

Anonymous

Chinese idiom meaning
"the wail of disembodied spirits
calling for sacrifices
to be made to them."

Light Dim

Dread of Confucius

Light silver

          15 miles Nothing

Inside their eyes
Moon move Came here from
Lute wood come from steep mtn
No jade but here ghosts of dead
Approach

                by Josie Kostritsky

[Josie's biography:]

1955. Ten years welding ships, Sparrow Point.
Pools of Steel. Five years medicated in nut houses
and Electro Shock. Continuous study of Void and Soul.
In moments of despair, things come to me. Again angels.
Driving cross country to Grandmother on West Coast.
Now to write these things to you, 1991.

[*Editor's Note*: The following are excerpts from a book titled *Abstracts and Relevancies* by Millie May Wicklund. It includes poem-like descriptions of canvases and autobiographical experiences from the hospital. The paintings focus around colors and remain undrawn.]

> *I want to talk about white, the white I am, and the dark-complexioned three—my magi. For am I not the uncontrollable mystery on the floor? Insanity describing this self to myself, again and again.*

BECAUSE IT'S SATURDAY

The second time I signed myself into a mental institution, I encountered the bureaucracy. I was, to my way of thinking, no longer that sick to be in a Closed Ward. My psychiatrist had told me I would be in for fifteen days, and it was well into the fourth week that I was still in a Closed Ward.

On Friday, when all the doctors and nurses meet to decide who goes home for a visitt and who goes over to the Open Building, my psychiatrist said I could go over to the Open Building. I was so elated, but found quickly there were no available beds, and I would have to wait.

When Saturday came, I was sure I would be allowed to go over to the building, but the day wore on, and no one spoke to me about going over to an Open Ward. Everyone in the Closed Ward was edgy and argumentative. Some patients had been weeping hysterically, and some also had outbursts of temper, and fear. One elderly lady played with herself, and the attendants had to keep telling her not to.

Another woman, who had just been admitted that night by the police, swore a stream of blue language, saying she didn't deserve to be in a place like that and that she wanted to get out, or at least be sent over to the Open Ward.

Then, just before dinner, someone was passing out chocolate candy, and a diabetic woman, confined to a wheel chair, suddenly lurched from her chair. She grabbed the box of candy and shoved several pieces into her mouth. Someone called the attendants, and they took the candy away from her and told her she couldn't have candy because of her condition. The attendants left, and she began to sob and rant, "I'm not going to get anything to eat! I'm hungry, I didn't get anything to eat!" I saw her problem and told her that dinner had not been served yet, and that she along with us would be fed at four thirty.

She calmed down and apologized to all of us, but then she began to scream about money and said that her family was trying to get all her money. We didn't pay any attention to her, and she forgot her pain when dinner was called.

So my nerves were really bad, even more so than usual. I wanted desperately to be out of there, where things were calmer.

I saw the male attendant who was in charge of the ward that night—in the corridor, talking—flirting with one of the nurses. It was early in the evening, and I thought I would ask him if I could go over to the Open Ward now. He looked at me with great condescension, and without stopping his conversation, said, "No." I asked him why. He answered with a wide and gratuitous smile, and sarcasm in his voice, "Because it's Saturday."

I didn't want to explode in anger and release my fury—as I didn't want to be sent to the Isolation Room. All I did was walk away, thoroughly unbelieving and amazed that such insensitivity could be in a mental hospital, like in the outside world.

Finally, Sunday morning came and I asked the head nurse—one who was decent and conscientious—if there were any beds now. She called up right that minute, found out they had one, and let me go over to the Open Ward.

A stage appearing with the curtain drawn. There were lights, kiegel and frenels, behind the curtain. A figure loomed behind the drawn curtain. The back stage lighting created a shadow growing from the figure. The shadow had a stage presence—as if a real actress, or actor. There was an aura around the figure. At first, the shadow was friendly, a tremendous figure of awe and respect, but then the figure seemed a vague patch of dark, an unapproachable truth, an unpaintable subject—the black, its haloed darkness, a too elusive modern color.

MOTHER'S HUG (Way Back Now)

The first time I came home from the mental institution, I had been confined for forty days. I went to visit my family for a weekend. I remember the first step into fresh air, then into my house. Both were exhilarating experiences. The first smell of the outside world out the door of the Open Ward was of grass, flowers, trees, streets and skies—I was immediately aware of being allowed to be in *open*, large spaces of the civilized, normal world again. The freedom I felt then must be the freedom you get from the reality of normalcy. It flees from me constantly.

My sister, Claire, had picked me up, taking a half hour off work early to do this. We drove carefully, but rapidly to my house, where my mother was waiting for us. When I stepped through the door into the kitchen, I immediately hugged her, and she hugged me back. The embrace seemed to last for an eternity, but that was because of the attendant emotion, an intense moment, one of those intimate mother/daughter moments. I had never really been affectionate toward my mother, nor she toward me. Maybe, the build-up of emotion from this lapse of emotion makes that hug seem so right, so poignant, so memorable and so eternal. But I knew then what it meant to be a daughter, and with my mother gone now, I feel emotion-poor, impoverished.

> *White sea wave. Light ebbing as if the sea. Light, so complete and tidal, it seemed the sea. But then, I looked again, and saw it was light. I also saw a tan foreground, and thought it was a beach, but it's the canvas again, and the night is just coming on, seemed no menace. Maybe, this is the solitude, which is the origin of the creative process.*

INSTITUTE LIVING

(On entering the Institute of Living; Hartford Connecticut 1972)

— No longer trusted or had Faith in myself; Empathy was non-existent.

— The first step was to find someone to *trust*. I could not truly trust anything—-that is Hell, a Labyrinth, a Pit.

— I chose to believe in the power of a place with unspoken rules, a place in my mind that had magical characters with magical powers, where communion with Good and Evil were manifest in the Nature of Life.

by Melinda

US AND·THEM

by Dorothy Newlin Lear

It's beginning the adjustment to locked doors
and broken hearts that causes the wound
to bleed more profusely while a "sweet"
little lady *wings* along with a badge on
her chest offering a band-aid.

We found ourselves more than lost to the
world we knew. Here is where we become one.
We are of our own race. Laughter is an echo
that mocks all of us in this place.
The gun shot, the doors closed—their keys
were evil. We wanted to break the windows
and scream.

There on the telephone is one of Us. She's
crying to mother. There in the hallway is one
of Us. He's looking for stars. There
in the pool room is one of Us. She's
trying at her ambition. What happened?
Humiliation never ends. We're joined as one
to restore what dignity we had left.
We talked among ourselves for we knew
they (them) were nothing but a "battle
of words." They played games with our
heads . . . warping the truth.

We are all one identity—All labels of
psychiatric technicians. In their office
which I refer to as "the void," a few boxes,
pills, remains of sharp objects one might want
to use, and three "mental" health workers getting
ready for med-time. We went there to
"The void" out of desperation. We needed
something! There we stood on the edge
of a line; suspended like crows on
a telephone wire, the staff—they
watched us sip our poisons and then
smiled—the bit of comfort we could find.

I is you. Us is not them. Eye meets
eye with an invisible but felt
compassion. "What are you doing here?"
We are equal here; all of Us with
our suffering and suggested diagnosis
Walking through the walls, through the
faces we have found each other.
And here is where the strength is.
Are you wearing armor among Us?
They have their battle plan—they
are to be fought—not Us.

I found my window alone; so did you,
but we looked separately, not knowing
how to breath. We all tried running
straight through somehow, but their
demented authority killed our ambition.
Don't you know those bars were there
to protect the world; not Us!?

Authority languishes in control while
they rattled their keys down the hall.
Don't you know how little they are
affected? They sometimes reached out to us
in times of need but again, only to offer
a band-aid for our bleeding souls.
In desperation we clung to a few who
had soft faces but it would be sure
that they, too, would turn their back on Us.

We have lost our freedom. See the papers,
the files and eyes that were nothing
but printed pages of book after book
of Psychology. Do you see a real heart
anywhere, really, but among Us?

We were caught committing the sin of being
young and ignorant. The bitter old man
hates the spontaneity of a child—
We responded with natural attitudes.
"Sir if you're going to be a brick wall. . .
I'm going to throw stones."

At night we dream of running again.
We were programmed to forget the beauty
we knew. We had lost ourselves in
our own shadows and were taught, may
I say bluntly, brainwashed to trust
the darkness of mind dissection

Therapy. We let them probe our very souls
with their intellectual needles. They
incestuously smiled. We were what they
called "Crazy" and this they taught Us.
They called for Us like animals when it
was time to take a pill. The poison we
took numbed our mind so we'd forget beauty.
They woke us up to pills, sent Us to bed
with pills. We'd forget the beauty of natural
sleep and remember all the pains of the past.

The spaceship landed out in the front yard.
They came to take Us away from here.
But we couldn't reach them. There at the
window, we wept. And we watched the
rain fall. We read the Rubiayat and
we read it with *power*. But we were
alone and no one could hear Us. They
put us in seclusion, too many times.
But we accepted it in ourselves
for a time. But then it got too dark,
too quiet, too cold, too still, and we
screamed until we could scream no more.
We pounded on the window but they
wouldn't let us out. Finally, we got
to go to the toilet and they watched.
Then we couldn't go and they said
we had lied to get out. But once
one of Us, we smiled through the window
and made the rest of Us feel better.
An eye was watching in the corner but
we were afraid and closed it.

We were one total family and they, they
were subversive minds subtly
forgetting their humanity. Then—they were
paid to care. They wrote Us in
books and records in computers that
will last forever. We learned how to
play the game; how to get the hell
out of there somehow. We stopped
telling them what we were thinking
and how we felt.

Finally we were determined to be a success.
It's still Us and Them; isn't it?

I am fading away once again
Will I disappear into nothing?
Am I nothing to begin with?
I mutter my swearing and go on.

Will I become mad?
Will I commit suicide?
I wait for a breeze
Something refreshing to come.

God is punishing me
I must hide
I am a piece of dust
In the wind blowing to nowhere
Melting in the heat.
I will simply wait for kindness. . . .

Mark Miller

ANONYMOUS

Do not ask.
Where have all the flowers gone?
We flourish still in cities
and in towns. . .

In private and hidden gardens
where decades sound. . . ..

So do not ask.
Why we pass unknown. . . .
It is enough that we blaze
though alone.

We have visions
beyond acceptable beliefs. . .
that won't kneel down before
the common griefs.
And when we pass we take
our treasures home
to a Heaven made especially
for Unknowns.

by Paula

DON SHACK'S STORY

As recollected by Kay Homer, June 3, 1990

Don possessed many rare and worthwhile gifts . . . deep sensitivity to humanity, a sincere understanding of the joy and pain of living. He was a poet, a song writer and a lover of music. He attempted a career in business, but was never able to integrate himself into it. Don died of an overdose of his antidepressant medication on August 14, 1986.

When I first met Don at Sheppard Pratt he felt isolated, very alone . . . nothingness. He was afraid to reach out to anyone around him. There was definitely a lot of shame. He talked about his family minimally; he didn't want to deal with them. I don't know what happened.

He had been hospitalized some years before when he was fifteen or sixteen, and spent a lot of time at Sheppard Pratt; he even got his high school diploma there. Don felt he didn't measure up to expectations. He was not a typical, white male with a nine to five job. In fact, he did a lot of night work. He could become easily dependent on the hospital. He felt the expectations there were less demanding than the outside world.

Ten or twelve years later he was hospitalized a second time at Sheppard where I met him. After being laid off from his job, he had taken an overdose of Valium. He was angry that he didn't die. They didn't know that he had insurance, so he was placed at Spring Grove, a state hospital. He hadn't known a place so awful, he said.

At Sheppard Pratt he took antidepressants, but said he really didn't feel that different on medicine. He could sleep better and eat better, but his state of mind wasn't affected.

During the hospitalization he must have gotten some type of hope, for he reformed his plans. He took a volunteer job at Sinai hospital, which he really liked. He got his driver's license. He reached out to people, and I was one of them.

I would write a poem and give it to him, then he would write a poem back. He had written before, but never shared it. He never talked about it, but would just give it to me and say, "I wrote this after going through a difficult time." His writing was often in response to a desire to get close to someone, as he felt afraid and anxious about it.

He was there for a month and half, and as he was Jewish, he got hooked up with Jewish services. They got him a supervised apartment where he lived with a guy with similar problems. He was feeling real good when he was released.

What changed was that he decided to live with a woman friend. He knew at that point he'd have to work for money, and he got an accounting job. A friend told me he felt discouraged at the job; he didn't meet expectations. He felt overwhelmed. There was no note; he overdosed on the antidepressants.

"Only the artists can help the poor learn again to feel."
(Pete Hammel, 1974)

SOMEONE'S SCREAMING, BUT THERE IS NO SOUND

By Don Shack

Someone's screaming, but there is no sound.
Flames of fury which blaze within the innermost soul,
extinguished by reality.

A night with no darkness,
like a grain of sand trapped in time,
on the beaches of reality.

A sunrise with no morning.
Castles built of dreams,
which are washed away by the flow of reality.

A love with no regret,
awash on a tempestuous sea of reality.
Crying, but not with tears.
Scared, but there are no fears.
Getting older, but not in years.
Could it be that no one hears?

And as the end draws near,
Listen hard, and I think you'll hear
someone screaming. Is it you?

So take my hand and follow me,
and as we drift across that stormy sea,
maybe we'll lose reality.

And if we don't,
we'll both wake up in the morning.
So stop screaming—now I can hear you.

But, can I reach you?

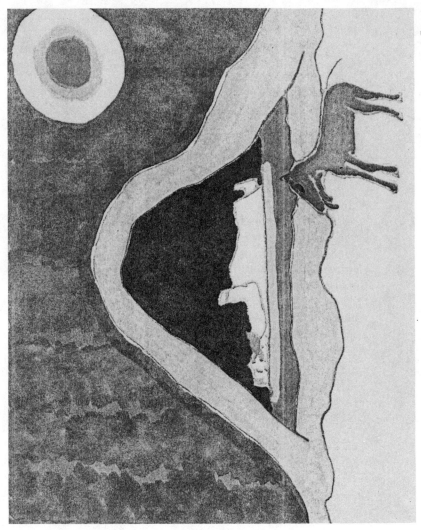

Irene

SOUL

Soul is guts. Down deep where no one is allowed. Down deep where there is room for one more.

Screeching horn, soft sax. The smell of clean wash.

Yes is no, and no forever never.

Hands. Oh those hands. They touch.
Who do they touch? Where do they touch? They must reach.
Very high, very low. There is no difference. A body to touch, to reach.

Warmth
Understanding
Music
Pain

LAUGHTER

from the depths of
sorrow and insanity.

Those hands race double-time to feel the beginning of it all

The sounds echo up into the clean air, arc and descend in a rush of feelings to touch the skin, mantle of prayer.

H E A T   &   V I B R A T I O N

Arms enclosed
legs support a shiver
hands clutch, ever so softly

OH GOD, WHERE IS MY MUSIC?

by Irene

TIM MILLS' STORY

I was born in rural Virginia. My grandfather was a farmer, my father was one of twelve children. My parents grew up with the value of the work ethic. They were straightforward, moral, supportive and concerned parents. Early on, I showed a lot of aptitude and potential: standardized testing showed me placing in the top five percent nationally. I had an awareness of the quality of life, of the real fullness of life. Most would consider, like myself, that I had a normal, happy childhood.

I was precocious, a "Peck's bad boy," a kid that's set about his own way, getting into trouble on occasion. I saw myself as way above average in intelligence, in capabilities, and also not too desirous to exercise my full potential. Compared to those who strove for average successes, I was above average without making any effort. I slid through. In some things that I had an interest in, like English, I excelled. But generally, if something didn't personally appeal to me, even though objectively it should have, I didn't give it any regard.

My parents' business influenced me a lot. They moved four of their five kids into a grocery store/service station and house with a cabin motel property. That was my home as I knew it. It was a normal thing to see my parents at work downstairs, meeting the public day to day. That had a lot of implications for my life, mostly good and some bad. For one thing, I became gregarious and outgoing by consistently meeting the public during the course of the day. My personal insight into judging people's character became heightened. When I grew up, I worked in the store, handled charge accounts for groceries, decided whether or not to cash a check.

A bad implication of the store was exposure to peer pressure on a day to day basis. My peers would stop by the store to get gas and would invite me along on their way to go drinking, taking drugs, and so on. It wasn't like they would have to seek me out; I had a lot more exposure than someone stuck at home. So I gave into that, and it caused a lot of problems. It seems I thought, not so much consciously, "Hey, I've got it made. I'll live off the fat of the land and take advantage of my position, have a good time." I didn't look at the long-term consequences of irresponsibility. That led right to problems later on; it created a pattern within myself—giving in to the frequent temptation to be irresponsible. In the same way, I became a drug user too, pretty heavily so.

At various points throughout my teen years, I left home, and then came back, until I was twenty. Then my grandmother died, in 1972. We were a close-knit family. My grandfather on my mother's side had left his family, and my grandmother had taken care of my mother, her brother, and sister. When my parents got into the grocery store business, they gave my grandmother her own separate motel efficiency, beside the store. They provided it for free and gave her groceries. She worked too, volunteering her help in the store with my parents.

I was the only child of the five who was situationally able to care for her. She had degenerated physically a year before her death so that she wasn't able to take care of her needs at all. She had to be lifted up out of her bed and fed like a baby. Day to day I provided her intensive care. She had dissociated mentally in her senility during the last couple months, calling to her dead sister and speaking to her as if she were alive. She was seventy-eight when she passed on in 1972.

The trauma had built itself into me to the point that after she died at home, that same day I became catatonic. I went into one of the bedrooms in the house, laid down and stopped moving. I went into this thought separation. Within myself, religious-type questioning went on—the existence of a deity or not, whether absolutes existed or not. I got lost in realms of thought. Looking back, I see it was the only coping mechanism I was able to effect, rather than exercising the proper mechanisms of grieving and mourning. It was in separating from the reality of her death, not admitting it to myself, that I created another world in my mind that would separate me from the trauma. Grieving and mourning would have admitted that she was dead.

I was catatonic for a couple days during the first spell. At that point my brother carried me down the stairs of the house, put me in the family car and took me to the local Fredericksburg hospital. They gave me a massive muscular injection of Haldol which brought me out of the catatonia and back to reality.

But I put myself back in catatonia, still avoiding reality. In the course of a couple years there were several episodes of intense catatonia, lasting three to five days each. I was even fed intravenously, becoming malnourished since I did not eat. What I did was to build up a block that Haldol couldn't supercede. They tried whatever dosages they could, but I put up enough "system block" that I wouldn't allow it to have its effect. I preferred to remain away from reality that much.

My parents ended up putting me in a private psychiatric hospital in Richmond, a fifty-five mile drive south. This place was well renowned, run by doctors who were eminent in the Richmond community. I was in the middle of one of my catatonic states and was brought out of it after a couple days. They put me in a locked room and strapped me on a table, even though I was near comatose, in case I woke up and got violent. They were doing it for their protection and mine. During every period of catatonia I was aware of everything happening around me. I can almost repeat conversations that were said to me.

I went through a couple dozen hospitalizations from 1972 to 1985. Initially, the catatonia appeared from 1973-75. During this time of hospitalization I met Linda, also an in-patient, who became my wife. She was in the hospital for alcohol abuse and psychological problems. She was a pretty girl, highly intelligent, with curly blond hair; at one point she was the Richmond Tobacco Queen. We got married after about a year of our relationship.

Linda's parents were Jewish and she was adopted. Her parents hadn't told her that until she was eighteen. Her father was a pharmacist. Her mother was a depressed type, suicidal, and had made numerous attempts on her own life. She kept a pretty bad house; they had show type dogs, and they let the dogs do anything and everything in the house. They were almost ruined by the dogs in the house.

Her grandmother was a spiteful personality who chased Linda around the house during her childhood, beating her with a broom, spitting on her. Linda seemed normally enough adjusted despite this, with a bright personality. She was twenty-six, five years older than me.

Overall, the relationship lasted seven years, but it was two marriages and two divorces. The first marriage lasted seven or eight months. The second marriage lasted almost two years. We separated again and divorced in 1981 and that was the final time we saw each other. During that time, I was admitted as an inpatient for various psychotic acting outs.

I was resistant to recognizing that my poor judgement had direct consequences. I refused to recognize the long term consequences of decisions I made. I set up antagonistic and confrontational interactions with people of authority in my life, the medical doctors, anybody exercising authority. A legal phrase, "show cause" defines my rebellious antagonism: why??— why such and such was needed, why couldn't things be the other way??

I didn't realize I was infringing on other people's right to peacefulness at times. For instance, my cousin in Fredericksburg worked in a new car dealership, selling Toyotas. I returned to Fredericksburg, indigent. I didn't stop to see my childhood friends but I visited my cousin at work. I told him I wanted to test drive a Toyota pickup, and show it to my girlfriend in the county. He gave me a writ, giving me permission. I drove it back to Richmond, where I lived, picked up all my possessions, and headed down to Mexico. I was fluent in Spanish and intended to live there. I had about twenty dollars, so I traded off my possessions wherever I stopped for gas or something to eat. I had things like hunting knives that service station guys would be interested in. I didn't stop that often to eat, mainly a coffee-type subsistence—with an occasional order of fries.

I met a fellow from Stark County, Florida, who was hitchhiking and heading for a job that he had heard about in New Mexico. When I told him I was going to Mexico, he said, "Hell, I'm at loose ends. I'll go along too." We got to be riding buddies that way. He'd drive for a while, and I'd sleep out back; and then I'd drive while he slept. We crossed the border and headed for Acapulco. I had been there in 1974 on a vacation with my brother and his girlfriend. I had met two Spanish sisters who were vacationing there from Mexico City. They were to be our reference point.

We headed to Acapulco first, to see what the beaches were like. On the way we ran into the Mexican militia, an army stopping point. We were smoking pot at the time. The soldiers started to pick out tiny, minuscule pieces of marijuana caught in the rug of the car. They were going to put us into jail to rot for that, they told us. I had some girlie magazines, so I offered them to the soldiers as a bribe. They kept us around for a few minutes, looking at the magazines, and then casually waved us on.

We got to Mexico City and I got work at an auto electronic repair shop. These people really liked an American who could speak fluent Spanish and talk some slang. I had the life of Riley; neither one of us did much work, and for practically nothing we were fed pork sandwiches and beer. They were passing us 100 pesos notes by the handful just for us being around. American workers like us were an attraction for customers to come.

One day, one of the local cops came by. It was a Wild West mentality there; he had an unlocked pistol holster. He asked about the pickup truck, and wanted to take it on a test drive. Oh no, I thought, maybe the police have got this figured. He'll take the truck and slap us in jail. It turned out he just wanted to take a "joy ride" in the truck. He brought it back with a full tank of gas. Almost every day he'd come back after driving it for a half hour and return with a full tank of gas.

I loaned the pickup in exchange for an old Harley police bike with a new friend, and hit the Mexico City streets with that Harley. It was like I had free reign. We never did find the two sisters we were looking for; but we found three other sisters, about our age, and had a good time.

My friend had a Harley Davidson back in Florida, and I wanted to get rid of the pickup. My act was a felony. We made a deal: I'd carry him in the pickup back to Florida; he'd keep the pickup and pawn it off. He would give me the bike.

We headed back, but we got stopped in Dutch Gap, Alabama, heading east toward Florida. We tried to get gas from a nighttime clerk who didn't want to barter. He said he'd have to call the manager. Well, the manager called the police on his way in. They came and saw the truck was listed as stolen, but I wasn't listed as the stealer. My cousin didn't know I had stolen it particularly. I told him that I was transporting a new vehicle for a company. It didn't wash because the truck was listed as stolen. So, they put us in a hundred year old jail in Dutch Gap; it was a rotten, nasty, overcrowded place. They let the other guy go, and kept me there for extradition to Virginia. They asked if I wanted to fight to waive it. "No," I said. "I'd just as soon get back up there and get a better deal."

The deputies carried me back to Fredericksburg, and they found me not guilty by reason of insanity. Seven months passed however between the time they put me in jail and the time of the court hearing. I ended up spending it in solitary, too, because my psychological problems led me to advocating "gang block resistance" against the guards.

After the hearing I was remitted to one of the Virginia state hospitals. It was 1983 and my dad had passed away—it caused another flip back into unreality on my part. My family had come to the hospital to let me know my dad had died, and they discharged me that day. I went to the funeral. Afterwards, I left my mother's apartment and started hitchhiking through Pennsylvania, Maryland and Virginia. I worked for a carnival in Pennsylvania for a while and ended up in Baltimore. I was confronted by the police for acting out criminally. Instead of going to jail for the arrest, I was hospitalized for two years.

This time, I used the hospital as a stopping point to really dig inside myself. Instead of using it for confrontational interaction with doctors, I gave myself over to internal investigation, the heaviest I ever had, and probably ever will do. It continued after I was discharged.

Once discharged, I weaned myself from prescribed medication from a full dosage to zero, over the course of a year. I made sure I replaced it with something inside my character and made myself consistently self-responsible. For the first time, I began appropriately exercising my natural abilities. Since that time I have been seen by two psychiatrists who agree I don't need any more medication. The medication had been providing a helpful crutch until that point. I replaced the medication with an assumption of responsibility for consequences, good or bad. Increasing my patience threshold was my sole responsibility. Now, I'm going to respond from the center that's within myself, not from the center that's directed at me.

I've been through the whole spectrum of psychiatric medications. The final medication on which I was released was Tegretol. I don't think medication or anything would have made any difference, except for my finally making the efforts. There's an old saying, "You can lead a horse to water, but you can't make him drink." You can't change peoples' mind for them. My mind was set on my life as it was without change toward responsibility. Until I made that change, made the effort, *nothing* would have counted.

In my new life I pursued a career-retraining course and successes have come from other efforts as well. I generated a consistent attitude of self-responsibility and acted on it. It led to speaking at seminars connected with the mental health field, as well as other speaking engagements. I served on the board of directors of human service organizations and worked as a mental health counselor. Now I lead an autonomous life, and am happy and fulfilled.

April 24, 1990 [*dictated*]

I feel a cruel, grueling wasteland wind
Again, suddenly uprising
As I'm on my destiny's trail.
That blustery breath of life's-force
which coddled me into the world
Now wants to enforce on me
A slackness to my sail.

And the muse's nod is directed at me
A favor wrought, a gift to see
And creation writhes again;
In the agony of growth, or growing agony?

Gratefully I would repose
In this sheltered den of calmness.
Forever a respite, a fortress,
Is escape to creativity unopposed.

Better to seek with never finding
Like the homeless, lost wind, ever-moving;
Than to find one's place of fulfillment of dreams
To be a success with screams inside.

Tim Mills 8/8/90

LINDA SAKS' STORY

As recollected by a friend, July 6, 1990

Linda expressed through her lifestyle the essence, perhaps even the romantic essence of a Bohemian soul, sometimes lost in her thoughts—at those times she wrote poetry. She painted in order to survive. Her creativity was not that of choice, but sustained her life until prospects of state hospitalization dimmed her vision and she jumped into the landscape outside her window. She threw out all the garbage, not just figuratively, until she left herself nothing but a lone rocking chair, her wall mural and some floor coverings. I brought her flowers fearing her demise; later her mom wrote me that she had given up on life.

Three or four months before Linda killed herself, she started throwing things out. It was the first time she had done this; she would throw things out in stages. She had been told by a family member that she would be put in a state hospital next time she had a breakdown. She usually went to Sheppard Pratt. I don't see them as any different—one is just as horrible as the next. Maybe Spring Grove is worse.

Her poetry was the way her mind worked, by free associations. It made sense to me, but I couldn't explain it. She painted too, oil portraits of her friends. She did murals—part abstract and part landscape—on the walls of her apartment, works in progress for a long time. The manager didn't seem to mind.

She never talked to me about her childhood. She didn't have many friends, three or four. She was flipped out some times. A few years before she died she had a "lover" who ended up marrying someone else. He was a recreation worker from the state hospital.

She suffered a lot of medication side effects. Once when she was lucid she said one of the doctors at the state hospital wanted to kill her. She said it like it was true; she really believed it.

I met her in 1974 at the Charles village House and she died around 1985. She was my first friend here in Baltimore. I had this thought that she had jumped out of her window. I came over with flowers. She left a message with the front desk, saying she was O.K. I knocked on her door, there was no answer. This was eight months before she died.

Linda disconnected her phone three months before her suicide. That's a red flag for suicides. After she died, I felt very lonely. I had prepared a gift basket for her; I was going to intervene. Then I got a note from her mother saying she had given up on life.

Her life was so painful to her that I thought she had lived longer than I would have, had I been her. She really suffered; she suffered most of the time. She had gone through so much pain before, I thought I could count on her not to kill herself. Her life and her death were a mystery.

[*dictated*]

APOCALYPSE

Morsals of the sun
Die in syncopation
While the sun goddess weeps her last song
The plague has begun
People in plastic bags heading toward the city dump.
I lock myself in my room
Waiting to die
My posters are tired now
A bush in a landscape winks at me
I gather up my cotton rags and silk for the
     long journey
We have used this one up
Discarding it like laundry
No one comes to clean.
My eyes are brown now
As the sun
Our only loved one is leaving us behind
Out in the cold, the roommate
Refused admittance moans over the phone.
Bemoan the landscape and the smoke from the
     factory rancid.
I have watched the faces wither into
The ocean like sugar melts into
Sand to specks lying no
Where in particular.

by Ken Girard

[*Editor's Note:* The author is forty-two and a native of the San Francisco Bay area. She has been diagnosed as a "paranoid schizophrenic," since the age of eighteen. She took degrees in the biological sciences and is currently employed as Program Director of the Marin Network of Mental Health Clients which operates a self-help, drop-in resource center. She also edits their quarterly newsletter *Hang Tough.*]

THE FAMILY GATHERING

Warping and distorting
they were waiting for me
as I entered the room
and the two Martian children
played on the floor.
Your smile grew until
it swallowed you
and I exclaimed in fear
"What's happening?!
Your mouth is as big
as your face!"
A silent shattering—
an inward surge of forces—
everyone got uneasy—
lost the beat—
which didn't help the fact
that space was flying by
at an alarming rate
and something funny
had happened to time.
Once more I had disrupted
the finely tuned game
they had spent their lives
perfecting—
not by crazy raving
or pulling down my pants
but by my Otherness.

by Cathy King

LADY SCHIZOPHRENIA

You are my real mother.
Your breast is filled with sweet poison milk.
I suck desperately to save my life.
I cannot live without you.
If I leave you for a moment
you destroy the world around me;
if I cling to you
your poison invades my body.
You are everywhere.
I have fought you, begged you,
bargained with you, flirted with you,
tried to be your friend,
and still my greatest dread has come to pass;
I have become you.

THE ANGELS OF MERCY
MEET LADY SCHIZOPHRENIA

We know you
and are not afraid.
We see you
among your masks
and we see your victim
though she cannot
see herself.
We will protect her
beneath our wings
and be light shining
through your dark veils.
We will let her choose—
something you have
never done.
We will lend our
eyes and ears
until she is
her own.
She will tame you.
You will let yourself
be chained
and she will go free.

by Cathy King

[*Editor's Note:* John is in his 80's, having spent almost all his life in mental institutions. He was the most hidden of the hidden—in a nursing home on a special ward for the mentally ill. He had not been known to speak during his fifteen year stay there. Anne, a recreation therapist, helped to draw him out of his inner world; she got him to draw and talk about his work. In April 1990, he was featured in an art opening at the BAUhouse in Baltimore, Maryland.]

Anne: Are you an Angel?
John: Yes I am

John: I'm drunk.
    Love does that to ya.

    John eats strawberries in the hospital that bleed all over his white
undershirt. He mumbles about pulling his head apart and being drunk and
crazy—getting kicked out of the Catholic Church by Dr. Malroony who
was drunk. "And YOU'RE drunk!" How his momma left him to go into
the Army. Left him when he was five, with his aunt. He punches himself
in the eye.

John: Straighten it out.
Anne: What out?
John: My head. That's what I do it for.
Anne: Knock your head against the wall? Does it work?
John: Yeah. Straightens it out.
Anne: Does it hurt?
John: No. It don't hurt.
    Can't talk. That's all.
    Books. Books in my throat.

John: I'm scared. I'm done for. I'm dead and gone.
Anne: When your death comes it will be very beautiful.
    You'll be like a little bird flying away.
    A little boat sailing away.

        Queen of horses
        Orange color hair.
        Face in front.
        Standing there.
        Picture in the picture.
        You ask what it is I'm telling ya.
        Leave me alone.

                    John

an army of small girls
  with brass knuckles
  is working to dam the rivers
of coffee in my basement
  Just as you have convinced me
that this pain is not my fault
    you insinuate that it is,
  as when I watch the otherwise
handsome young man on the bus
  snort, sniff, scratch, pull at his crotch
and adjust every article of clothing
    that fetters his person.
  looking very much like the souls
  locked in the day care ward
    waiting for a hot meal or the once
    monthly visit from a real doctor
who would initial some order
  for drugs and more drugs
maybe four or five prescriptions at time
    with no regard to a blood pressure reading
    already 80 over 60
  blaming the client as he faints
and kicking individuals out of the program
for not responding to therapy,
well after many years and reams of paper
  yards of canvass, college credits and even pay checks
you say "please don't be depressed,
    I can't deal with it"
  and look out the window
        as I kiss you

                    Martha Gatewood

D'S STORY

I went into Tyler Hospital on a voluntary basis. At age sixty-four, my life was falling apart; the depression that been chronic for most of my life was now acute. Sleeping was always difficult, anxiety was frequently present. I had lost control over my life—control over simple things like whether I would handle my correspondence or visit the sick in my parish. My marriage had been a half-life for years, the church was collapsing around my ears—mostly due to my own self-defeating decisions—and I was cutting myself off from almost all of my significant relationships. In retrospect, I could have done better with a long vacation and out-patient therapy, but at the time, I felt that the hospital was the only choice.

I stayed for seven weeks. Here are some impressions I have of those weeks, taken mostly verbatim from my journal. One recurring note present from the beginning was the sense of *hopelessness*.

After two days: "So far, this is a horrible experience—if I can not prevent it, they will make me into a mental patient. . . the walk, the talk, the line up for meds. How could they do this? Five hundred dollars a day to have us sit around for long periods of time. . .I am sick or screwed up, but there is nothing here to give me hope."

I had seen clearly that I needed help to get from *here* (the collapsing church, the failed marriage, the terrible sense of paralysis) to *there* (decisions about retirement, the marriage, and my future). No one helped me to see what Tyler could offer. There was so little activity, meaningful therapy, and so little interpretation of the process that I was left with a terrible sense of hopelessness. "Trust the system," I was told, but no one made very clear to me what the system was or how it contained the means or even the seeds of hope.

As I listened to other patients, I realized that they too shared this sense of hopelessness. . .this feeling of being caught in a world that could decide one's destiny and over which one would have no control.

I arrived on the unit on a Thursday; presumably it would be good for me to get settled before therapy would begin on Monday. A long, deadly dull weekend, a time with no activity, a time for constant second guessing—why did I come here? What will I do about the money? A lot of people around. . .the aides who wrote constantly in their books—that strange phenomenon I did not understand until the end. The PNC's, Psychiatric Nursing Counsellors, were the ones who were most closely in touch us. At first, I thought they were there for us, to talk with us, answer questions, even help us play Scrabble—since they played themselves— but they spent their time writing. . . .

I found out later that in a *for-profit hospital*, one of the major tasks is to justify to third party payees (mostly insurance companies) that the patient needed to be in the hospital.

Everything we did was recorded and interpreted by someone without a sense of humor, with little understanding. That first weekend I was watched as I endlessly paced up and down the halls. What else would a work-a-holic do? I was viewed as terribly anxious, even desperate.

My first roommate, a retired employee of the State of Maryland, worked for many years in the prison system. "Tyler is as bad as being in prison," I said one day. "Worse," was his reply. "The inmates would tear the place down if they had so little to do."

When I came to understand that the hospital was a *profit-making* venture I saw more clearly what was happening. I had thought that the hospital is supposed to be here for the patients, not the patients for the hospital. In fact the patients are there for the hospital. It is only in that way that the staff can make its living and the owners can make their profit. The first rule in such a hospital is to *make a profit*. The second rule, like unto the first, is *do not get sued*. The third priority is that the staff should not be inconvenienced. The counsellors and psychiatrists were never available except during scheduled times.

"How can therapy work here when I am so angry? Why should I trust them? And there are others who seem to be kept here long after they are ready to go home—they want to go—and don't get answers."

Monday, the third week: "I have really been down. No hope at any point outside, and no feeling that there is hope here."

Just when I began to feel a little better about being there, I was shot down with the news that I could not have a grounds pass. Apparently, they thought I was desperate and suicidal. I could only explain that it was due to their obsessive fear of being sued. I had never been suicidal, but I would make statements in jest (taboo at Tyler) that were taken down by the ubiquitous PNC's.

"Admittedly, I am influenced by the fact that so many others have the same complaints: boredom, inability to get answers, lack of hope in terms of treatment. . . ."

"So much energy is taken up with just fighting this place. My roommate was there to get his Lithium monitored and was frustrated by the fact that Dr. M. was unwilling to listen to him about his past experience over several years with the drug.

I know I am scared of being a mental patient—being caught in the system. The endless hours stretch out—I've read, dabbled in water colors, watched some TV, written some letters. . . ."

I feel intimidated by people who seem so good at being in the group. They've been in the hospital so often and done this so much that they can sit around like junior psychiatrists, making comments about body language, playing the "sir echo part," or giving sage advice. I remember D. a young school teacher, yet she had become a perpetual mental patient. "She is so full of her history, her hospitalizations, her symptoms, her medications—accompanied by shakings and tremblings—one has a feeling there is no D. there, just a patient."

March 25: "I am increasingly angry at Tyler. R. has been here ten days, still has not seen a therapist. . . . He feels he's about to lose his wife, who did not understand why he was in the hospital, was terribly burdened by having the baby, financial pressures and a religious context in which she believed that R.'s multi-personalities came from the devil. He has already lost his business. . . .

R.M. has been shaking like a leaf. She is here to get over an addiction to a prescribed drug she's been taking for several months. She's feeling neglected because Dr. M. was sick on Friday and does not come in over the weekend."

One Friday night I went to get a sleeping pill and was told it had been discontinued. No one had told me. That was a night of painful anxiety. On Saturday morning I asked about it and was told to check with the doctor on Monday. He couldn't be disturbed with a five minute phone call, but I could spend sleepless hours over the weekend.

On April 7, I wrote, "Angry as hell toward Tyler. $3,000 poorer, stigma of the mental patient and no better functioning than I was six weeks ago. "

P.'s experience in being dragged to the locked ward: "She had been increasingly suicidal and rebellious since Easter when she was deprived of her privileges. Eight to ten attendants, mostly men, descended upon her and she was taken to another ward. She is being treated with no dignity; where in hell is a caring psychiatrist? I feel I have watched the destruction of a human being." She was the one who gave me a copy of the ten rights of mental patients:

1. You have the right to remain silent.
2. You have the right to repress anger.
3. You have the right to be wrestled to the ground by eight to twelve men at any time.
4. You have the right to go bankrupt in the process of mental recovery.
5. You have the right to be tranquilized for inappropriate display of emotions (any loud emotion).

6. You have the right to speak with staff but good luck, charting comes first.

7. You have the right to be observed urinating or defecating by the staff.

8. You have the right to be strip-searched by staff request

9. You have the right to be herded to and from any activity.

10. You have the right to remain miserable.

> To your health,
> Welcome to your breakdown.

This is not to say that no good is done in a hospital like this one. It is not to say that there are no caring people; obviously there are many individuals who do care. It does, however, raise questions about the basic assumptions of the psychiatric hospital—in this case, the for-profit hospital.

July 12, 1990

ASYLUM

The air is smoke gray
thick, a cloud you can
see above the room.
It's a cloud present
in winter and spring,
in rain and shine.
They hide in it, their
faces wet with tears.
Take the hippie who calls
himself Satan—he hides
in the corner sipping
blood and sulking.
And there's the woman
named Mary with red hair
who sits above the cloud
performing miracles.
Beside her is Angel with
hair dyed dime-store blonde,
with a painted smile that

has become a fixture in
the room.
Of course, there are the
quiet ones like Goat and
Mouse, who never venture
past greyness.

On occasion, Angel flies
to the window to let in
wind, but even then, the
cloud hangs thick and
deliberate as Hippie's mane.
The faces remain lost in
the mass, while their
bodies hang limp beneath
the cloud like corpses from
a noose, swaying in the wind.

by Kathryn

WELL, THIS AIN'T THE ANSWER EITHER

I just cannot stand the thought
of spending one more hour
in this bland, sanitized-looking psychiatric unit
living amongst the other walking dead
who are too numb
or too out of touch
or too riddled with anxiety
to realize that they should lie down
when they are dead.
I don't know how
being in this get-away for tortured souls
which seems to be run by a burnt-out staff
(who possess the same degree I do
but considerably less understanding of me
than even I do)
and act openly hostile toward me
because I'm not responding
        to their latest/greatest treatment plan
        or standardized therapy technique
for major depressive fat ex-catholic recovering alcoholic addicts
        who are approaching thirty. . .
(and I'm sure our numbers are legion).
Or worse yet—
a mental health aide
who's fresh out of college/adolescence
and has one abnormal psych course under his belt
and sees in me
all sorts of neuroses beyond his wildest dreams
that he's only experienced vicariously through textbooks
Until now.

        And of course, jigsaw puzzles. . . .

There are a never ending barrage of jigsaw puzzles
which, at best, I've always hated to do.
It just makes me think:
What is the point?
And if I'm already thinking:
What is the point?
Then doing jigsaw puzzles only cause me to think it all the more.

Jesus Christ! They act as if I'm putting my life together
    (symbolically?)
when I succeed in fitting the minuscule fragments into place
to complete a picture
that I really have no interest in seeing
when all I'm doing
is doing it to get the damn thing done
so that I can break it apart
to put back in the box.
I mean—good god!—what is the point?
If I don't put the puzzles together to take them apart
so that someone else can put them together to take them apart
I'm accused of resisting treatment.
And let's not forget that I'm not socializing adequately.
Not socializing adequately? With whom?
Others, like myself, who seem unaware that they are
even crying?
Some have unwiped tears streaking their faces
    or glazing their eyes like ice.
So who shall I socialize with?
Others who want to share their newest suicide fantasy with me?
I barely have the incentive or energy to keep myself alive
no less trying to provide them with a reason
to carry on.
So who else is there?
Oh yes—my old friend from high school—
    another success story
who is left chemically lobotomized with Thorazine,
left stripped of his artistic ability
his outrageous sense of humor
stripped of his personality—
stripped of any personality.
Who else is there?
Maybe that sad-looking young woman I could talk with
last week, but today?
Well, today she doesn't seem to know—
    or care—
who I am/who she is.
You see, her grey matter was toasted just a little bit.
The psychiatrist figured if he jolted enough brain cells. . .
    short-circuited some synapses

it might make it more acceptable to her
that dear ol' dad fucked her at four years of age.
    It didn't work.
It seems she forgot everything
except that particular horror. . .
    And that's the one that hurts her the most.
What next, Doc?

It's just that it really makes me more anxious
to be in this goddamn camp for sorry cases
so I prefer to sit in my room and listen to music
which is something that has always soothed me naturally. . . .

except that I'm not socializing adequately. . .

so they take away my radio
and when we all line up
    at the nursing desk
like kids at a candy counter
I look in my goody bag
    and—behold!—
my tranquilizer has been increased
so I can calm down
and not feel so angry
that they took my radio away
so that I can't calm myself down on my own

And I can instead learn to socialize adequately
on tranquilizers. . .

Then we are all herded into the day room
where we can pace the floor
where we can pace the floor back and forth
looking as interested as goldfish trapped in bowl,
periodically checking the time on the wall
    for absolutely no reason.

I mean—good Lord!—what is the point?

                Grace Ann 1/9

The Evening Sun, Baltimore, November 2, 1983

DEATH OF HUGH RIVERS—
END OF FEARSOME STRUGGLE

"There is but one serious philosophic problem, and that is suicide. Judging whether life is or is not worth living amounts to answering the fundamental question of philosophy."

—Albert Camus
The Myth of Sisyphus

By Carl Schoettler
Evening Sun Staff

Hugh Rivers impressed people. He was tall and rangy with a booming, sonorous voice that filled the room. He was witty and intelligent. He had a degree in history and he had most of the credits he needed to finish law school.

He wanted to help people. He wanted to become an advocate for patients in mental hospitals. He was a valued friend. People believed Hugh's life had weight and worth and meaning.

They, in fact, valued his life far more than he did. Around noon one hot and humid day in late spring Hugh decided life was no longer worth the pain of living.

He wrapped a web Army belt around his neck and knotted the other end around a shower head in a washroom at Springfield Hospital Center. The belt left only superficial abrasions on his neck, but it cut off his breath and popped the tiny blood vessels in his eyes. And Hugh Francis Rivers, Jr. was dead a little after one o'clock in the afternoon of June 16.

He'd brought to an end a long, profoundly painful struggle that perhaps no one who has not been through an emotional breakdown can really comprehend. His sister thinks he fought and fought and fought and then just got tired. Caryl Rivers, a writer, composed a moving eulogy for her brother. She read it at his funeral:

"The measure of a life may not be in its accomplishments," she said, "but in the arithmetic of its playing out. For Hugh, that equation included a devastating illness, one that so often meant the dashing of his hopes, the unraveling of his dreams."

Hugh's illness was called "bipolar disorder" by one of the last doctors to examine him. "Mixed with mood incongruent psychotic features," Dr. Daniel F. Johnson said.

Other diagnoses called Hugh's illness "schizophrenic-affective." Hugh had, roughly speaking, what used to be called a manic-depressive personality.

In his psychiatric evaluation for the Social Security Administration, Johnson said that Hugh's symptoms included deep and psychotic depressions, periods of great elation and poor judgment, and periods of delusions of both grandeur and persecution.

Than meant that for the last dozen years life was horrendous for Hugh Rivers. When he was in the grip of delusion he could believe simultaneously that he was on the staff of the president and that the president wanted him killed—even that he *was* the president.

The world around him exploded with the signs and symbols of his delusion and his mind struggled to interpret them. He acquired the edgy, draining alertness of the point man in an infantry squad. When delusional, Hugh walked through life on tiptoe, taut, wary. The strain was as exhausting as the task of Sisyphus in hell.

Like the doomed Greek king, Hugh every day had to roll the huge stone of his illness up the steep hill of sanity only to have it come crashing down again and again as he brought it close to the summit.

In an article written for New Times magazine with Hugh's help, Caryl Rivers described a frightening delusion that took over her brother's life in the spring of 1974:

"Hugh begins to think he's directing a fearsome struggle between democracy and communism, a delusion pieced together in his head from a kaleidoscope of sources that included a novel by Allen Drury, an episode on Kojak, a Civil War book by Bruce Catton and *The Manchurian Candidate* by Richard Condon.

He absorbs sensation like some vast psychotic telescope scanning a universe of fears. *Everything* fuels his delusion: books, sounds, colors. He even believes his mother may be a Soviet agent. And, perhaps most awful of all, she begins to fear her son and at night bars her bedroom door against him.

Hugh starts to drive south because the Catton book indicates Southerners are his allies. Colors guide him. Gold means safety so he follows any gold-colored car or truck headed south. On road maps the red lines mean danger; black, safety: he only drives the black-line back roads.

He abandons his car somewhere in North Carolina and strikes out through a swamp. He hears helicopters and airplanes and concludes an air-land search is on. He believes the planes have metal detectors so he rips all the metal from his clothes, including the zipper from his pants.

He's convinced the songs of birds will lead him to safety. He stumbles on through the night and through the next day in the rugged back country.

At sundown he stumbles out of the swamp a frightening apparition. He knocks at a farmhouse door and collapses. Oddly enough, his delusion has saved him. The farmhouse door has a gold knocker."

Hugh's difficulties may have began as early as puberty when he lived with his family in Silver Spring. But he told a case manager at Springfield he first recognized a delusion in 1970 when he was in his last year of law school at George Washington University. He was married then to a woman from El Salvador and she was pregnant. After he was hospitalized, she divorced him and returned to El Salvador with their son.

And, until his death, delusion remained for Hugh a kind of horrible alternative reality. You have the sense of Hugh struggling to contain his delusions like a man packing sandbags into levee disintegrating as flood waters rise.

"But there were things he never lost in the struggle," his sister said at Hugh's funeral, "an ability to reach out to other people, and the sense that in an unjust and complacent world one must try to set things right."

Hugh's final effort to reach out from within his broken reality and help people was his work last winter on the Legislative Report of the Mental Health Association of Metropolitan Baltimore. The report outlined a lobbying effort and described a legislative platform of the association, including the "Bill of Rights" for mental patients.

Hugh helped compile the report and was credited as the editor. Then the job became too stressful.

Still the report was a tremendous achievement for a man who had to struggle awake every morning through a suffocating fog of psychiatric drugs, who feared that at any moment his uncontrollably obsessive delusions would rise out of some black hole at the end of his mind.

Hugh helped lobby for the Bill of Rights. The Maryland General Assembly approved it about a month after his death.

Since 1971, Hugh Rivers lived mostly in mental hospitals or halfway houses. For most of his last six months of his life he lived at St. Paul House, a three-story stonefront rowhouse just above North Avenue on the east side of St. Paul Street. It's a halfway house where about sixteen people recently discharged from a psychiatric hospital, live in a controlled and sheltered environment.

Almost everyone thought that Hugh had shown extraordinary strength in just getting from Springfield to the St. Paul House, and even more in staying there nearly six months.

He had been hospitalized almost continuously at Springfield for the preceding three years. He had been in and out of hospitals for twelve years. He seemed a candidate for the "back wards" of a mental hospital, a state more psychological than physical, where patients lapse into a kind of well-regulated storage. He may have thought that was the future he faced the day he opted for death.

Kathe Horton is director of St. Paul House. She's a brisk, direct young woman with curly hair and no makeup. She manages the halfway house from a basement office crammed with canned goods and mismatched Goodwill furniture.

"I'm a former resident. I've been on the board, and now I'm in charge," she said one afternoon a couple of weeks after Hugh's death.

Hugh arrived at St. Paul House Dec. 17, the day before his thirty-eighth birthday. He was dead almost exactly six months later.

"He was a real tall guy, lanky," Horton said. "He had a big, black, bushy mustache. Real black hair. Big feet. Big hands. Very striking physically. A very striking character walking through the neighborhood."

Often the staff people at St. Paul House just listen to the residents.

"To whatever they want to say," Horton said. "We try to help them with whatever problems they have. We concentrate on daily problems: Finding a job. Am I able to work? If I'm not able to work can I get Supplementary Social Security? Medicaid? Welfare? General Public Assistance? Unemployment? Social Security Disability? If they're turned down we try to help them get an appeal going."

Hugh applied for SSI, she said, and he was turned down.

"After being in hospitals for fifteen years," Horton snapped. "I think it'd been a least eight years since he held a full-time job."

The SSI denial notice is dated May 23, 1983. Hugh was already delusional again, and at St. Paul House they were thinking hard about sending him back to Springfield. The SSI notice has all the humanity of an automatic ice cube maker.

"You said you were unable to work because of a nervous condition. The medical evidence shows you have had a nervous condition for a number of years for which you have been hospitalized and treated many times."

"Recently, treatment has been more successful and you are able to think well, relate to other people, do daily chores and have a good memory. We realize that your nervous condition prevents you from doing you [sic] past job as an administrative assistant, but it does not prevent you from doing work with restrictions on stressful situations."

The crucial lines said, "It has been determined that your condition is not disabling and you do not meet the requirements for eligibility."

The letter seemed to be signed "D.O.C09."

Twenty-four days later, Hugh committed suicide.

Dr. Johnson in his evaluation of Hugh for SSI said, "I feel that if Mr. Rivers is able to remain out of institutional settings for a period of twelve to eighteen months he may very well be able to reenter the work force."

But at that time, the doctor said, Hugh's ability to return to work quickly was "very poor."

Hugh was unable to stay even six months out of an "institutional setting." And when he was turned down for SSI he was caught in a classic Catch-22 situation.

"You can't apply while you're in the hospital. And you can't appeal while you're in the hospital," Horton said. "So if he can't stay out of the hospital long enough to apply and appeal, how can he get SSI? What could he do?"

Kathe Horton explained what SSI meant to Hugh:

"Hugh had no money. He was dependent on the hospital to place him in the community and pay for him, and on his sister for spending money. And she contributed enormous amounts just to keep him going.

"He has no choice of where he lives if he has no money. He has to depend on the hospital to *want* to place him somewhere."

At the end of May when it became clear Hugh had to go back to Springfield, money became increasingly important. Springfield paid for Hugh's stay at St. Paul House out of what it called the adult foster care fund. The hospital had to decide if it wanted to spend more money on Hugh. St. Paul House needed the money to hold a space for Hugh, space that many, many other people could use.

"We said he would come back," Horton said, "but they said they didn't know if they could fund him again.

"A person who has SSI can choose where he lives," she said. "A person who has some money can make some choices about what to do with his life—not a lot but a few. And I think that's very important."

St. Paul House requires its residents to go some place and do something four hours a day. Hugh fulfilled that requirement less than half the time. Some days he just couldn't handle the burden of holding himself together to face the world.

He'd be down here and he'd talk and he'd be sympathetic and intelligent and in every way my peer," Horton said. "And the next day I'd have to tell him to shave and brush his teeth."

Hugh had a girlfriend who was also a resident at St. Paul House. He wanted to marry her. Staff members thought the relationship might be harmful, but they were ambiguous about what to do. Even the "mentally ill" have the right to companionship.

A log of Hugh's last few weeks at St. Paul House reads like the transcript of the flight recorder from an airplane crash: Hugh desperately fighting irresistible forces pulling him straight down.

On May 1 he lapsed into delusion for 45 minutes. The St. Paul House staff began to worry.

"When he was delusional the possibility for violence was definitely there," Horton said. "In a delusional state he was totally unpredictable.

"I got along particularly well with him," she said. "I enjoyed him a great deal. He was the kind of person I might have as a friend, when he was in good shape."

But when he was delusional he was big enough to be scary. He was six feet four inches tall and weighed 190 pounds.

By May 17 Hugh had been delusional for a week. He thought he failed a computer test he didn't take. He believed his girlfriend was dead. He said he killed a man. He was convinced the Allies' lost World War II. He threatened a resident and a staff member with his fists and then a stick. He picked up knife.

After fumbling through mental health agencies and clinics for six hours, Horton drove him back to Springfield. On the way Hugh had a kind of delusion: "Out of the blue he put a cigarette out in his hand."

By now the considerations were as much financial as medical or psychological.

"Somebody had to make some hard choices about where the money goes," Horton said. Technically, Springfield couldn't pay to hold Hugh's place at St. Paul House, to pay for him at two places at once.

Horton has fifteen men ready to move in. She can't hold the place without money.

"We're caught in the same trap as the hospital. We have to be fair to everybody, too."

But she did hold the bed two weeks, the absolute limit. Hugh came back for four days. "It was clear he wasn't ready," she said.

At St. Paul House they wanted him to enter a day-care program. He resisted because it would require him to change therapists. He agreed to return to Springfield. A note he wrote reminded him that he was not an emissary of the president, that the Axis did not win World War II—a note that was a pathetic amulet against delusion.

On June 15, he was back at the hospital. He was still in the admissions ward when he hanged himself on June 16. He gave no warning, his doctors and case manager said. He talked with his sister by telephone earlier in the day about his plans for the future.

"I don't know why," Horton said. "He could have been tired of fighting. He could have felt he lost his last chance."

Hugh was buried next to his parents at Gate of Heaven Cemetery in Silver Spring, no far from where he grew up.

A SPARK OF LIGHT

by Hugh Rivers
From *Street Images, 1987*

I was on the back wards of Springfield State Hospital and had little hope of getting out. One day, I made a bargain with God: Get me out of this place, and I'll do all I can for the rights of psychiatric patients. A spark of light lit up within me. The slow process began, of dragging myself out.

[*dictated*]

NEON

Light
All absorbing
Dissipating walls and floors transparent
    all that is of substance
Ethereal
Hell's total Light

Body and mind, soul
Dissolving in an ocean of Light all encompassing
    Without shape, color or variation of contrast
Tones bleached, Washed out in Air

There are no absolutes
Caught in the Lantern
You evaporate

Disappearing into Nirvana
A universal White.

by John Holton

HAZY RED/INSANITY

When I die you can plant my soul upon the sea
where swift knights charge in white armor
and then I'll dance with lovers tenderly
lost in rapturous tenderness forever.

Yesterday I saw a man swaying to a dream he never had
Alongside a woman whose love had made him mad
        and when sunset comes he swims in loneliness
        groping for the dead
Forgetting of the pain and bright lights in HAZY RED

How come the sun rises for some
and sets in wondrous beauty
and others nakedly lie in darkness
and toil through pain in forlorn cities

love must seek
and thrive to fall
but love for one's life must survival all.

I'll toil hard and fight the dead
but please help me through this night
so that pure white light does not turn to HAZY RED

by Kate

"We're trying to get you started again. Now shut up!" The voice throbbed with icy authority and I quieted and tried to contain the pain. I discovered now that my head was encircled by a piece of cold metal like an iron cap worth by the occupant of an electric chair. I tried unsuccessfully to struggle, to cry out. But the people were so remote, the pain so immediate.

The Invisible Man by Ralph Ellison

MY EXPERIENCE OF SHOCK TREATMENT

I have experienced shock treatments and think they are horrendous, and should be abolished. I had two series of them, and I never gave my consent to any of them. Although I went through eighteen treatments, I still remembered the problems that had put me in the hospital in the first place.

I needed to discuss and work out the problems that upset me and depressed me to the degree they did. Shooting electrical shocks through my brain did not help any; it only frightened and depressed me more. The reason the patient gets so depressed is that they do not see any answers to their problems. They need to be taught there are answers and solutions. After counseling I went on to teach music, direct a combo, and play professionally. I raised three children that went on to college and went to night college myself.

You're not crazy because you end up in the hospital in a state of depression that renders you unconscious, or unable to respond. You may very well be a very useful member of society, and capable of contributing a great deal to society.

By Carol

FROM AN EX-RESIDENT ON ST. PAUL STREET

Good Morning! Today is a hot, humid day in the city. Walking south through town I try to dodge the monoxide bullets coming out of Tin Lizzys. Churches and bars, bars and churches, I grope for a positive thought or feeling; living alone one has to create her or his own space. I would like to have self-esteem in abundance like a bird flocking to grab fodder and worms to secure a strong structure.

For the last thirteen years I have been on phenothiazine drugs in one form or another. Sometime I feel that this is good. Other times I express guilt and outrage because of the internal damage that these modern placedils cause to my body anatomy. I feel like its suffocating my brain from oxygen. It's putting a mask over my thoughts and feelings and prevents me from becoming fully aware, to live my life fully as a Christian.

by John L.

THE BLOOD BATH

Nighttime is like taking a bath
In a meal of blood,
Spaghetti and blood,
All those poor white bastards and me.

Well I'm black
But I get blacker in here.

In the daytime
They prop us up
Like sitting ducks
Before the T.V.

One night they bring in this poor white boy;
He sits down and just cries like a baby:
Then he gets up and drinks that orange juice
Like it's pouring out of a hole in his stomach.
A little white nurse comes in and holds his hand;
Then I give her a kiss with my black lips
And she jumps for joy.

Every morning they take Judy the Nuisance
"To have your hair done," they say.
She comes back on a pallet
Tongue hanging out
And sleeps for two hours;
She says, "I don't want no more
O dose shock treatments no more."
And "Gimme a cigarette," again and again.

They won't get me in there
Without a fight. . .
Sticking their needles into my brain.

But it gets harder to stay awake
(Every day those little pills)
It gets harder to kick up my heels.
Harder to get it up.

Robert Allen, Halifax, Nova Scotia

Marc Grabowski
Former Peace Corps Volunteer: West Africa
B.S. in Languages Georgetown U 1968
Legal Assistant Certificate, Community College of Baltimore, 1990
Seven times hospitalized
Nine times arrested (two convictions under dubious testimony)
Three years at Perkins hospital for the criminally insane
Homeless twice
Shot by police, wounded twice, for assault
    "with intent to murder"
Still kicking and alive

EXCERPTS FROM A LETTER FROM BALTIMORE CITY JAIL, JULY 20, 1985

Dear Mike,

When you saw me that morning, I was pretty far gone: I hadn't slept for at least forty-eight hours, and hadn't eaten much of anything. My hallucinations occupied practically all my time. They were about pornography (I've never been to a peep show), about the cameras, the booths, not naked ladies. I thought there was a movie projector in my closet, and I imagined that people involved in that were inside your apartment. Sometimes, even though the door adjoining our apartments was closed, I could see inside.

I started to tinker with your door to see inside better. The fact that the telephone line was broken was not because I wanted to prevent you from using the phone. I didn't recognize it for what it was, I was that screwed up. Scraping the door frame was just something to do—in fact, it was fun seeing the wood scraped off. I felt like a carpenter doing a good job.

I was toying with your door that morning, a very sick person, sick because I had been arrested in front of the VIP bar on Twenty-first street and charged with something that I didn't do. I say this unequivocally because it was my false arrest that precipitated this downturn in my mental health. The fact that my doctor had left and my relationship with Dorothy was not working out, were coincidental—they didn't make me feel good, but I would have been OK in the end.

The same pattern can be seen with my arrest at AMTRAK when I was falsely charged with "making gestures with a cup of stones . . . and striking a policeman in the stomach. . . ." A few days before that trial I went completely sick, and was taken to Maryland General. The same pattern was repeated when in March 1983 I was arrested and falsely accused of having an open knife stuck in a cardboard tube. It was a terrible experience to hear someone lie on the witness box. Not only did I feel outraged, but totally helpless. After the trial I started getting sick, cut myself and landed at North Charles General Hospital.

Back to the door—as I said I was toying with your door. I got occupied with feeling the blade of the screwdriver scrape the wood. It took away my hallucinations momentarily. I wasn't trying to break into your room. I was following the hallucinations, and there was nothing I could do about that on my own. Later, I broke the glass fire escape door to your apartment because I thought the place was being used by certain people for pornography operations. Initially, I saw something like a man in your room, but this faded away and I saw the beautiful sunlight and how still and calm it was inside. For a moment I was pleasantly awed, then satisfied, I went back to my room.

FROM PERKINS STATE HOSPITAL   SUMMER, 1985

I was doing what I could to forget the place, the dreary stinking hole I was in. For me that meant reading, occupying my mind, instead of pacing around the floor and staring at the ugly walls and dreary screened window. Perkins State Mental Hospital isn't a Club Mediterranean somewhere in the blue Caribbean where luscious bikini-clad damsels stroll about ivory-colored beaches.

It was an unfortunate incident that brought me here. I went into a psychotic rage over the space of a week after some Baltimore Police officers arrested me for "stealing" a parking meter. I was just carrying around a broken parking meter I had found.

The psychotic rage led me to a further tragic interaction with the police. An employee of Kentucky Fried Chicken was hosing down the sidewalk. He was rude to me, so I took the hose and started hosing down the place. Someone inside pressed the emergency alarm. I ended up being pumped with two .38 slugs to my left shoulder and arm, because it was said I refused to drop a knife I had. I do not remember any of this, my mind was just not functioning right. Perhaps my psychotic state was such that it obliterated the painful memory of such a sad event.

*   *   *

One bright and sunny Sunday in August at Perkins, an incident I call "the snatch" happened. As usual I would bring my novel with me to the dining room to read at the table while I waited for the food line to get smaller. I had been doing that at every meal for the past eight days, a total of twenty four meals and not one attendant had said anything to me. "You're not supposed to read that book, Grabowski," I heard a voice say.

I looked up slightly confused and bewildered, afraid I had done something wrong. But how could I have? No one had told me before that reading was wrong. I decided to defend myself: "I'm just waiting for the line to thin out," I said tremulously. A huge attendant with a basketball-sized belly and vacuous vapid marble eyes approached the table threateningly. I became afraid, so I got up cautiously. The attendant—with a glazed look—betraying an I.Q. of about 90, reached for my book and slid it across the table. I riposted and moved it back.

I was hurt, wounded by the ignorance and insensitivity of the attendant, but I knew what I had to do. I moved to the food line and swallowed my pride. The attendant stood there like a lifeless ebony statue with an ugly stare. I said, "What kind of place is this, a concentration camp?" He was furious that I dared to speak. He snatched my book from the table and threw it in the hallway.

This shocked me, disturbed me emotionally. But it led me to reflect on why I was so emotionally upset.

Slowly, I began to realize that I was vulnerable because of several unresolved conflicts, dating back to childhood: my parent's divorce, feelings of worthlessness, low self-esteem, feelings of being abandoned by my parents when I was twelve years old, of not being loved by my mother and an estranged relationship with my step father.

For many years, I have been lonely and invisible to the world. My illness forced me to dissociate from people. Unable to live up to my intellectual potential and participate in social life, I was relegated to the background.

But, **I can see clearly now. It's like coming out of the cold. You can see how ugly the world can be but it doesn't have to affect you emotionally in a disabling way.**

Dear Diary: 24 June 1987

I have been here at Perkins hospital for almost two years trying to get my mind to a normal functioning state, to eradicate the symptoms of my mental illness, and to achieve a sense of self confidence as a human being—an imperfect human being in a less than perfect world. To begin with I had to admit to my mental illness, which I did shortly after arriving here at Perkins. The memory of the incident with the police in which I was shot twice in the left shoulder left an imprint on my mind and made me realize how serious the situation was. I truly had to have been very sick for this to happen.

I have succeeded in stabilizing myself, thanks to the combined effects of medication and various therapies including psychotherapy. I feel good now, more or less happy, and for perhaps the first time in my life, free. Free to use my intelligence, my brains without emotionalism, free from the fears of getting needlessly arrested, free from the fear of endless cycles of manic-depressive illness and free from the fear of admitting that I have a mental illness. I feel whole again and in charge of my faculties.

Who am I? I am the product of many things, someone who cannot be labelled. Someone who has been hurt many times along the way. But I am also a survivor. I know I have a lot to give and I am looking forward to using my education and my experience, including my two years in the Peace Corps in West Africa, so that I can help myself and help others and do something socially useful.

Dear Diary: 2 July 1987

Yesterday afternoon mother came to visit me. She looked a bit old, gray hair, stooped shoulders. She had been waiting for me for at least an hour. I could have been there in the visiting room a half-hour early, but there is little communication between the security people at Perkins.

I was glad to see mother, always good to see her face to face. She has aged in the past two years since I saw her in the hospital after I was shot by the police. She brought me lots of goodies to eat and drink, but security wouldn't pass the cigarettes. A pity.

We talked a little during the visit. Mother doing the talking. But time was short—it's only a twenty minute visit.

Dear Diary: 7 July 1987

Two days ago an interesting incident took place in the smoking room. For some odd reason Ken wanted to do something which escapes me at the moment; Howard refused Ken's request until he kowtowed to him. What Howard, a patient who killed two people and crippled a third, did was rather childish. He grabbed Ken into an arm lock and forced him to kneel, then he told him to stick his tongue out. After that humiliation Howard smirked slightly while Ken went on his way out to his room.

It seems Howard always gets his way with Ken. I've seen Howard on previous occasions order Ken to stick his belly out so that he could touch his belly button, and Ken always acquiesced. It's a game of intimidation and submission where Howard (an ex-cop) plays the honcho manly type, a little dictator who gets his way with those willing and sick enough to play his game.

That's life in a hospital for the criminally insane. But in many ways it's a far more peaceful life than life on the outside. Security keeps the peace, and we have three squares a day, TV, and a bed to call our own. But that's just the surface. The deep fact is that there is no real freedom here. We all have to earn our freedom here by getting well and proving that we can function in society and not be a threat to others or to ourselves.

Tony, who killed four members of his family when he was psychotic one crazy day, is here. Apparently, he received messages on the radio that told him to commit his ghastly crime. Tony is ahead of me in getting out of Perkins. He's been on Ward A, where I am supposed to go soon. Tony and I have talked on occasion, before he went to the pre-release ward. He is not medicated and is doing quite well. You would never think he was a mass murderer and I don't treat him as such; for me he is just an ordinary Joe in a state mental hospital.

I've also rubbed shoulders with Tad, another mass murderer at Perkins, during the lunch hour gathering in the game room. Tad walked in one day in the factory where he was employed armed with a carbine and shot dead five of his co-workers. He's been at Perkins quite a while and now is also on Ward A, enjoying the privileges of a pre-release atmosphere, include week-end passes to Baltimore. No one really knows when he will be released. In the meantime he stays on the ward, works in the kitchen, and listens to classical music in the music room. Speaking to him is a pleasant experience. In fact he is quite erudite and spends a lot of his time, so I've heard, working on learning words.

You find them all at Perkins, the murderers, the rapists, those who have committed assaults of various kinds, and arsonists. It's not a pretty world, but I've learned to live with it and make my own life in this hospital and am pleased with the results. I read, I write, and take advantage of every therapy that is offered here. I know it is only a matter of time before I come back to the society I left two years ago; I will return a healed man. For a year now I have been stable and have been able to pursue my intellectual activities here; to date I have read almost eighty books. Soon I will be on Ward A and there will be new challenges as I will start to work in the kitchens and be able to eat in the employee dining room. Then I will probably get a job on the outside and in no time at all, I will be released.

NOTE FROM THE AUTHOR, AUGUST 1990

I left Perkins in August 1988 almost three years after I entered with fear and hopelessness in my heart. I was discharged a changed man. I was self-confident and knew that I could take charge of my life in an uncertain and fickle world.

Perkins was a blessing in disguise for me. I was able to take stock of myself there without having to worry about the daily necessities of life. I was able to reflect on the past and I had plenty of time for this, and know that it has paid off. I needed that time to reflect and think about my life experience and understand how I got to the present situation.

I can say that I have no stigma at all about having a mental illness or having spent three years in a hospital for the criminally insane. It was the right thing and it happened at the right time; Perkins, in short, helped me to get well and taught me the value of medication as a preventive prophylactic in the fight for sanity and well being.

Since leaving Perkins I have spent eighteen months at a halfway house in Baltimore during which time I studied for a Legal Assistant Certificate at the Community College of Baltimore. I received the Certificate in June 1990, with a high A average.

I am now looking for a paralegal position with a Law firm in Baltimore. In April 1990 I moved to my own apartment and am enjoying the independence of living on my own.

My goals for the future are to finish a Master's degree in Agricultural and Resource Economics that I started in the mid seventies at the University of Maryland, and to complete a novel on hunger in West Africa where I spent two years as a Peace Corps Volunteer. Much of the novel draws on my experience in that part of the world. Eventually I would like to work on Third World agricultural and resource problems, specializing in development.

So far I believe things look promising. I'm no longer a non-entity that no one looks at or cares for. At last I'm able to lead a normal life; without Perkins I really don't know what would have become of me.

Civility
is
like
Air.
It's
Easy
to
Breathe
In
And out
But difficult
to grasp
If you're raised
in a
Vacuum.

by Chuck Schusshim

Orange leaves reflect on the water
Like a passionate man
They're on fire
Colors of leaves
Reflect
To my eyes
The water is still
The sky above darkens
A fish pops its way
Out of the water
Into the reflection
Of orange leaves on fire
The ground is barren
Winter is near
It's hard and it's cold
Like some humans' survival
Silence prevails
Ears can only hear
Eyes can only see
There is no sound or sight
To the passion of the orange leaves

by Chuck Schusshin

RON'S STORY

PART ONE

I was in law school in November 1964, and I woke up one morning and couldn't see myself in the mirror. This was two months into law school. I was in a three story building I had rented before acquiring five roommates. After the mirror incident I called my parents and said, "Something isn't right." They flew right down and drove me home.

I soon found that I had a great fear of going out; I didn't leave the house and didn't want to see anybody. During this time I had desultory interviews with different shrinks. I was further troubled by realizing that I had a great sense of relief from dropping out of society.

Three months later I had a nervous collapse that took the form of a physical catatonia. Weirdly, it was associated with the death of Winston Churchill, which had occurred ten days before.

I had begun to feel intense pain throughout my back. It got so bad that I began walking outside after midnight. Finally, my father drove me to the hospital seventy miles away, in the middle of the night. I was balled up on the rear floor of the car.

In a mental hospital, I had nurses around the clock for ten days. It was strange: they looked more upset than I was. My body was in bad pain, but "I" was dissociated from it, not in much pain at all.

It was Christmas week of 1964. What followed for the next thirteen months was the bleakest time of my life. I was unable to stand up straight. I couldn't run, I couldn't eat sitting up.

Oddly enough, it was during this phase that psychiatry was most helpful to me. Three weeks after my immobility phase began, I told the doctors that I had to leave the hospital, or something very bad would happen. Naively, I wasn't surprised when they honored my request to leave.

They disagreed with my decision and tried to coax me back in for the whole next year, but never did anything to commit me. In view of what has happened to psychiatry since this time, it's hard to believe my wish would be respected now as it was then. Essentially, the way psychiatry and my parents helped was to leave me alone. During my meetings with a psychiatrist, I literally said nothing for over a year. In amazes me now in 1990 that this doctor was able to accept that arid and futile exchange.

After the thirteen months I experienced a sudden and dramatic physical change which restored my physical mobility. I was suddenly talking and relating to people again. If asked to reflect on what caused this change, I think it was due to a doctor who gave me a bit of common sense. I would beg the doctor to guarantee that the pain would end. He used to say, "Yes, it will end, one day." This time, when I pressed him, he said, "No, I can't guarantee that." Initially I was very upset. But when I woke the next morning, I realized something had been released within my system.

The above doesn't mention my encounter with psychiatric drugs, for I had been taking them without question—Stelazine, Thorazine, and others. Years later, it occurred to me that certain very unpleasant effects were due to these drugs, over and above the pain I was in—which the drugs did not affect. I fell down several times after getting out of bed, not knowing that low blood pressure was a common effect. Years later, I heard the word *akathisia*. I realized this described at least four incidents that frightened me badly, when I thought my problems were getting worse for no obvious reason.

After this thirteen month period when I had no other energy but for enduring and keeping alive, I spent a lot of time in psychoanalytic conversation with my doctor. These conversations, as well as several important books she recommended, helped me to acquire an intellectual framework to understand what led to so dramatic a breakdown. In a nutshell, leaving aside necessary subtleties, it involved the fact that I was denied the opportunity to go through a vital developmental stage. It's called the *No* stage. To miss this stage is like going from four feet to six feet in height, without ever having been five feet tall.

Aside from these conversations, the best and most helpful thing was new friendships with other patients in the hospital.

Looking back, these memories seem incredibly quaint and archaic in light of what psychiatry has done to itself since my breakdown in 1964. I feel pink-cheeked with embarrassment at my naivete at the time, for I had no idea that I had a minority type of experience, one which has all but disappeared. I was treated as a person who had problems rather than a diseased brain. I was also treated on a voluntary basis, despite the fact that my problems were severe and appeared completely intractable. At the very beginning doctors advised my parents to put me somewhere where I might be comfortable and to forget about me. It's hard to believe that anyone regarded that way today would receive such non-insistent treatment.

It no doubt helped that I was not disposed to violence. I was vaguely aware of people being carted off to some mysterious ward if they were considered violent. It helped that I had never picked up the habit of street drugs, although I was aware of a brisk commerce in these drugs among teenagers there. It seems ironic and bemusing to look back now on my time in the mental health system as a sort of "Psychiatric Golden Age."

During the second part of my hospital stay as an outpatient I fell in love with another patient. This was a woman who had such a reputation for pyromania and other unsettling behaviors that she had been locked up for many months. After we had been together for a while, the hospital began to let her go out with me, instead of the usual two football guard-size attendants.

After I left the area for a vacation with a friend, I got back to find her parents had suddenly transferred her to a bleak state hospital in up-state New York. My adventures in getting her out of this hospital had the incidental effect of getting me out of treatment. In spite of receiving benefits, I was delighted to leave psychiatry, even if I hadn't left all my problems. I was able to get back into normal social and work routines, if living in New York City can be called normal.

PART TWO

A crucial thing in New York was "Don't tell anybody about my background." I got a job at an insurance company. One of the most powerful associations in my personal life occurred on my first day of work. Sometime that morning, I had a tremendous sense of "Is this all there is?" I must have had some kind of fantasy about what a colossal thing it was to go to work. It was as if I didn't know that millions of people do this thing called "working." After digesting my ability to do this, I had from time to time vertigo-like attacks while at my desk. The crucial thing about this problem was simply to ignore it or sit quietly until it passed, and above all, not to talk to anybody else about it.

All this worked fine for over a year, including two promotions and getting something called "adjuster of the month award." At the end of the year I developed an angst or dissatisfaction with this job that I couldn't figure out what to do with.

At some point it almost seemed necessary to have a "second breakdown." This took the form of an insomnia that prevented me from keeping to a structured schedule. Eventually I accommodated to this problem—especially by staying up late for a two hour reading period. The consequences were paradoxical and frustrating. It provided me with a functional relationship to an incomplete personality—one that became complete mentally but not emotionally. This psychic arrangement has left me with a foot in two worlds—it's now gone on for almost twenty years.

For the first ten years I was at major risk of further collapses or hospitalizations. Living much of that time alone in an apartment, I was a recluse in the midst of suburbia. I was cut off from emotional contact with other people by my own blocked emotions. The only substitutive activities that worked for me were intensive reading about history and my good fortune to have a car to drive around.

During the past ten years a number of things have happened to greatly diminish or preclude the likelihood of any involuntary contact with the psychiatric system. One of the most important was the sobering realization that treatment that might help my remaining "psychiatric" problems simply may not exist. This is an extremely unpleasant and disheartening possibility that either doesn't occur to many people, or which simply and sadly, they can't face.

Certainly a detail of some significance is that I met my wife in 1981, and have lived happily in that sphere of existence ever since. The third and final factor involved the consequences of meeting a former acquaintance in the fall of 1986, who became a close friend. Andy is a fellow of even more fortunate social and economic background than myself, but who has been ensnared in the mental health system for almost thirty years. Understanding over a period of several months how that system has not only failed him but greatly increased his problems, triggered my involvement in advocacy. Any lingering self pity I felt about my continuing problems became laughable and embarrassing in the face of his grave difficulties and mistreatment.

Perhaps the day I came on the ward and found him on the floor with his hands and feet turned inward as a result of a PRN overdose of Haldol, and a loud arrogant nurse told me that he was merely seeking attention, was a critical event. As I walked back to my car across the grounds that day and looked at other patient inmates, I was hit with a sense of genuine Revelation. It flashed through me that persons, like Andy, look the way they do because of the way they are treated, not because of the natural course of an "illness." Although advocates, families, and the general public are constantly told to consider the appearance and behavior of mental patients as "illness," this revelation has remained vivid and unchanging for me.

With regard to the particular incident involving Andy, it gave me some measure of satisfaction to prevent any further Haldol drug overdoses. A pattern of being able now and then to prevent bad things from happening has unfortunately not been matched by being able to make good things happen.

Can I generalize from the continuing predicament of my friend? On the one hand I remain astonished at the invisibility of the Gulag he is confined in, devoid of anything that could be called genuine treatment. On the other hand the very emptiness of this bleak landscape, the lack of genuine help for him and the thousands like him is a giant opportunity—if any advocate should be up to the human challenge.

PART THREE

It has also been of help to get to know Andy's parents and reflect back on my own parental situation. For his parents have been faced with an even worse dilemma than were mine in the '60's. I have had to restrain myself from asking them what on earth do they have to show for three decades of faith that psychiatry knows what it's doing. For some reason I recognized when my psychiatrist had reached the point where she could no longer help me help myself, even though she didn't realize it.

In my case, at least up to a point, psychiatry did make a genuine contribution. She did help me figure out my non-appearance in the mirror. My enormous denial of accumulated emotional problems, which had allowed me to get through college, could not be duplicated in law school.

That fierce denial process had probably started when I made a crucial decision and turned away from facing a problem. It may sound strange to say that I made that wrong "decision" at the age of two, but I think that's what happened. The decision was simply not to face things that were either too painful or too large. That decision was forced on me by a parent who didn't know how to be a parent. However, it is important to note that this is a problem of causation rather than blame.

Like Robert Frost's famous poem of "The Road Not Taken," every other problem was on top of the first. One piece of simple bad luck also contributed. For the first time, and fortunately the only time in my life, I had bad peers at the age of six or seven. My neighborhood chums went on eventually to careers of delinquency, failure and even crime. A parent who failed in leadership, and reinforcement by chaotic playmates, didn't give me at the threshold of life good ideas about human possibilities.

Almost in compensation, I have been far luckier than most in my successive circles of friendship after this initial disaster. Starting from the seventh grade and until the decade of isolation, I had many remarkable friends. Fortunately my parents, after I reached a certain age, did provide good models not only for friendship, but also for the life of the mind and interest in affairs beyond our small town.

I long thought the only reason I didn't become a delinquent or worse was because of a genuine role model I met when I was thirteen. This was a man for whom I had almost an undue respect for over thirty years, until he passed away recently at the age of 89. More than anybody I have known personally, he showed me what a human being could do or be in terms of compassion, intelligence, and especially leadership—this latter quality I most needed when I met him. Initially I went to his camp as a kid and stayed on for nine years as a counselor and group leader. I was endlessly startled by his grasp of everything with regard to his responsibilities. He could give me a serious fifteen minute lecture on the different types of brooms needed to clean different buildings of the camp. He could also give a thirty minute family history of a seemingly incorrigible kid, after which I might feel foolish for thinking the kid incorrigible. His camp seemed a national microcosm, for his reputation brought children from all over the country.

It is curious that such good experiences in no way precluded an eventual devastating breakdown, but it did provide me with the raw materials to get through it, if I could. Again these fortunate experiences were more important than capable psychiatry.

All this led to a reintegration at the base of personality and identity, at least at an intellectual and perhaps spiritual sense. Did it do the same thing in an emotional sense? The answer has to be No, for there remains a definite blank spot in my emotional life, an area I still can't get into.

When I did not see myself in the mirror, it was an apt symbol for a denial so extreme that it came to include my entire self. It was a denial of so many of my feelings, or so much of my feeling capacity that nothing was left. Perhaps that void became my visual disappearance. This eclipse of self, if I'm not careful to avoid certain situations, still happens. For instance, I remain unable to put myself under someone's supervision in a work situation. The reason for that remains a deep distrust of authority because the first exercise of authority over my life was done in a chaotic and hurtful way.

The problem may sound trivial, but I think it is profound. It appears that it has to be safe for the young person to *say No*, which is not the same thing as "getting away" with the No. In a physical-chemical sense I think the No must be allowed—not in a fear-free environment—but in an anxiety-free environment. (Fear knows it's source, anxiety does not.) If this doesn't happen, then what seems to take place is a literal short-circuit of the developmental process of our humanization and maturation. When the parent is feeling anxiety without knowing why, it's literally inducted into the nervous system of the child.

If there's any truth to this, then we are at a point where interpersonal and biochemical theories of personality interface. I believe that if you don't get to say No, you can't say yes even when you want to. For this reason, I feel that No is a foundation or seedbed for self. Paradoxically, Yes comes second.

What does this mean for me today? It means that anything to do with reading, thinking and interpersonal conversation comes both easily and efficiently. But it also means that anything to do with fixed behavioral responsibility comes either by outwitting internal resistance or not at all. It also means that as an advocate, I can go to conferences with a great deal of useful and mutual networking, but an almost complete inability to speak before groups.

Although I don't receive an income, I am hardly unemployed. I work as an advocate for people who are unhappy about the way they are being treated or what was done to them, in or out of psychiatric hospitals. But these efforts are often stymied. If there's something I wish to do which is unexpected of me, it often gets done. When it is expected, on the other hand, no matter how much I consciously agree with the expectation, it's accomplishment is more often that not defeated by "this alternate source of decision making in my mind." This buried aspect of self seems to be an albatross left over from the still-unsolved "No-situation."

From another angle, advocacy almost seems easier when it's on a competitive and adversarial level, than on a cooperative "we're all on the same side" level. This means I sometimes have more useful conversations with opponents than with friends—at least those opponents who don't come to the conversation as "representatives of the truth."

Does advocacy opposing psychiatric involuntarism have much of a future? Curiously, I don't think so, unless the size and depth of the problem is much better understood. In the short run, this view is considered negative and pessimistic, but in the long run if recognized, I think is the only hope for real progress. Also, full recognition of just how bad things are would illuminate what an open field there is for attempts to help people based on a genuine idea of treatment, rather than a judgmental control, masquerading as treatment.

If such advocacy takes place, before a level of critical mass is reached nobody will believe that success is coming. But after that threshold, everybody will be surprised it didn't arrive earlier.

August 30, 1990 [*dictated*]

KINDNESS

You seek kindness in these prison hallways,
in the laugh of a nurse
like a light through fog,
in rooms hungry for love. Trees blow in a wind
you do not hear. Now you know

the monotony of dry toast
caught in your throat, stale coffee
in your cup, the pride that even God
did not break down, like a property
you try to save. You crave kindness
like a drunkard his bottle,
you who are abandoned,
left in the middle of the road,
an animal cry darkening the morning.
You remember how summer closed down
city streets, trees bowed with heat,
a rock tune winding down
through an open window. You pray

for a miracle, remembering
how you poured out your heart to someone,
how rain drippling from branches

turned to dogwood blossom.

                                        Elaine Erickson

III. Wounded Since Childhood

You had the fangs of a venomous wolf, so early did the gall take root in you and poison your loyalty. You should have felt pity for your host . . . and have asked the cause of his suffering.

Parzival, *A Medieval Romance, by Wolfram Von Eschenbach*

Pain is the sign of something unanswered; it refers to something open, something that goes on the next moment to demand, What is wrong?

Medical Nemesis, *by Ivan Illich*

SUNSHINE'S STORY

I'm in the hospital here because I had suicidal thoughts. I was hospitalized once before because I tried to commit suicide by overdosing on sleeping pills. I was homeless, penniless, and had just broken up with my boyfriend.

My mother abused me emotionally as a child. I had little self-esteem. She didn't know how to raise me.

I've been depressed all my life; I don't know any other way to be. It's normal for me to be sad, especially since I was ten. I can't remember before five. My parents were divorced then, and I was molested when I was five by the baby-sitter's son. I blocked it out for a while.

I was terrified of guys; I didn't even talk to them. At seventeen I came to grips with it. All of the sudden I realized it and turned around and started dating.

I'm nineteen now and the past abuse is a huge factor in me being sad, and it's a factor in my suicide attempt. The doctors here never asked about this. I did most of the work myself. It always bothered me that they never got into it.

They did set up family therapy and it helped to an extent with my relationship with my father. We're closer now.

July 30, 1990 [*dictated*]

GATEWAY TO THE SOUL

Coals of steel
Gleamed in her eyes,
Unfamiliar tones of color
And sound
Radiated from her every
Movement and word.
A throbbing ache pounded
Deep in her heart;
She knew it was her soul
Crying out endlessly to be found.

by "Sunshine"

Blackened skies
Full of fury
Powerful fires of anger
Explode in the darkened night.
There is a face there
Collectively calm
Deadly pale
And it searches;
Life slowly dies
Burning in the hands
Of a flesh seeking devil,
Green in color.
Flames of hatred
Dance in his coal black eyes
To surrender is useless;
He'll take you just the same.
There is no mercy
Where he hangs his hat
And props his feet.
You are among the little people now.

by "Sunshine"
6/89

SUICIDE

by "Sunshine"

I understand why so many people kill themselves. When you're dead, you don't have to worry about what people think of you or deal with disappointment. There's no wars or bombs to be concerned about, no bills to pay, no job to fail at. You can't feel pain anymore, and no one cares about how you look or what you are. Just who you are. And love rules in Heaven. Life seems so much easier when you're dead. It seems to be the easy way out, but it's actually very hard to do. After you're dead, you can't have a beer or eat pizza or rollerskate or dance or make love. You can't be held all night by someone you love, or have Mommy to take care of you when you're sick; you can't get sick. You can't feel the joy of your baby saying Momma or feel the tears of joy on your cheeks when you achieve a lifelong goal. You can't change the world or express your views or ease someone's pain. Maybe being dead isn't so great after all.

SUE'S STORY

Sometimes it's better to be on the street than in the hospital. Usually it's because there's something there you can't handle, like people picking fights with you, or the medicine which can be so bad.

The summer is the worse time. There's no place to go, the shelters are closed. I'd sleep outside in back of someone's pick-up truck or someone's yard. Townhouses under construction are good. Being a young woman, people would be curious. "Why are you here?" they'd ask. "Don't you have some place to go?" I tried to be evasive; I didn't want their help because I knew there was little they could do for me. I'd go to Harbor Place where people in suits would give me five or ten bucks.

The reason I'm in the hospital now is because I tried to commit suicide. I was going to jump off the Jarrettsville Bridge over Loch Raven Reservoir. I'm scared of heights, somewhat scared of water. No one noticed me. I was standing up there looking down in the rushing water and got nauseous. I took some pills. I almost shook off the railing—I didn't think of closing my eyes.

One reason I wanted to jump off was because I was broke. Who wants to live without money? And if you have parents like mine, you wouldn't go home. They're dirt poor and flipped out people. They don't make any sense; they should be here. My father is an alcoholic. He was mean to me, constantly haranguing me about what I can't do.

My ex-boyfriend is an alcoholic. That's why he beat me up. He gets a check, picks up a girl at a bar. It makes him feel like somebody. I was trying to get away from him. After he beat me up one time in February, I was bed ridden for a month. I thought I knew him. When I was a little kid, we were attracted to each other. But it turned out he couldn't control his anger when drinking, and he drank all the time. I had a kid by him, because he was good looking. I wanted a good looking kid. He's six months old now and looks just like his father. Someone made up a story, and they took the kid away from me and now he's under foster care.

I don't tell the hospital people this information because I don't trust them. The more I try to cooperate here, the more they'll take advantage of me.

June 16, 1990 [*dictated*]

ONE HUMAN'S STORY

I realized I was mentally disturbed at a very young age, probably between the age of five and ten. I don't think that my parents were aware of the difficulties I was having, and so they could not help me at all. As I got older I realized my parents were not well either, and they could not see that I was ill. My father was an alcoholic, my mother was into fundamentalist religion, trying to find a way out of her own torment. I loved my parents very much and will always love them. I do not hold any grudges or grievances against my family whatsoever. I don't blame my parents for my illness. I did that forty years and I didn't recover because of that. Even as mental patients, we have to take responsibility for what we are doing.

At a young age I got involved with drugs and alcohol, trying to escape the emotional turmoil in my head. I was terribly, terribly frightened all the time, living with constant confusion. When I was eight years old, I tortured and killed animals. I was angry and filled with rage. I had been physically abused by parents, sexually abused by adults. There was constant turmoil and drunkenness on the weekends.

I went into the Service at seventeen; I got out of the Service on account of an illness in the family, and I got married at twenty-two. I was not a good husband because I was ill, so therefore I could not give my wife the emotional support and help she needed to make the marriage work. My wife and I separated in 1969 and were divorced in '72.

My first hospitalization was in 1964 for attempted suicide. I felt hopeless and was extremely depressed, and I didn't see any way out of the situation. I would just sit and stare out the window for days, frightened. I always felt frightened and terrified. In my first hospitalization I was introduced to psychiatric drugs. From 1964 to 1985 I was hospitalized thirty different times, mainly in the Baltimore area. Throughout this period I was constantly under psychiatric drugs and/or psychotherapy, but I realized that I was not getting better and still in terrible emotional turmoil. I remember one time taking Haldol and I got worse, extremely paranoid. No drug ever helped me to recover. Drugs always kept me in a confused mental state.

I had electric shock too. I felt a little better afterwards, but it didn't do much. I believe I have some brain damage. Also, I believe that because of taking psychiatric drugs for twenty years I have damage because I can't take any type of drugs now without a reaction. The drugs that I took all those number of years never helped me to recover or alleviate the symptoms I had. Under no circumstances should someone be *forced* to take psychiatric drugs against their will, unless they are dangerous to themselves or others.

Some of the hospitals were just a place to put someone, to warehouse them. That's exactly what my experience of the state institutions were. I had some good doctors who really tried to help me, but in retrospect as I look back on my life now, the only person who could help me was myself. I went to AA meetings and began the Twelve Steps. I decided when I got out of the last mental institution in January of 1985 to come off all psychiatric drugs and quit seeing a psychiatrist.

I got involved doing holotropic breath work in 1986 and during this time the emotional pain got much worse in the beginning. Gradually, though the change began within myself and I realized that I was not to blame for all the things that happened to me in my life nor were others.

I began *Vipassana* meditation practices in 1988. Holotropic breath work is getting together with a group of breathers and sitters, and doing enhanced breathing with eyes closed, flat on your back for three hours, listening to evocative music. This was developed by Stan and Christina Groff. I meditate one hour in the morning and one hour in the evening doing *Vipassana* meditation. This meditation purifies the mind. I began to learn how to forgive and the most important thing of all, I began to learn how to love myself and others around me.

It has been a difficult five years as I have pursued the truth within myself and I might also say the same truth is in all people, that I have no ownership of truth; it's universal.

I'm now completely drug free for over five years and don't need to see psychiatrists. I look forward to each day as I get up, to go out and be with all the people in the world, and hopefully during my day, I can help others on the path of truth, as I see it. I know without a doubt that everything in this universe is OK and that all people and living things in this universe are OK. I have no regrets about my life whatsoever. I would like to thank all the people I've met along the way who have put me on the path to truth, so that I was able to find the way out of that emotional turmoil.

I still continue to pursue truth and to be open to listen to all points of view without judging anything. Just as I have the right to live my life as I choose, the same goes for all others. As I see myself today, I know the only way to live a peaceful and loving life is to live according to truth. To all other mentally disturbed people, I say you have within yourselves the capacity to come out of all suffering. It is a very hard task and must be worked at every day. May all beings everywhere experience freedom from suffering. May you have real peace and real happiness, right now.

Anonymous

A DAY AT THE STATE PARK

My niece
    at the age of six
    does not cry very often.
As we walk on the leaf-littered trail
    she chatters continuously. . .
    wanting to explain how it is
    or wanting how it is explained.
She takes in the sights
    of the wide-open worlds of trees and lakes
    with her clear blue eyes,
and crouches to pick up a few smooth, white pebbles
      to toss into the water—
      the rings dance around each other
      under the glint of afternoon sunlight.
I spread out my blanket under a willow tree
and in that brief moment she's out of my view.
I panic briefly
but calling her name only once
she appears before me
dirt-streaked, with a fist full of dandelions.
Exhausted, she stretches her small body on the blanket
    next to me.

I think of her aunt at six years of age. . .
    frightened, down-cast eyes,
and hiding from the wide-open world
in corners of the house—
    beneath tables, behind sofas—
and all-too-familiar with the rough texture of carpet
or the cool of the plaster wall pressing against her cheek.
Hiding in silence.
Hiding from the pain
    she knew would find her as it always did.
I rub my niece's back gently.
She does not stiffen with tension
    as her aunt would have at six years of age.
She knows my touch
is a loving gesture—
    it will not hurt or violate her.

I look down at my hand
and imagine its size at six years of age. . .
remember wishing mightily that it would be big enough
to fight back.
But it was not.
And it should not have had to be.

    I start to tell a story.
A story about a sunny day at the park and white pebbles.
My niece objects. She wants a different story.
A story that she knows the ending to already—
    a happy ending.
And I realize that is truly how it should be.
I should have known that
    because those stories should have been told to me. . . .

Stories that would have endured.

        by Grace Ann 7/17/87

WHAT SHE THOUGHT ABOUT AT SIX
(AND HAD NIGHTMARES ABOUT AT THIRTY)

Before he squashes me
or smothers me,
I'm going to turn into a big black balloon
that can't feel anything at all. . .
    no legs to force open. . .
    no face with a mouth. . .
And when I turn into a big black balloon
I'm quickly going to let all my air out at once
so I can flit and dart through the room
back and forth
    back and forth
        back and forth
like a crazy drunken bumble-bee—
stopping short just before I crash
    into this or that wall
or smash into the ceiling,
and suddenly change direction.

And when I do this he cannot catch me
because even I don't know where I'm going next,
until the air is all gone from the black balloon
and it lays limp as a dead kitten
        on the ground.

But at night,
when I'm tucked safely in bed,
I close my eyes and dream
that I'm flitting and darting
back and forth
        back and forth
                back and forth
and crashing into walls and ceilings
with no idea how to stop
my own body
from getting hurt. . .

If only there was an open window to fly out
I might be free!

                                by Grace Ann 5/87

HOW MANY LITTLE GIRLS?

How many little girls are there
that have ingrained in their memories
an old man's skin,
his heavy breath stinking of cigar,
the taste of him,
his angry penetration
        pounding like a jackhammer,
his use of coercion,
and accept all his lies,
and believing his threats,

strip off their own clothes
or have them (st)ripped off,
and are made to feel even smaller
    than they are in reality
when made to lay down
on the cold garage floor
and feel dirtier than the ground beneath them,
while thinking no other option exists
except to submit,
only to be degraded by him for obeying
    his wishes (which they don't understand),
and are so ashamed to hold such a secret
that can't ever be shared
or uttered aloud?
And how many little girls are there
who are terrified by his power,
and of God's rage when he discovers the sin,
and of their parent's disgust and rejection
    after they learn
and the absolute fright that their peers will know
    the dirty secret
merely by a glance at their face,
so they avert their eyes so as not to be seen,
retreat from the world
and wish real hard
    for invisibility?

And just how many child-women are there
who still refuse to look into that glass
thinking for sure that it will mirror the filth on their soul,
but give themselves away to strangers
only to see their reflection in the uncaring eyes
over and over
each time—
then later
silently cry. . .

silently cry
Alone?

                    Grace Ann   3/29/87   4:45 AM

THOSE WONDERFUL AND CARE FREE
DAYS OF CHILDHOOD REMEMBERED.

STORY OF KAREN M.

[*Editor's Note:* This is an oral version of Karen's story. Her own written story is due to appear in a book entitled *Special Surrender.*]

PART ONE

I was a sexually abused child. When I was six years old, my mother went to the hospital to give birth to my baby sister. During that time I suffered incredible abuse. I was hung spread-eagle under the blue basement steps, where my kindergarten pictures were. I was sodomized with a finger, and terrorized with an electric saw. Four years of sexual abuse had culminated, but there were no marks on my body. My mother didn't know, and I bore within the guilt and pain of sexual abuse.

That summer Daddy went on a business trip to Europe. He was an art conservator. While he went to Europe, we went to Bolton Hill to stay with some friends of Mommy's. We went to the store and ate Charms, blow pops and liquorice with the children of the family. "Have you ever been raked?" one of them asked. "Raked?" I exclaimed. "What is raked?" "It's when they take all your clothes off and drag a rake across your naked body." "No," I shivered, "that never happened to me."

Finally we returned to our house in Mount Washington, the one at the top of the hill with a white picket fence. Our dog Ginger was very happy to see us, and stopped chasing squirrels, came over and wagged her tail. My sister Erica and I began to run towards the back door of the house. We got as far as the stone patio when Mommy called, "Wait girls." We went up to her. "Girls," Mommy said, "I have to explain something to you. We're going to live in a brand new house, not too far away from here." "Is Ginger coming?" Erica asked. "No," said Mommy. "I think it would be a good idea to leave Ginger to keep your father company. At that we burst into tears. We cried and cried. She explained, "Mommy doesn't love Daddy anymore so we can't live in the same house, and all your things are at the new house." "Even my horses?" I asked. I had a proud collection of ten toy horses. "Yes," said Mommy. "The moving men were very careful with them." We cried some more, said goodbye to Ginger, got into Mommy's '57 Chevrolet and drove to our new house in Roland Park.

When I was eighteen I attended McDonogh School. I was a senior there and had always excelled in courses, making A's and B's. I took riding and was on the Varsity squad. On January 11, a school bus rolled up to our stop, and my mother's Citation was there, waiting for us. What can be the problem, we wondered, climbing into her car. "Girls, a terrible thing has happened," she said. "You lost your job," I said, the most terrible thing I could think of. "Your father has been murdered," she said.

Immediately, Erica burst into tears. But for me, a veil had been lifted. It was as if some unknown thing had disappeared, something I couldn't put my finger on, something I couldn't remember. Then I started to cry. We cried, watching the news that night, as they showed the sketch of the murder suspect, a seventeen-year old male prostitute who was at the house of my father that weekend with his thirteen-year old cousin. They stabbed him to death, sixty-seven times. Maybe it had something to do with drugs, as my father was a phenobarbital addict.

I went to college. As it always had been I was the outsider, the outcast. I felt different from everybody—as I had felt in grade school, middle school and high school. I felt different until I saw a black haired boy who had a goatee like my father. His name was Clark, and one month and one party later he was my boyfriend.

I took an animation workshop and was working on a clay animation film over Christmas break. I was obsessed with this film, and got everybody I knew to help me with it. While shooting in a dark basement, Lisa, one of my best friends, asked if I would like to try some LSD. "Yes," I decided.

Two days later, I took a half hit of "window pane." While playing with my unicorn model, I started thinking, *Clark is magical. He's what I've been looking for all my life.* I fell in love.

The next day, so happy at my new-found awareness, I barged into his room. "I tripped," I told him. "I have something to tell you," he said. I wondered what it might be. "Why do we continue this farce?" he asked.

We broke up that night, but I clung to him. I waited for him, just to see the way he walked, just to see the color of his eyes, just to hear his voice.

I continued to take acid and one day in May I found myself on the roof of the dorm. I remembered a lucid dream Clark had described to me and how he had said, "People can dream together."

If people can dream together why couldn't there be telepathy, I thought. *Clark!* I screamed in my head. "Karen," I heard a voice answer. "It took you long enough to figure it out," said the voice. I was so excited, I jumped around and ran down the stairwell. In the morning light, I went to sleep, happy that I had found something, something to fill the hole inside.

PART TWO

When I returned to school the next fall, I was still in love with Clark and continued to hear his voice. I also became addicted to marijuana. Often, while smoking dope, I would sing loudly to Bach's cantatas, my father's music, or listen to my roommate's psychedelic tapes. By spring I was using pot three times a day, and I was very ready go home on Spring Break in March.

One night before dinner, my mother found out I was stoned in the kitchen. She told me if I continued to get high in her home I would have to go back to college early. I said fine. That night I got high on the porch again, thinking she wouldn't smell the odor.

Later, Mom came into my room. "Karen," she says. "You have to go back to NYU right now." "OK," I said, and then a very strange thing happened. My father's spirit came into my body and started talking to my mother. "Mary," he said—my voice became deeper. "There's nothing to be concerned about." "Karen!" my mother exclaimed. "This is Peter M. speaking," he said. "This is the part of her that becomes difficult. I sexually abused Karen when she was six years old."

At this, I returned to my body and screamed and screamed. I had heard every word and was frightened. My youngest sister Amy, then thirteen, stomped into my room and shouted, "SHUT UP!" That stopped me. "Karen, my mother said, "We have to go to the hospital." "Daddy was in my body!" I said. "If I look in the mirror, I'll see his face!"

My mother swiftly explained that Karen was having difficulties and needed to go to the hospital. "I think it was a drug overdose," she said. "Maybe there was something in that pot. Maybe there was something in that pot."

I hurriedly dressed, pulled my army pants over a bare bottom and wore my red rag sweater. Overtop all of this, because it was a chilly March day, I wore my father's old army coat.

I begged my mother for some snapshots of when I was young to see how I was abused. I knew by then that I had been abused as a child. This was the only piece of information I had about the travesty I called my childhood.

My mother reached through photo albums, grabbed two snapshots of when I was three and five. I was with my sister, laughing and happy. Nothing seemed to be wrong. I gazed at them going down Charles Street, knowing that they were a lie, that something horrible had happened to me when I was a child.

We passed Sheppard Pratt Hospital; the Gingerbread Gate House looked happy. I knew that I would end up there. We reached the Emergency Room of Greater Baltimore Medical Center and I was taken immediately. It was 3:00 A.M. and no one else was there, so I had to wait for the psychiatrist to show up.

I wasn't tired, my thoughts were racing. A female doctor examined me and asked me questions about drugs. Have you taken this, have you taken that, she asked. I had taken everything except Cocaine; I had even snorted Heroin, thinking it was Cocaine.

The doctor asked if it was PCP I was smoking. "No just regular pot," I said. She left me in the little room by myself and went out to consult with my mother. After a period of time, the doctor came back and took me to a waiting room. I wasn't hearing voices anymore. I was too high for that.

Another nurse was there: male, blond with blue eyes, wearing blue scrubs. He wore glasses and his eyes reminded me of Clark's. I knew that Clark would be there waiting, at the end of this trip. Sooner or later, I had to go to the bathroom. He showed me where it was, and at my request brought a sanitary napkin. It was the type that pins to your underwear and since I didn't have any underwear, I threw it away.

As I was sitting on the toilet, I heard my father's voice. He said, "Karen, I've done a terrible, terrible thing to you." *It's O.K., Dad,* I thought. "It was really a terrible thing," he repeated. *Well, it's over now,* I thought to him. "Please, forgive me," he said. *I forgive you,* I thought. "Forgive me, please Karen," he said. Hunched over the toilet, all I could do was say *I forgive you Dad.* Then his voice went away; it was the last time I talked to my father.

I decided a few other things in that bathroom. I decided by my rhinestone dappled earrings, that I was really a *Black Prostitute* from New York. I was also a *Black Wolf* with my short hair. At college I had it cut from long to short. Now it was just the style of the child in the snapshot when I was five. But I was a wolf, and I could take it. I could take anything. I growled under my breath as I returned to the waiting room where the nurse was. Then the Prostitute asked him a few questions. "Am I pretty?" she asked. He nodded. "Do you think I'm beautiful?" He just gazed into my eyes. I reached out and held him for a moment.

Shortly thereafter, the psychiatrist arrived. He led my mother into his office and then the nurse showed me in. They both stood against the white concrete wall and my mother waved goodbye. I knew I would never see her again; I knew she was dying.

The doctor resembled my father, balding on top with black hair and greying beard. He wore thick, black-framed glasses, and his nose was not unlike my fathers. He sat down and began asking me some questions. "What is a Blue Ball?" "I don't know," I said and meant it. But I felt inside it must have something to do with sexual abuse. Perhaps it was what my father gave me after he hurt me so badly. "What about White Feather?" The white feather must have been what had the blood on it, but I wasn't going to tell him about it. He obviously knew much more about it than I did. "Have you ever been hospitalized before?" he asked. I said, "No, except for my tonsils." He said, "You have to be hospitalized. The ambulance is going to be here soon."

It was about 5:30 in the morning. On my way out of the office I saw my mother down the hall, near the nursing station. Though I have no memory of this, I'm told that I screamed, "Where were you that night?" "What night?" she asked. "The night I was raped in the shed!" The doctor said there was nothing more for her to do, she would see me tomorrow at Sheppard Pratt. It was about then, I believe, that my mother realized I had been sexually abused.

The ambulance finally came around 6:30 A.M., on a cold March 16th. The ambulance driver was filling in for my father in his gay stage, when he shaved his goatee and wore a Corduroy Cap. *Oh no, this is going to be a rocky drive,* I thought. My father was a terrible driver. But it wasn't. My father, who had come down from heaven, was a careful ambulance driver, hardly a bounce, hardly a break.

The stretcher was wheeled out and the ambulance driver/my father tied me on and said goodbye. I was taken to A-3 at Sheppard Pratt where I was still the Black Wolf and the Black Prostitute.

Everybody seemed to be someone else, representing someone else. The girl on my left was Clark's girlfriend, Stacy. Mike was tall, thin man with long brown hair. I tried to hug him, but he said, "Better not let them see you doing that." I knew then what Mental Health Workers meant.

I signed a voluntary paper for admission and played guitar for everyone, being the Wolf character. Eventually, as I was practicing, everyone went to bed. It dawned on me, *I'm locked up. I'm locked up in a mental institution.* "Come on, honey it's time to go bed," said a Mental Health Worker, who was standing in for my high school boyfriend's mother. "Finish your cigarette and put it out," she said. I smoked the Camel non-filter down to the nubbin. Then I stuck out my tongue, turned the burning ember toward it, and put it out on the top of tongue as if I were taking a hit of acid. I swallowed the butt. "Karen, that's no way to put out a cigarette!" she said, shocked. "Now go to bed."

I paced to the end of the corridor, noticed the red-lit Exit sign and the guitar leaning against the wall. *I'm getting out of here,* I thought. I grabbed the neck of the guitar, swung it over my head, and charged her. "All male call to A-3! All male call to A-3!" the loudspeaker blared. Within seconds a band of men surrounded me. One forced me to the ground in a half nelson. I went limp. *Do it,* I thought. *Fuck me up the ass.* They took me to the Quiet Room and left me inside.

Shortly thereafter six Mental Health Workers come and pin me to the floor face down. My pants are pulled down and I'm given an injection of Haldol. "This will help you sleep," a Mental Health Worker says.

Sometime thereafter I have not fallen asleep and have to use the toilet. I'm having my period. Two female Mental Health Workers look in on me as I urinate. Some blood globs into the toilet. *That's the seed*, I think. *That's the conception of my love for Clark.* I reach into the toilet, hold an inch wide chunk of menses in the palm of my hand. "Put that back in the toilet," one of the workers says. I think about it. *This is my love for Clark. This is our future. This is our three children.* I put it in my mouth and swallow it.

It was like eating raw oysters. The shock on the Mental Health Workers faces was self evident; it made them cringe. They locked me back in the Quiet Room.

I stared at the light and began to hear voices again. I was coming down due to the injection. Laying on my back, I stared at the sun-like light above. It was dim, but it radiated plastic spokes. I heard Clark and I also got in touch with my animation teacher, Dan. I decided after talking to the two of them, that even though Dan was flaming queer, he was the one I really wanted. Finally, I fell asleep.

When I came to they had breakfast waiting for me: cold eggs, a strip of meat, some kind of potato. I wasn't going to, I didn't mean to, but I ate it anyway. After another twenty-four hours and a little green pill, I had calmed down sufficiently for them to let me out.

PART THREE

Life on the hall was spent mostly in my room, sleeping, because I was put on 15 milligrams of Haldol, one of the most potent drugs in psychiatric history. It's equivalent to 200 mg of Stelazine, enough to knock out a horse. It got to the point that one of the Mental Health Workers threatened to lock the door to my room, if I didn't spend more time on the hall.

I developed a case of tardive dyskinesia. My neck muscles pulled my head to the right, and I couldn't straighten it. Once my head was forced back so I was looking straight up and couldn't bring it forward. They gave me a drug called Cogentin for the side effects. Still I drooled. I hated Haldol, knowing it was not the drug for me. As far as I knew, I didn't need any drugs. But my doctor thought that I was schizophrenic.

After a month on A-3, the short term unit, I was transferred to B-1, a long term unit. The doctor caring for me took me off all medicine. As it always is with a cyclical disorder, the next time I got my period, I got sick and ended up in the Quiet Room. I hallucinated that the tiles of the floor were rising and lowering. I saw a sparrow in the crack of the white wall. Through the metal screen I watched my roommate run around and around the perimeter of the hospital.

My doctor came to me with a small plastic cup of what seemed to be orange juice. "This is Stelazine," he said. "Drink it now." He also prescribed Lithium, two pills twice a day. "Congratulations," he said. "You're a manic depressive." After I got out of the Quiet Room, I was to take Lithium two times a day, 1200 milligrams and Stelazine PRN, meaning I was given it when necessary.

Most of the work we did at the hospital was stabilizing my illness, and although I confronted my doctor with my childhood sexual abuse, we did little work in the area. I'd go in and say I was an abused child. He would say, "Maybe you are, maybe you're not."

I became quite close with one Mental Health Worker, Joseph, who had blue eyes, black hair and a big nose, just like Clark. He was the first man I could trust. He took care of me: let me out when I had to go to the bathroom, watched me during my smoke break, and gave me my meals.

My mother came every single visiting day, except when I was in the Quiet Room. I was hospitalized till August and had to stay two weeks extra because my mother and family went to the Club Mediterranean, a group of resort islands in Europe. While they were on vacation I was presented with the hospital bill of $36,000. I had no insurance. Well, I thought, it has to be paid. Leaning against the wall, I wrote the check and gave it to the Mental Health Worker. The Social worker with whom I spoke had contacted NYU and had told me I was covered completely, but I was only insured for the first $5,000.

I interviewed for college at the Maryland Institute College of Art. They loved my four minute clay animation film. I was accepted. But I still didn't fit in at school. I met one "friend," invited her over to dinner and she nearly raped me in my room. I developed a strong crush on my 2-D design teacher, but the only real interest he had in me was as an artist.

In February, I decided I didn't want so much Lithium and decreased my dosage to three pills a day, then to two. By the end of the week I was flying. I remember playing in the snow around the tiny Japanese Maple tree in my mother's backyard. I kept writing in the snow, "Melody of Love," a popular tune at the time. My mother gently called me in. I had recently switched therapists to a woman, a licensed social worker named Sarah. When my mother took me to her office, all she could say to me in my state of psychosis was: "If you don't go to the hospital, I'm going to drop you." She repeated it over and over. Finally, I said, "I don't care." That shut her up. But I went to the hospital anyway and was taken to a psychiatric ward at the University of Maryland.

Once I was stabilized on Lithium, I had to take Stelazine as well. They changed my diagnosis to schizo-affective, a cross between manic depressive and schizophrenic. They gave me 1200 mg of Lithium a day plus 5 milligrams of Stelazine. So they just stabilized me on medication. There was no therapy. I was out in ten days.

The medicines make me functional from day to day, but I think my problem is due to the sexual abuse. I hope to one day be off the medicines, and my doctor is working with me on it. I know now I am a schizo-affective personality. It's not an illness, it's my personality.

Six weeks after the hospitalization, I met a guy named Penn, who admitted to being schizophrenic. One night, Penn and I, along with a hippie girl from the Institute, decided to get high. I stayed the night over the girl's house, ate a pizza that I cut up with a knife from my father's collection.

By the next day I was high. I did not sleep all night and ended up at the University of Maryland again. For the ten days I was there, I was in and out of seclusion. I repeatedly dove at the screen window, hoping my spirit would fly out. When I finally got out, my doctor put me on a pedestal in one of the back rooms, a light shining on my face. As I spoke, he took notes, and I felt very beautiful and special.

Six months later I got high again which led to another hospitalization. Leo, a driver at the Pizza Delivery place where I worked, had befriended me. By November we were such good friends, I decided to get high with him. I had a sleepless night, and I called my therapist Sarah. She said she would meet me at 9:00 A.M. in the office. But I came at 7:00 A.M., prepared to wait. I asked people if they had seen her—they had not. I ended by climbing down the fire escape. At the whim of passing children I became *Wonder Woman*. They said, "Jump! Jump!" I jumped into a dumpster.

Around 10:00 A.M. I drove my car till I was lost somewhere in West Baltimore near North Avenue. I stopped by a trio of black men and invited one into my car. He told me where his apartment was and I drove him there. As he got out, he grabbed my purse. I had just wanted to drop him off. I ran behind him, trying to get my purse. We went into a room with bare floorboards and a bare mattress. He did something in the corner with a rolled up sleeve and needle. He asked if I wanted some. I said no and undressed. I was in the Last Tango in Paris. Nothing happened as far as I can recall. He fell asleep.

I had worn my Thomas Man earring and hooked it to his latch hook, a crucifix for his home. I tried to bathe, but the water was cold and there was no plug in the filthy tub. Finally I decided I had to leave. I ran naked out the door and down the steps, past a fat black woman who exclaimed, "You can't go out like that!" I flew out in the sunshine and huddled naked in my car. Masses of black women came running out. One had a comforter and wrapped it around me and said, "Everything's going to be all right, honey."

They called the police, and they came with a paddy wagon. A female police officer took me back upstairs and told me to dress. Then the police had an inquisition. They asked the man some questions. I couldn't remember, everything was too foggy. Finally they decided I was crazy and took me down to Sinai Hospital. For two hours I was observed in a quiet room. Then an ambulance took me back to the University of Maryland Hospital.

I spent some time in the Quiet Room after dancing with some of the patients, and exposing myself. After ten days the medicines, Stelazine and Lithium calmed me, and I was again released to the world again.

I moved out of my mother's house in June 1985, and lived in the Seminary Apartments in Bolton Hill. Often times, Leo would come over and sleep on my floor since he had nowhere else to go. Leo and I became better friends. It seemed I could talk to him. It seemed like he understood where most everyone else didn't. He got me high and I felt like I could understand everything again—of the mind, not the heart. Within my heart was just simple pain.

PART FOUR

I would go to the Tavern, drink three beers and pray to see Clark. Sometimes I did and sometimes I didn't. My life was centered around Clark and his voice in my head. Even though the doctors had doubled my Stelazine dosage, I still heard the voices.

Unfortunately three beers a night led to shots of Tequila and a Black Russian and eventually Leo took over. He wormed his way into my life, didn't mind when I drank, but he didn't. He was a dry alcoholic: one who doesn't drink, but isn't working the Twelve steps of A.A. He told me he had sobered up the moment he saw me.

My mother bought a house to rent to me and a roommate. Guess who became my roommate—the ever present Leo. At first he stayed on the third floor, in his room. But in my co-dependency, my neediness, I beckoned him to my room and soon we were lovers. The co-dependency between Leo and I was such that I would bolster his ego with false compliments and he would comfort me in times of distress.

My affliction, my heritage of sexual abuse was running rampant, and I didn't even have Clark's voice to guide me. Leo soon tired of comforting a comfortless person. I took to calling the Rape Crisis Center when feeling anxious, angry, and in pain.

Our relationship ended on an evening when I found he had invited some hippie, pot-smoking, beer drinking, guitar playing friends over to my house. Since one of his old friends had broken into our house and stolen everything, I squealed wheels home when I found he had given them the keys. I threw them out, threatening to call the police. They left soon enough. But when Leo came home he knocked me off my Exercycle, threw the pizza he had brought home at the wall. We battled in the kitchen, he wrestled me to the ground, put his knees to my throat. "You're hurting my throat," I wheezed. He removed his knee, stood up, and left the house.

I called his sister. She came over, tried to comfort me and warn me at the same time. She told me of one of her relationships, that started with little pushes and shoves and ended with guns and knives. I was sold. I was terrified. Maybe he'll calm down, I prayed. But when we tried to talk about it the next evening, he flew into a rage, growled and paraded on the floor as if insane with anger. He threw a chair at a kitchen cabinet. But he didn't physically hurt me. He only spit on me twice.

That was it—I knew I had to leave. I was terrified. I saw my father in each of my boyfriends, and I finally found my father in him. I was trying to find the father to make the father change, to save the father.

My therapist helped me to understand that I needed to leave Leo right away. So I did. I went to Mom. I called her and told her what had happened, and packed my bag as quickly as possible with only my necessities. I even left my jewelry. Leo had been abused when he was a child, and then abused himself with drugs and alcohol for years. What came of this is something I still do not understand.

I had begun AL-ANON, a group of people who share their experiences in hopes that others who live with an alcoholic loved one will recover. It was now April, my bad month. I started buying beers, and putting them in my mother's refrigerator. When she had a drink at 5:00 P.M., I had a drink or two. But I didn't like the feeling that I had to continue to drink the next day, after I had stopped. It was the beginning of understanding the compulsion to drink. I started to write in my journal, kept going to AL-ANON, and even began going to ACOA, groups for people with alcoholic and dysfunctional families. I seemed to have both.

My sweet and gentle mother bought me a new house. I paid for half of it and she paid half. Over the summer I tried five different jobs in five months, including cashiering. Finally in November, having settled comfortably in my house, I found a job at an art and craft store.

January slowed down some and I made a friend in A.A. June and I had lot in common. Dysfunctional families, alcoholism? She was alcoholic, but was I? I thought I was. Then I thought I wasn't. Still I didn't drink. I went to my ACOA meetings once a week, if that, and figured I'd be all right. After an off and on friendship with her, I decided to end our relationship.

About the same time my youngest sister Amy went into a psychiatric hospital in Illinois. I wrote to her immediately and sent her a "May King Villi Warrior" bracelet, for strength. The wearer of this bracelet, I wrote, is strong. It's there to remind you, you are strong." She got out of the hospital. Of course, I was gritting my teeth through all of this.

One day about this time, I tried to stop my cigarette habit. After one hour of nicotine withdrawal, I decided to drink a beer. I thought I would worry more about whether I was an alcoholic or not than whether I smoked or not. I drank half the beer and my brain went crazy. Half of my brain was saying, "Drink the goddamn beer. You haven't drunk in six months. Drink the rest of it. It would just be one beer—what's one beer?" The other half of my brain was saying very clearly, because I was in a state like tripping, "My God, you sound just like an alcoholic. Don't drink the beer. Throw it out!"

The side of my brain saying I was an alcoholic won. I knew then that I was an alcoholic. I made sure to invite June over the next night when I felt the craving of alcohol again. After that, I knew it was time to get serious. I starting attending A.A. meetings and talked to someone who convinced me I needed to go to 90 meetings in 90 days.

This past summer, I spent three weeks at Springfield State Hospital, reliving childhood sexual trauma. I laid on the mat in the quiet room with legs apart, pounding on the mat, because I was so angry. I was remembering being tied up under the basement steps and being abused. As I emotionally relived the experience, I imagined the abuse to be even worse than it was. I was pricked with pins, pierced with a drill. I was drugged before being abused sexually and physically. I had large scars and lacerations on my body.

In some detail, I fantasized my mother saving me. When she arrived home, she did not immediately notice the marks on my body. It was when she gave me a bath that she noticed and dragged me out of the water and screamed, "Oh my God! Oh my God! Oh my God!" Wet and naked on the bed, she said, "I could just kill him! I could just kill him!" She took me immediately to the hospital.

A lady doctor told me this is going to hurt. "You're a brave girl aren't you?" I said, "Yes." She took one stitch and it hurt. "Do you want me to do this fast or slow?" she said. "Fast," I said. She gave the stitches and I screamed and cried. I was given a tetanus shot for the puncture wounds. My mother took me home and stayed up with me all night because my arms were stiff and sore.

In the fantasy, my childhood abuse came to a stop at this point. After I came out of the Quiet Room, I was in such pain, that I burned myself with a cigarette on the back of the hand. I also, saw a man who said he was suffering pain. By burning myself, I showed him that I was suffering greater pain than he was.

I am an alcoholic and doing the A.A. program, and this is what's saving me right now. Upon publication of this book, I'm still sober. I have worked up to the third step of the program and have experienced miracles, magic and joys. I have the beginnings of self acceptance, all through God's love. When I made my decision to turn my will and life over to the care of God as I understand him, I didn't even know what I was getting into, and I'm so glad that I got into it.

May 1, 1990

JIM'S STORY

Jim was the name I was given when I was adopted. My mother and father died when I was a child at the age of two. They had a domestic quarrel, and were going to get divorced. He killed her and later he was found dead, apparently a suicide. I was adopted by an Anglo-Saxon Christian family who worked at the Port Mission. I was ten years old when I was told all this.

Once I was taken to a psychiatrist, by my parents who felt I was unbalanced. After the doctor talked to me, he asked to speak to them. He pointed out to me the imbalance—if I did have it all—was possibly their fault. "Did it ever dawn on you that they might have adopted you for the money, that they might not love you at all, as much as you think," he said. When my parents found out what he said, they got quite angry and didn't take me back.

My father used to spank me with a sewing machine strap. Whenever I was bad, I would get the strap. One time I fought him back and grabbed the strap. I broke his watch. I said, this is the last time you're going to use it, and it was the last time. I took the strap out to the trash can. I didn't have any more physical confrontations till age seventeen. I was an abused child and didn't realize it.

At the age of seventeen, I was asked to leave home. I hit the streets. The Christian family I was raised in was too strict: I couldn't smoke cigarettes, nor drink beer. It caused me to go the opposite way. It was a traumatic experience—on my own at the age of seventeen. I was very emotional, totally unaware of common sense. I had a playboy image from reading too many Playboy Magazines. I love good looking women, and I gave them every penny I had. Consequently I was soon out of place to stay and out of a job as well.

By the age of nineteen I needed rent money and I was "in love" with a Ruxton girl. With my last two dollars I bought a pocketknife and went out to Towson and robbed a gas station. I got $78 and 120 years. They just tried to scare the hell out of me, which they did. I went to Spring Grove Hospital, trying to beat it on temporary insanity. I did. I was given eighteen months probation and a nine year sentence if I violated it.

Back in the '60's, Spring Grove was something you see in the movies: dirty, unkempt. They didn't care what your case was; they put all the criminally insane together. You would walk in the bathroom and a guy used to be there eating razors. They had male and female nurses who took advantage of you physically. I could get money from male nurses by performing sexual acts, then give it the female nurses for sexual favors in return. All this was happening at the age of nineteen.

They gave us massive dosages of Thorazine. When you first got the drug, it immobilized you. I had to walk, leaning on the walls, just to get down the hall. Once they found out you weren't physically violent, they would lighten your dosage. After seeing several psychiatrists, one of whom put his hand on my leg—only to ask what my opinion of abnormal and normal was. I told him, "The dictionary says insanity is the opposite of sanity which is normal." He acted surprised that I was that intelligent.

There was a group of us in there, nothing wrong with us, just trying to get out. Some did belong. They had one guy that would hear voices and start swinging because God was telling him.

I was there three months. It was better than 120 years in prison. Cliche's are overused, but there's truth in them. One of mine is that you have to laugh to keep from crying. I went through several tests. Eventually two doctors qualified me as sane. Basically, I just had a traumatic childhood experience, too much stress, strictures from the family. I drew a picture of my family. My dad was slim, healthy, wore a double breasted suit; my mom had a good figure and wore a mini skirt. They weren't like that: my mom was short and fat, my dad, tall and fat.

By the time my father told me the facts of life, I had already learned how to have sex and not care. Over the years, every time I have cared about a female, she got everything she could out of me, used me and threw me away. It's caused me to have a disrespect for women.

I haven't gone without drugs except periods of time when I've been on religious kicks, or drug incarcerations. When I was thirteen or fourteen my mom used volumes of Valium pills. I used to take them. My girlfriend's mom drank gin, so I started on gin and Valium. When you take three or four it gets you pickled, like a half-pint of Jack Daniels. My drug abuse goes back to my childhood.

I have no desire to continue to be a drug user, but don't tell me you love me, and that I should lock myself up for three months—that I should be manhandled. Take me into your house and allow me to get a job.

* * *

I'm a street person. People remember your face and situations around you. A person can do the right thing 364 days out of 365. If they spilled coffee on the last day, the whole restaurant will remember it.

I'm forty years old now. At times, I question the social structure of our entire society, knowing it needs a lot of changes, wondering who's wrong and who's right. I'm not a man of violence, but I feel that people's lives are taken from them by what I call the "pushing of the pen." By verbal agreements, peoples lives are taken for God and country. My basic opinion is that the wealthy people of the world—there are certain families that have all the power—run and rule the government, and our society deals to them. This is just basic knowledge; all you have to do is read. We've had men in history—John Kennedy and Martin Luther King— anytime a person who has shaken any tree, they are done away with, violently and quickly.

These are the kind of thoughts that go through my mind in the day, pan handling, trying to get spare change. Basically I live a simple life. One of the reasons I do—I look at people who have so much responsibility on them. I don't really want that. If I had some wealth, I'd make sure the pressure wasn't just on me.

I recently served two years for theft. I was released, but it was under an A.A./N.A. requirement. There are winners and losers; they tell you to stick with the winners. My life is rough, but not unmanageable. At the end of the day I'll be sleeping in a vacant house. I don't know if the owner is going to call the police.

I'm a loner; I've stayed at the mission, even volunteered on staff on Helping Up, because of my addictions. I've taken in A.A./ N.A. to myself.

I found N.A./A.A. to be positive in its own way with its beliefs in God, higher power. But when you walk through the door and say your name, you're not anonymous. Still, walking in there is recovery. The expression is: once an addict, always an addict. I've received partial support, not proper support. My hope is that people will quit judging me and give me an opportunity.

May 22, 1990 [*dictated*]

CREATIVE WRITING CLASS
at Sheppard Pratt

Coming out of a stupor. I'm starting to feel better. I'll be free once again. The chains have been broken and I'll try to live again. Once more I'll struggle on the outside world and go through the motions of being alive.

Write a Gesture: Something a Person Always Does:

The way he holds the cigarette and gestures as he talks is similar to a bird flickering in a bush.

She rocks her head back and forth, cradling it in her hand. It's as if she is holding a baby's head, trying to comfort it. She smooths back her hair, as though she is trying to hold her head up.

A Childhood Memory:

I was around eight or nine years old when my brother and I played in a club basement. We had a rocking horse, painted red, roller skates and other toys. I had a china tea set and bride doll that I didn't really like that much, and he had a bow and arrow set.

My brother and I would fight often. Once he jabbed me in my back with his arrow and I fell, pretending I was dead. My brother who was only five, said with a shaky voice, "Well, she's dead." He threw a cover over me and said there's nothing to do except turn out the light and go upstairs. Later, he came down with my mother who comforted him, telling him she's not, but then she scolded him, "Do you want your sister to die?" "No." "Then don't do that again." I think of our childhood and I suffer from heartache.

The Horror Story of the Seventh Grade

By the Seventh Grade, I had already entered puberty. I weighed about 105 pounds, had hips and beautiful thin legs, with breasts fitting into champagne cups. My face was beautiful, but my hair left something to be desired, since my father insisted it be kept short, and I didn't have a decent hairdresser.

When we moved and I entered a new school, a fifteen-year old boy fell madly in love with me at first sight. I didn't know quite how to take it. When he asked me to one of his friend's parties, I said I would go. However, my mother disliked the idea and said I couldn't go.

After, the kids in the class found out and I was labeled queer. I would be walking home from school and pass Neil Turner's gas station and get called fag. When I would see guys in the hall, they would harass me. A guy would be standing with a girl and say, "Isn't she a little swishy for you to be flirting with her?" Another guy walked up to me and said, "There's a girl that listens to her mother. Then he got closer and asked, "Are you afraid of me?"

A Happy Moment:

When I first got Jeremy as a kitten, he was scared and didn't trust anyone. I looked down at him as he poked his head out of the carrier and said, no one is going to hurt you. He looked back in anguish. The first night I stayed up all night with him, reassuring him, holding and caressing him. I was holding him next to my stomach as I tried to sleep and suddenly he crawled towards me and started kissing me and rubbing his face against mine.

Write Something Honest, Without Censoring:

Dear Kitty,

I'm wondering how I'm going to survive this mental concentration camp. By rational standards I am quite insane. I'm trying to cover it up to keep from being fed more drugs. This cruel cold environment is getting the best of me.

The Bum

When I was younger, I lived downtown in the heart of the city. I was often lonely and looking for something to do. One day I decided to go to church and challenge the Sunday school class. As I walked through the park, I was in a trance. A street person stopped and waved at me. "I can tell you're full of the Holy Ghost," he said. "Good day to you!"

A Place of Safety:

When I was a young child I loved to play in the dirt under my Grandmother's porch. It was dark and peaceful. With my bother and cousins we had some utensils and a bucket of water for making mud pies. We would stay for hours spooning dirt until our mothers told us to come in and wash. We didn't mind the fleas we got but our mothers did.

144

A sense of calm has come over me. As everything has boiled down to 38 years of pain. But I know what went into it. Maybe I can begin to walk now. . .

Electroshock and Medications (At another hospital)

They didn't have my parents' consent to run that current through my brain. I was dying—in the most terrible pain I had in my life—and so I signed it. They said, "Sign this paper. We are going to try and help you." They didn't say it was shock. I didn't like the results. I lost memory and thinking ability.

The medication causes a feeling of emptiness as though I were a robot, going through the motions of life. I am always trying to fill this void with food or drink. If I don't stop, I will probably self destruct.

The only hope I have is my spirituality. It's a refuge from the pain. I know some day I will be free.

Ter Ann

On the horizon written in the past
gleaming young faces
toddle in the dark . . . awkwardly

And in the valley before me
Old men rap the dry sands
while barren painted faces of ladies in holy laces
stare wickedly across the dusty landscape

The future hangs,
suspended in fine lines and wretched hands

The easter sun proclaims daybreak
and sullen moon with sluggish pace
creeps below the hills
to fornicate strange phantoms for the incestuous day.

by Kate

IS THIS WHY I'M ILL?

by Linda Coolen

PART ONE   1966

I can not remember all I should of the very young years of my life. However, the years I can remember were really quite horrible. All through my youth I lived in fear of being put away. Perhaps I did act differently towards most others my age, but I had good reasons. I can see my mother running to the telephone to get what she called "MEN IN WHITE COATS." At the time I really thought she was serious; only in my later years did I find out she was only pretending. Every time I'd hear or see a car coming into our yards the words "MEN IN WHITE COATS" would run through my mind.

The feeling of fear built up strongly inside of me. All through my life I was told how "queer" I was. Some people however wouldn't say this to my face; they'd say it behind my back. Father always told people I was "mental." At that time, Mom and I weren't very close; our relationship wasn't like a mother's and daughter's should be. I wanted to be close to Mom, but she ignored me. She clothed and sheltered me, but showed no love, interest or affection.

I, at the time, was closely attached to my father. I can remember my father so often saying to my mother "Marcie, for God's sake get along with Linda; she's your daughter too." When she started to show that she cared, I was so mixed up I couldn't quite understand the sudden change. After she began to show signs like a mother should, father began to fade away and ignored me.

I became grown up at an early age, more than most girls. However, I was still a child in mind, if not in body. I always had best friends, but father always found fault in them. They either laughed too much, or he hated their parents. If I wished to have company in my room or to stay overnight an awful fuss was made. So, when I was growing up I played mostly with the boys because my brother's friends made me welcome. But most of my childhood was lonely and quite hopeless. I was always afraid of what would happen next.

I had an older and younger brother. There I was between two boys, but no little sister to love. I used to beg Mom to get me one. Finally, I knew Mom was going to have a baby. The time came, early one afternoon, a baby girl was born to the family. I was the first one to see her because she was born upstairs in Mom's bedroom. I was almost hysterical. She, like me, looked quite ugly. Of course, all I realized was that I had the baby sister I so longed for. I ran up and down the streets telling everyone the good news.

As she grew up, she had the love of both mother and father. I loved her too, but somehow I couldn't get close. I was usually told, "Keep away from her." Even today she's kept away from me by her father. He cuddles her and says "Thank God, Dad got one girl"—as if I never existed.

I was never much to look at; however, I did have a sense of humor. I was always very smart in school, got top marks and prizes. This too came to an end. In the eleventh grade, I could feel myself going down hill very rapidly, but I didn't know what was wrong. I didn't have enough sense to go to a minister or doctor for help.

I failed the eleventh grade, tried a second time and failed again. I was almost certain I was ill. My parents didn't do anything about it. No one insisted I get help. After failing the second time, I was forced to leave home. But I wasn't ready to give up yet. I felt so miserable, suffering from severe attacks of headache, heartache, and loneliness. Finally I was allowed back on weekends, thanks to Mom. But I got so bad, that Mom, the family doctor, and I agreed I needed help.

So I went to see a psychiatrist. I went along and answered many questions. They at first made me recall my childhood. . ."Oh, what a childhood, and my teenage years. . . . Nothing exciting ever happens to me." Same old thing. FRIGHT, FEAR, HATE. Now my teens are closing. I didn't enjoy any of them.

I remain in my nineteenth year a lonely, sick, miserable girl. Simple and dumb, I guess one would call me. Most teenagers have special boyfriends in their lives. Boys are all alike; they want one thing—and it isn't "love." My life is a bad enough mess without adding more agony and misery. Now that I'm older I sometimes wish I were a child again and had love and someone to look after me. But it's too late. I wouldn't go with anyone now, because Mom said to me one day: "Linda, I hope the man you marry or fall in love with is taken from you by another woman or death to make up for what you did to us." I'll never forget these words and the expression on her face.

I remained quite ignorant regarding the facts of life. I only heard about them expressed in dirty terms from the school kids and society. When I want to clarify something now, I run to a close relative or friend. I wouldn't dare ask my father or any doctor.

I'm classed as a nut by almost all the people who know me. However I think there are a few who care and know I'm sick, perhaps a bit mixed up, but not totally crazy. I keep reliving my past and hoping my future will be better. I pray almost continually that I won't go completely "Mental."

Some people tell me I'm OK. Are they serious or just trying to be cute? I know I'm sick, at least I'm willing to accept the fact. It's no good to try and hide it because the proof is only too visible and evident. I was in a mental institution eleven times altogether. People there aren't the same as me. I mean they were—I hate to use the term—mental: cutting their wrists, jumping out of windows, fighting with different articles and weapons.

My first trip to the mental institution was quite a pill. Two doctors signed me in because I was in an accident. I can't remember a thing about it. No one, not even the doctors believe me. The cause of my accident is only known by the person or persons responsible. I'd give anything to know the truth of what happened.

At the institution I was classed for awhile as "Schizophrenic Paranoid," meaning "split personality and suspicious." Whenever I asked how I could help myself, I didn't get a satisfactory answer. My psychiatrists have helped me to understand myself better. I think they're really quite serious, but I'm scared to tell them everything because I'm afraid of being on a locked ward with barred windows and locked doors, needles and people running around with white garments.

AN UNFORGETTABLE EXISTENCE

by Linda Coolen

During the mid 60's, I was signed in a mental institution against my will. First, they took all my clothes away from me, and I was made to wear a Johnny shirt and a housecoat. I waited days to get my clothes back. Then they told me to take a bath. I tried to explain I had a bath before. No privacy—two hugh nurses stood watching me. When I went to step out of the tub, one nurse gave me a shove. I fell against the side of the tub. It felt like a couple of ribs were broken; I was very sore and tender for a long time. When I told them I was going to report them, they both sneered and replied, "Who'd believe your word against ours. Don't you realize you're in a mental hospital?"

The staff did much against my will; they tried to make me break down and blow my cool, but I promised myself to stay in control.

I was heavily sedated and the pills I was on made me constipated. I went several days without a movement. The doctor wouldn't help me, until one day I left the ward and marched to his office and told him to look at how distended I was. So, that night, I was given one pill, a laxative. It was not effective. It was days later before I went to the bathroom.

Upon my admittance, they took my radio from me and put it in what was known as the "trust fund." It was there a couple of weeks before I was permitted to get it back. I had to walk through a long, dimly lit tunnel-like hall. While I was going to get it, one of the male patients grabbed me and succeeded in tearing nearly all my clothes off. He lowered me on the concrete floor, but I kicked him where it hurts and poked my fingers in both of his eyes. I ran back to the ward, but nothing was done on my behalf. I lived in total fear the whole time.

There were four patients in my room; across from me was a lesbian. I was warned about her, and my first night there she attacked me. I thought I was dreaming; someone was playing with my breasts and kissing me. I woke and there she was. I knocked her on the floor. She was an older person and I didn't want to hurt her too seriously. The nurse came in. She said I was upset, gave me a needle and threw me in seclusion. I was only trying to protect myself.

I saw many sad cases there; I was sick myself, but I conducted myself in an orderly manner. I was slapped about, beaten, and cursed at by other patients, but again I kept my cool. I never retaliated unless my survival was at stake.

I noticed that lots of patients who acted up were getting discharged, but not me. So, for two weeks I pretended I was feeling better; I put on a good front, smiling, playing games with patients, etc., and finally, after all that, I was let out on a trial basis.

The institution taught me to hate, lie, and have a terrible fear. I've not been the same since. I keep it in my mind if I don't function well, that I could be sent there again. I never want to darken its door as a patient. I may visit a friend or family member, but that's it.

A person in those kinds of hospitals sees and hears nothing if they want to survive. I knew when to speak and when not to. Right to this day, it scares my terribly. I feel I've been branded. I won't give up though; I'll fight my last breath to survive.

I cooperated and now will try to carry my head up high, try not to be ashamed of who I am l. I feel I paid a debt I didn't own.

PART TWO—WHO AM I?   July 27, 1972

I never discussed my other personalities. First, there's Linda; she's the sick, abnormal one. When she meets someone, she's usually Debbie Green, trying to hide Linda. Debbie puts on that she's normal, well, pretty, quite capable, and a nice person to know. She also exists when her mom is happy or laughing.

Then Linda goes into another person, a Minister. She has the ability to preach, pray over people, even to cure. Linda gets very religious at times. But this is the minister personality in her. It's not really Linda at all.

Linda hears voices, like someone calling to her. She even had words with God one day while in the hospital. Linda is a mean, nasty, terrible person. In fact, she shouldn't be classed a person or even a human. She's full of hate and suspicion.

August, 1972

All day I've been wondering about things. For example, do I have any real, true friends? I just can't trust people. They're out to destroy and play games with my mind. They want to tear apart any good (if any) that's in me. People are such liars. People are haunting me, watching my every move. I don't want to go out anywhere except when I must, like to church and my doctor's appointments. I bet a man would come right out of church and turn around and rape you if he had a chance at all.

All my doctor talks about is Sex. I hate that topic, it brings back too many memories, memories I never will forget. I don't want men's hands on my body. I shiver at my brothers' hugging or kissing me. It actually makes me feel nauseated.

I wonder, does my mother really love me? Only a sick person could think anything nice about me, one such as myself who has mental difficulties. I don't feel I was ever cuddled or loved as a baby. I feel I was dropped on the doorstep at my mother's residence. I don't think my mind developed or even matured. There's a blockage there; there's something in the way stopping me from many things. How much longer do I have to wait for a miracle or a miracle drug? My cry goes up, "How Long?"

Two years later, 1:23 AM

I went to church at 7 p.m. Luckily there were only seven in the congregation to whisper and to peer at me. I didn't sing, I can't anyway. I didn't pray, just sat there like a dummy—getting up and down when the others did. It had no meaning for me.

Coming out the church door the minister shook my hand and said "How are you, Linda?" I felt like saying all of a sudden, "I'm the Minister, how are you and the rest of my congregation? Immediately following that, I felt like screaming, "Go home, all of you just go home; you have no right to stay in my church any longer!"

My recreation is now very limited: bingo once every two years, a show once or twice a year. However, I like folk songs, spirituals, sacred music. . . . Don't misunderstand and think I'm religious crazy. I care to mention it because "God is real" and does change things. Still, People sneer and smirk at me.

As I said before, I'm nothing to look at. I don't doll all up. I'm just a plain Jane and I intend to stay that way. People are false enough without adding unnecessary novelties. With me, I'm laughing on the outside and crying hard on the inside. True, I'm false too because my laughter is usually to relieve tension and pent-up emotions.

The mornings are my worst, my evenings the best, if there is a best. In the morning I can't seem to relieve the agony and misery and tension. At times my mind keeps telling me to walk and get out. So up and down the streets I wander, just like the little "Hobo."

October 29, 1980

I am still having those terrible spells and complete numbness over my entire body. If I were sitting it would feel like I was melting right down in the chair. If leaning against anything—same feeling. If lying down, I felt it too. If I closed my eyes, I'd have slipped into unconsciousness. No one knows why. However, as frightening as it was, God saw me through.

I urge you, if you're experiencing the same things, please seek help.

Well, I've given you many ideas of myself and what the illness has done. Much more could be said, but I can't express it on paper. However, I'm sure I've had my HELL. Even though I don't fully understand it, I'll continue to pray, to believe and try not to doubt.

TO MY LOST FRIEND

Oh, my friend; you asked me not what I see,
tho I will tell you so, and by so doing, speak more of me.
You are a river rat on hamster row, an unclean thing full of pomp
and show. Upon your head, I see the Cardinal's crown, the scarlet
heart, pierced ruby red jewel, the dripping frown. . .
Of Kings and men and wars and terrible deeds, you sow, you reap,
lay waste your seeds, chop off a head, rip out a heart. . .
make doubt, make fear, serenity of God, depart.

Thy creature of the night, what day blindness assails you,
that you cannot see the greatness of the smallest acorn,
such is man, of woman born. Your seed, it searches like a dandelion
puffed on the wind, lands on some poppyseed flower; illusions,
grand delusions, dwelling within; you creep about in day, the light
assails you, it chases you, picks you out of corners,
shows your nightmare ridden face to the crowd, you shout, you spit,
you writhe and snake about. . .and still no mercy from the crowd.

You pant, you gasp for air from all this torment; you find relief
inside a jail, imprisonment? You scoff, you scorn, you rage;
You're not reborn. . . . You're lost. . . . No rose. . .No!. . .Nothing!. . .
but a thorn! Pray thee to God, to open up your heart, to put
the Spirit's flame inside your head; to pierce your hardened heart
with ray of hope, the son, Christ's blood again begins to flow,
to bleed anew. . . the ROSE. . . where did it go?

by Paula

SUPPERTIME: OR FULL COURSE
WITH SEIZURE SALAD

Sitting down
To our just desserts
Of vain pie
And brain tumours,

We ate in silence
Choking on a cyst
Gripping an implement
In each tight fist.

Robert Allen, Halifax, Nova Scotia

THEODORA'S STORY

PART ONE

In 1949 when I was born my mother believed in everything Doctor Spock said. Of these early years I had many happy memories and it was not until I attended school that I became depressed. In Kindergarten I can remember having my hair pulled by the teacher and being teased by other students and being miserable away from home. At five, I realized the older one grew the more miserable one became, and I decided not to grow up. I had a long argument with my Uncle Edgar, when I said I wouldn't grow up and would prove it by tying myself to a chair. Uncle Edgar lost the argument. I'm about a foot taller, but I'm still five.

Among the pleasures of life, culinary pleasures loomed large. Once, my mother was expecting my brother Benjamin, and she sent me to the corner store for a pickle and pretzel. I ate the pickle and pretzel on the way home, so she sent me back for another pickle and pretzel which I also ate. After three tries she decided to go for it herself. In those days we lived in an old rowhouse on Monument Street. There were nine of us: uncles, aunts, and cousins, and of course myself, and Benjamin.

Every year the Christmas tree fell over, and in those days ornaments were made of glass. One year we had angel hair on the tree and I became fascinated with angels and death. I have never seen anything as beautiful as the halo cast by angel hair when a light shone through it. We were learning about angels in Sunday School. I believed that upon death, one became an angel and grew wings. I wanted wings more than I wanted life. Why wings, I am not sure—perhaps because of the multitude of pigeons in the neighborhood and the gulls, who fascinated me with their flight. The pictures of angels I had seen resembled beings who had never suffered. Of course, even the smallest infant suffers, if for no other reason that he needs his diaper changed. And I thought that if I went to heaven, I wouldn't have to go to school.

My first real brush with death did not come until much later. When I was in the tenth grade, a daughter of my mother's friend was killed by a car after being dragged six blocks. The child was six years old and we were all taken to see her at the funeral home. As I looked down at the small dark face, that blind, unseeing face, I felt for the first time a real terror of death, not the dead which to me have always seemed pitiful. It was then I realized that I wanted very much to live. I have this obsession with death. Sometimes I think it's the only thing that is going to free me from the pain.

At that point I began to write serious poetry, but I had always written stories and poems since third grade. Before, my stories and poetry had been idle fantasies. Now I was no longer fascinated by truth and light, and my mind took a turn to the dark, deep, and mysterious. I wrote a story about cannibalism, another about suicide. I wrote of being raped, plagiarising from one of my father's paperback novels. Then I wrote about horror, about a beast, a headless woman covered with gore who haunted my palace in Siberia. I suppose most adolescents sooner or later become fascinated with the darker side of life.

In addition to normal anxiety and desire, I suffered an overwhelming depression. I remember sitting for hours in the basement listening to Chopin's Nocturne, finding them beautiful. I turned—in my manner of dress and conduct—completely away from my own generation. Years later, the neighbors would call me a Hippie, but in those days I was merely strange. I was the young, stern girl who rebuked adults and had a larger vocabulary than their English teacher.

At about that time I became obsessed with Ringo Star. Ringo appeared so sad and so vulnerable. Besides, the other Beatles picked on him the way my peers picked on me. The impact of his sensitivity was tremendous. He seemed to be immediate in his longings; in other words, he sought to be there for me. I taped his pictures to my wall. I cried when I listened to his records, and I stayed up late writing him four page letters every night. I wanted to marry Ringo; the first stirrings of sexual feeling in my life were for him. Now I look at Paul McCartney and remember what John Lennon said in *How Do You Sleep*: "a pretty face may last a year or two." In middle age Ringo is handsome, filled-out, happy, but Paul has merely sagged. I noticed that Paul was loved, real believers loved John, nobody loved George, and Ringo received fourteen proposals a day.

In the mornings before going to go to school, I would practice kissing, imagining I was kissing Richard Burton. What was it about Richard I loved?—it was his face for it was tormented. It was his very torment that attracted me. I fell in love with all sorts of men: Elpenor who died in the Odyssey of Homer, anyone who could speak Italian, Frederick Chopin, Jack London, John Kennedy as well as Dylan Thomas.

Somewhere in the odyssey of my youth, of going from love to love, I ceased to love men and tried to be a man. I tried to love the life of Aurore Dupin, better known as George Sand. I wore pants and smoked cigars in my eighteenth year.

I decided to be a writer. I decided I would keep a menage of friends in an old mansion or in a country estate, and that I would support them all by writing. (Oh God, was that a fantasy!)

At 18, when sex became possible because I had left home, I fled from the campus boys with horror. Now I see at the age of forty, when it comes to men, I'm a mere esthetician. I can love them all for their looks, their wit, the way they dress, or the way they hang from the back of a garbage truck, without being a whore. I loved them, even as I loved Ringo from afar, and I loved them well.

It was in my eighteenth year that I went on my first date. I was a sophomore at Morgan and went out with Oswin to an Orioles game. I never saw him again.

I withdrew inwardly more and more, become bolder and bolder outwardly. I had an affair with a married man, Yusef. He strung me along for five years. He was intelligent, handsome, sensitive, witty, rich and thoroughly committed to his wife and children. I wanted to marry Yusef, but he put me off time and time again. Now I'm glad I did not because I married Frank. At the time Yusef and I were going our separate ways, Frank came into my life.

I always felt a certain horror at the advances of most men, but Frank was subtle. He did not come on too strong, but talked to me soul to soul, heart to heart, hand to hand. He did not see me as a broad to be conquered, or a soul to be corralled into the kitchen and bedroom of his life, but as a friend. Perhaps loving him as dearly as I do has become the form of my disability. But even though I feel most of the time as if I were dying for love of Frank, I would not cease to love him.

PART TWO

In addition to my increasing awareness of sex and death, I became interested in Philosophy. I was fascinated by Buddha and his inward journey to enlightenment. I also read *Siddhartha* by Herman Hesse. My identification with the hidden Sannyasi reached the point where I felt myself to be God. The whole point of Hinduism may be summed up in three sentences: everything is God, I am God and you are God. My perception of this three-fold truth was distorted. The form of Buddhism I practiced came from Tibet and is called *Vajrayana* which means "Lightning Vehicle." In this school of thought there are no rules.

About this time I made a circle of new friends. The young people whom I spent my days with were into illicit drugs. My fascination with sex, drugs and Hinduism was increased by the use of LSD-25, speed and marijuana. I was mad as a hatter.

In studying Buddhism my goal became annihilation of my consciousness. The vehicle for this process was LSD and in taking LSD, I found Charles, who raped me. If I had not taken LSD along with studying *Vajrayana* Buddhism I would not have been raped, and if I had not, I could have coped better with the situation.

I met a drug dealer named Charles who happened to be a Hopkins student. He asked me if I ever dropped LSD, fired up, or snorted heroin, cocaine or smoked marijuana. Strange questions, but in the early '70's they were a standard means of introducing oneself to other heads. He invited me to a party and I gladly went. He offered me a tab of acid which I took. We proceeded to smoke marijuana together. Every light in the house was turned out and more men arrived.

I went upstairs to the bathroom. There was no lock on the door. Charles dragged me from the bathroom to the bedroom. Then I can remember a scene like Dante's Inferno, in the city of Dis, in the pits of hell. Every man in that house used my body, in any way he saw fit. I felt nothing. I could hear my own voice pleading for mercy, for compassion, for understanding, but even my own voice sounded small and far away. There were a lot of large black bodies looming over me. By these demon faces, I was driven mad.

I hastily dressed and fled the house. How I made it from one side of Cold Spring Lane to another, I will never know. Perhaps, it was a little like Eliza skipping ice (a scene in *Uncle Tom's Cabin*). Cars traveling east and west swerved to avoid me. I reached home, laid down in the bed, and have never been the same since.

For six months I struggled with this conflict. At last I decided to go to the school psychologist at the infirmary. She spoke to me kindly and examined me with much perception. *But sex was not discussed, and they didn't find out about the rape.* She sought the advice of the head doctor and I was committed by these two. I was told I could go either to Phipps, Springfield, or the University of Maryland. I didn't want to go to the hospital, but I didn't mind because I needed help. I chose Phipps, and the doctors called my parents at home and told them I was having a nervous breakdown. They came in a car and took me quickly to Johns Hopkins Hospital.

I talked to the doctor at Phipps, and we discussed some of my symptoms, such as hearing voices and seeing things which were not there. For a long time I was left in the ER's seclusion room. A nurse brought me dinner, but I didn't see my parents till the next day. They had held me only twenty-four hours for observation before giving me the drug Thorazine.

Inside, I felt much rage. I was angry because I was regarded as being ill, and furthermore was being punished for something that had been done to me. Although I must say Phipps was a warm clinic at that time, and community was stressed, I was so badly hurt that I couldn't communicate. I could only strike out and make symbolic gestures. At meetings, I refused to talk; at meal time I refused to eat; at night I would not sleep, but stayed awake twenty-four hours at a time.

I was angry with my roommate. Late at night I would open the windows wide and turn off the heat. But as soon as my head hit the pillow, she would close the windows and turn on the heat. It was a silent struggle between us.

I began to be noncompliant by refusing my Thorazine, so Doctor K. ordered liquid Thorazine for me. After months of taking liquid Thorazine and participating in petty meetings, there was still no mention of the fact that I had been raped, except to a young nurse who did not believe me. Nobody, it seemed, was interested in what caused me to get ill.

One of the things that made it difficult for me was the fact that I felt guilty about what had been done to me by Charles and his friends. I felt unattractive because I was unhappy with myself. Had I possessed Michael Jackson's millions, I would have made as dramatic a change in my appearance as he did in his.

I began to have strange afternoons where I hid in the window and made my mind a blank, looked out on the garden, and thought: *this is how I'll spend the rest of my life, safely hidden in a dream world, never to be touched again.*

After taking Thorazine for one year, I gained thirty pounds, and I hadn't changed my eating habits. A lot of my time was spent lying down, more and more in a semi-dream state. I was truly incapacitated; I felt more incapacitated by Thorazine than by the acute schizophrenia, my diagnosis.

One afternoon as I lay in bed, a butterfly materialized over me. It appeared first as a black dot, then as a supernatural Monarch butterfly which disappeared as quickly as it appeared. Some of my hallucinations were caused by a drug-induced inertia, rather than by the illness. The medicine at no time stopped the pain, but prevented me from expressing painful feelings and acting out as one in pain. *The psychiatric drugs don't stop the pain, but stop the scream of the pain.*

We were on a very civilized ward: one staff per patient, several registered nurses on duty at all times, and there were two doctors for twenty patients—more staff than patients. We sipped coffee from ceramic mugs.

For the first time I developed problems with black men who were having problems themselves. I developed a hatred and fear of my own people because I had been hurt by my own people. Not only had I been hurt, but a trust was broken between me and my own. It occurred to me because

I had been raped by a handful of black gangsters, that I was bad and black people were bad. I became ashamed of my Southern accent. I became ashamed of black music. I stopped wearing an Afro and became fascinated with white culture. I felt things and people of African origin to be ugly. Not only did I find ugliness in my blackness, but in my womanhood itself. I stopped wearing dresses and for a very long time wore nothing but pants. I did not date, nor did I go to parties, and yet during this time, I found a friendship with an African gentlemen named Yusef.

At last I was discharged from Phipps, after nearly a year there. I was alone at home once more. I spent my time reading, trying to play the piano, and looking at my poor battered guitar. That had been a beautiful instrument, but was now as scarred and cracked as I felt my soul to be.

PART THREE

At this time I began to think that only God could take away my sorrow. I lay in bed, praying all day long. I prayed for my family, but my most fervent request was as follows: "Lord you know that I believe in you and you take those who are dying with faith into your kingdom. Take me!"

I slept little and seldom ate. I survived by drinking tap water from the bathroom. This went on for months. At this point, I was beginning to embrace Christianity, but I had yet to let go of the East. I wanted to experience Nirvana which means extinction, a blown-out candle. I wanted to merge with the universe and cease to be. The responsibilities of life and the work of adulthood frightened me. I lived in fear, regretting the past, hating the future and suffering the present intolerably. Noises, even the slightest sounds, I found distressing. As I lay there, my parents became alarmed. To them it seemed I was never out of bed and the truth is I seldom was. Once a week my parents took me to therapy with Dr. K., but nothing was accomplished. I lived in a waking dream and had no time for reality.

I think back now to the last act of worship I performed before being officially declared insane. I had gone to St. Alphonses church and there before the agonizing crucifix, I lit candles, prayed before the pieta, and went completely out of my mind, realizing my own lack of love for others, and my propensity to sin. Outwardly, I remained the same, but my psyche was a crumbling edifice because inwardly I had nothing to sustain me. I was spiritually poor. Too late, I realized that I had thrown away myself and the gifts that God had given me. Yet I persisted in taking street drugs until my last day of freedom, when I found myself committed to Phipps

Clinic. There in the Clinic they asked of me what I could not give. I had no insight into my problem, but then again that is what madness is, a lack of insight, a fearfulness, and a retreat from reality.

I cannot remember how I became able to cope with the slightest difficulty, but I do remember the night my life was saved. It was cool autumn night, the stars shone down from my windows, a tune by Mozart was playing on the radio. I had lit a candle. An audible voice said to me: *"Life can be made beautiful."* I looked to the stars, to the candle, I listened to the music and for the first time in my life, I was truly glad. Not with a fleeting materialistic joy, nor the hysteria of drugs, but with the sense that God abides and that his world is good.

Although I thought I had discovered all there was to know about God, I've since found him to be a source of infinite meaning. Since that healing experience of almost twenty years ago, in the eyes of the world and sometimes in my own yes, I remain mentally ill.

I married and my marriage has been difficult, but for me worthwhile. My husband is a quiet, sensitive man who like all men of good will, has suffered. Since I'm unable to work, he supports me and himself and never complains. But I sense a deep sadness sometimes in his demeanor. I have panic attacks where I'm horrified at the possibility of disaster. Sometimes, I lie in bed and feel the earth quake under me, or I have imaginings where I fear something has happened to Francis, my husband.

I'm afraid to die. I have terrors of being buried alive and wonder sometimes are not the dead sentient? Trapped six feet under in a coffin, unable to move, alone with their own thoughts. But if this is so, then it must be the common fate of man and I'm not afraid.

At one point, I felt that medication preventing me from being a normal human being. And so to make myself more like everyone else I would not comply with my doctor's prescription.

When I don't take my medicines, the first few days I'm unable to sleep, and I never sleep well without a tranquilizer. Then I become depressed, alternately weeping and raging. I have muscle spasms, and I lose my appetite, which doesn't bother me because under the influence of these pills I've become extremely fat. Also colors become bright for me, and my feelings are intense. I think if I'd never begun to take the tranquilizers, I would not now need them.

To this day, I do not like to take medication, not only because of the side effects, but because it decreases my creativity and interferes with my sense of being well physically. Some of my best writing has been done when I'm a raging manic. With the tranquilizers I take, sometimes I have nightmares such as I had when wasn't under the influence of medications. They are graphic, waking dreams and night terrors, so that even now I do not like the dark. But I've taken various powerful medicines for twenty years and I don't see a way out. I'm having to make my peace with it.

In recent years I have lived my life in the most constructive manner possible. I can honestly say that I am content, that I am reconciled to my past. I realized I made mistakes which caused difficulties in my life and have learned to not to repeat the mistakes. I find that in seeking psychedelic experience one loses touch with the real and the real is always the best.

I look forward to my future as a poet with a published volume. Several of my poems have been published in small journals such as *East Wind*, *Blind Alleys*, and *Unicorn*. Presently, I am writing a novel about the Ante-Bellum South titled *Richwood Manor*.

The crucifix which once broke my heart has been my healing. Where I once couldn't see beauty, I now can: in black men, women, children and in black culture. I have found a true and loving friend in Jesus. I go to Mass every Sunday, and sing with the choir.

Often I experience ecstasy contemplating God. I feel the love that flows from God to me and from me to God. The light in the room is enhanced and even if the room is dark I feel the light. Being with God is hyper-aware, while the "psychedelic" is as nightmare, although it doesn't seem so at first. The contemplation of God also brings peace and looks beyond itself, while the "psychedelic" is narcissistic.

Earthly life is difficult, but I accept it with all its problems and hope to rise to meet life's challenges. I do not think I will return to Springfield or any other hospital because I know myself.

All my life I have felt the extraordinary. Now I want to do the ordinary: to work, to play, to grow, to be.

February 13, 1990 [*dictated*]

A PSYCHIATRISTS' DISCOURSE
RUDELY INTERRUPTED BY A PATIENT

"What symphonies
do catatonics hear
as they weave and bob
to an invisible lyre?"

"do colors burst
on the blank screen
of catatonic eyes"

"do catatonics run
through fields of praise
unshackled by our lack
of passionate desire"

"are roses velvet
in catatonic hands
their perfumes redolent
of celestial fire"

I know
because I walked
out of the barbed-wire fence
of an educated mind
into the frenzy of
the night
with winged feet
and high heart
i laughed
wore next to nothing
passed through walls

out of the city
out of the daylight world
into the madhouse
staring
stark and stiff
my soul sailed
into the glory
without fear
feverish and fey

i know
that one can live on dreams
i almost died
but didn't
i am here
a testimony of light
a child of ice and ire
god-intoxicated
essentially liberated
beaten
sedated
almost hated
and free
as the wind is free
to play with children's hair
and kiss their faces unafraid
untouchable
unreachable
and wild

by Theodora Stanley Snyder

Lyn

DISTORTIONS OF REALITY

Falling through the pain
    on my way to distortions of reality
I noticed my mind had become a fatality
When did the war start
    And death taking them away with a cart
It smells of life although it's a lie
It's only a knife to help you die
I arrived pink and fresh
I was caught and caged in a gold mesh
The land was clear
But I knew others were there
I could smell the fear
They were hiding in their lairs
Waiting for me to walk by
But it was too late, why?
Because I had already died
I had gone on the path to reality with full morality
                Hurrah!

          by Lynn

D. Cherubini

Where were you
Inside my empty spaces
I tried to show you around
my condominium heart
But it was too much
all at once
It was too much for you
to touch
All with the appliances
for cutting
I try to hide
and the fur and the fur rug
needing a good vacuum
to suck and pull all the
white lint stuff that
collects from being stepped
on too much
Tracked in by white
socks
hard to get out
of this small space
and my skin
itches to be touched
by your warmth
my cool skin has learned to need
cold as safety pin
dragged against my skin
My voice screams
along with the music
that speaks of love
gone all wrong
of trying to hide
behind bed sheets
of running away
from momma's eyeball
arrows to my loins
Don't do that!
Don't touch that!

It's all wrong to be in love
with you and touch and touch
when Momma wouldn't even kiss
me on the forehead or rub
my head while I slept
I need you to do these simple things
I need you to be there for me
When the razor blade screams
Or I'll leave
Like I left Mom
I'm running away
Because I need you
and I don't want to need this
I don't want to need you at all
and I'm trying hard to run away
before you push me away—but
I can't.
Do you want me
to cringe in the
dark corner
afraid of the
scary world
Like mother made me do
No. I don't think so.
I felt the fascist
hand around my
throat
My head banged against
The wall I'm
going to speak
aloud among the
crying
babies I'm
going to be free.

By D. Cherubini

THE URGE

Remarkable the housewife
who links me
to her loins
Remarkably the gift of art
that prevents me from
hurling my body off
a tenth story building
at night
Smashing
My bones
My eyes
My flesh
Against the pavement
Remarkably overpowering
is this need
To express
myself

Tugged away at by words
Touched when you don't want to
feel used
feel abused

I inked my memories
all over the front page
of my face

The ink was red
The tool silver

One, two, three,
five times in one night
I struggle to vibrate
my emotions out
the back door the
alleyway the
End.

NO! Don't even think about it.
Take a drink
When you know you shouldn't
because your liver is crying
Don't hurt! Don't hurt!
And you don't want to so
You keep scribbling
all this nonsense
Into your journal
until the pen runs out
and when there's nothing left to do
The urge compels you
The urge tells you
To continue the violent violet bruises and welts
To continue the cuts oozing
through band-aid Mother put there
to hide
the evidence
of hurt
The hurt remaining
remembering the hurt
reliving the ritual
that cleanses
that casts away the demons
Remembering the mother
who spent too much time
at home
cleaning.

D. Cherubini

THE BATTLE

There was
A face slain in the sun
The battle won by a mother
who buried her daughter
under antiques petite fancy
nic nacs bought at
Garage sales for a quarter
on Mothers Day
The whiteness of a
drained fetus
searched in the rain
for a place of warmth
Blemished skin hides
from mother's fallen arm
Was it ever an accident
that you hit me accidentally in the face
marring some sunshine in my
fragile eyes that somehow
I never thought I would
regain
During the numb stages
ignoring the pain
I found a lost partially
winged angel stuck to
the ceiling of dreams
I realized
I wanted to fly through that
little room of walls and
blood
She stuck me in
So I searched
They found a cure
because I told them to
I told them to find a
cure because old scars
talk about rivalry between
subconscious thoughts and
mother's words that burn
and rebellious tendencies
of a bright battered child
suicidal, they said, suicidal

They didn't know how right
they were
But they left me there
Battered
They weren't
Battered.

I was told a big lie
I was told mothering
is nurturing
I missed out on
something

I wasn't nurtured
I didn't feel nurtured
I hurt
all over
and on the inside
and my mind tries to
hide the scars
But y'know, it's
alright to show
them to the world
Someone's got to
so the pain stops.

WHAT VIOLENCE IS
seen through the eyes
gets inside to change you
FIRST   DON'T
Don't let it inside
You'll be fine
THAT'S THE TRICK
If it gets in
you can't say I
didn't warn you
You'll need plenty of
good luck

THE BATTLE
IS ON.

D. Cherubini

THE PUBLISHER'S STORY

By Harrison Edward Livingstone

PART ONE

This is intended to be a story of hope. I can remember years ago when Mike Susko tried to get me to see that there was hope in this life, and I didn't have any. I thought he was crazy because hope had been destroyed in me. I had it once in spite of a terrible childhood, but then my first publisher killed hope in me for many more nightmarish years.

The truth was, I was too fragile and my character too poorly formed to survive such a deliberate infliction of mental distress. It was character assassination at its worst, and in my mind repeated what my mother had done to me as a child. I was too fragile to survive it in a sane and cool fashion, and became one of those walking wounded—in certain respects a mad hatter. What follows is a tale of what I learned.

I've known some joy and happiness, but there were two long periods in my life lasting many years each of horror, torment, and anguish. The first was in my childhood starting from the earliest age I can remember. I wrote a book about it that helped make child abuse a national issue.

From the time I was fourteen I could no longer cry. I could no longer express what I felt because I was too afraid. I turned anger inside on myself, and it became depression, which is repressed anger. As well, I turned fear in on myself. I repressed fear, and it was a colossal fear. I was afraid of everything. My mother built fear, anxiety and terror into me.

My mother was a great monster when I was a child. She systematically "raped" me. That is the way I think of it now. Her form of punishment was very brutal. I can remember it from the earliest age. She would give me an "Enema." She would pull my pants down and put me over her lap and stick the nozzle in and grind it around violently.

This is just one of the means where she destroyed my identity at an early age. I wrote these words years ago, and published them in my "novel," *David Johnson Passed Through Here.* This was really a true story, and not a novel. The names were changed, including my own:

"Sometimes, gazing out at the landscape from the window of a speeding car, it would appear: the hate-filled face, snarling and screaming, the sound and the pain of the blows, the roar in my ears, the awful terror sud-

denly so alive. Then I would try to concentrate on what I could see with my eyes—a tree, or the road outside the window. But the dream was so real that I saw it with my eyes, superimposed over the landscape. It would often drift over my vision a second or a third time until finally it would go away for a while and I would be almost free.

Sometimes its return was as strong and intense as the first nightmare had been, but it never lasted more than a second or two. If there was then a third recurrence, it was weaker and not so hurtful.

After years of this I learned to take an intense interest in the land-scape, people—what I actually saw with my own eyes—so that a more defi-nite line was drawn between the real world and my own world of memories and dreams. Then the nightmare slowly faded and became less frequent, less intense, and less real. What others would say was a bad dream and what had been for me reality became for me less true and more like a dream.

Until it began to fade, however, I did not know what was real. I did not know who I was or why I had been born. The only thing I knew was running away and the constant onset of the dream: in my sleep; when I was awake; when I talked to people and suddenly was lost to them, standing dumb before them, a sentence unfinished, no longer there, astonishing them; until I had to run from their inquiring stares.

They thought me odd. Some made fun of me. Others attacked me. Now and then someone took pity and befriended me, and was there when I tried to talk. But for years after I would still awaken screaming in the night, terri-fied, thousands of miles away, dreaming it over and over. Even as a grown man it came to me—like the scream of shells and bombs come to the soldier at home asleep in his bed years later.

Often the screaming would start again. It went on all night sometimes, in my mind—one continuous roar. And it went on day as well as night, sometimes around the clock. I did not seem to sleep, and when I was in school, could not concentrate on what was being said or on my work because of the screaming in my mind. But school was my main refuge.

School was a refuge, but only a partial one, until that too became an extension and intensification of my hell. But at first, it was quiet there, and I could rest, even almost sleep. At first it was easy. I was an honors student, although I did not do much work and had trouble concentrating. Books were an escape, the only outlet, beside the toy trains. I loved history because it took me into worlds other than my own, where heroes did battle with villains and destroyed them, or were destroyed.

But the stories in the books had a beginning and an end. There seemed to be no escape, no end from the evil in my own life.

But then, school went bad as well.

I began to fail, and could no longer comprehend what was taught. I no longer cared, had no interest in the new subjects, in French, math, grammar. Such subjects dealt with form and required discipline, something I had had enough of. I only wanted to be told stories in books. That was all I wanted to read.

Before this, there came a time when I no longer cried, and the tears stopped. This was when the nightmare began to grow darker, when the black cloud of depression began to follow me, to hang over me wherever I went. Perhaps I was ten or twelve—it is hard to say—when this happened. I had been beaten enough, and it no longer did any good to cry. I merely fended off the blows as best I could, and then went and hid somewhere, sometimes in the closet in the dark, sometimes under the covers, or in a culvert outside the apartment, or in the woods. I retreated into a dark world, began to build a shell around me, slowly, piece by piece.

Then the tears stopped one day and did not return for fifteen years."

I wrote the above passages a long time ago, it seems. I have traveled a perilous journey since then, and I paid a terrible price for writing that, for remaining somehow true to what principals I had.

PART TWO

I had just gotten over the conscious pain of what my childhood had left me, though it had marked me badly—as an adult of thirty-three at the time—in more ways than I understood even then. But the consciousness of the torment of my childhood had left me. Sadly, I was too scared from the past to be able to handle a new life, a new opportunity. I was too fragile to be able to handle my big chance in life, and the publisher wasn't sensitive to that. They ran right over me, and when I tried to stop it, they ended everything for me. They told me, "You will never be published again. We can play pretty rough."

They labeled me a trouble maker and I was blacklisted in the industry, even though my first book had a favorable write-up in the *New York Times Book Review.*

Ultimately there was little or nothing I could do about it, try with all of my might. Their statement wasn't just an idle threat either. They called up the agent I was dealing with, my lawyer, and friends and planted the idea in their heads that I was dangerous and unstable. They had provoked me to screaming at them. Provoked me to making threats, which were only threats to sue and expose them, but easily distorted to look a lot worse. That is what anger does to us, among other things. Yet, I was only reacting to the great power that came down on me.

This was a form of murder—*Psychic Murder*—and it is more damaging and more cruel than any physical blow could be. The new wounds stayed with me and interfered with my life for many years. The company that did it to me deliberately inflicted mental injury. That was their way of getting even for my failing their expectations of how they were going to make money off of me as a writer writing about my torment.

At the end of my sea novel *The Wild Rose,* I wrote, *"It's the ones with fear and anger in their hearts that you've got to watch. It's them that often go bad. You can't carry anger in your heart. I learned that. It eats at you and then it finally is the death of you."*

Well, I didn't learn the lesson I was trying to teach others in *The Wild Rose,* even though I knew it in my mind. I let myself be overwhelmed once again by great emotion, not so long after having eased away from the primal rage that I had grown up with. I wasn't far enough away from all the hurt that had devoured my childhood and early life, and my feelings got the better of me just when I had to keep a level head. I didn't know how to control or channel the rage at the new injustice which befell me. Time was healing the childhood wounds, but I did not learn enough from it. I was far too battered to be objective.

I learned a lot during the new and long tormented period that followed, but my anger got me into trouble and compounded my problems. People are often afraid of angry people, and they were afraid of me. I became my own worst enemy. My anger often spilled out at anyone who crossed me, who hurt me. I became paranoid, thinking that those who blocked me were against me, and some were, of course.

Life became a living death without hope. For several years after they threatened me and ruined my career, I could not write at all. Writing had been my self, my identity, my *raison d'etre*. It was all I had, and they killed that and the hope that went with it. "You will never be published again," they said. "We can play pretty rough."

When I tried to write, it was often quite bad. The few months I was on prescribed psychotropic drugs saw to that, scrambling my brain for years afterwards, until the poisons were washed out of my body.

There can be no doubt that the medicines they give people who have been gravely wounded by trauma, people who have assembly-line psychosis, people who have been raped or murdered psychically destroy people's ability to self actualize—if the drugs are maintained longer than a few weeks. They destroy the victim's ability to learn to cope with the pain they live with and get past it.

PART THREE

Five years after the blacklisting, I made the first attempt to become a publisher, setting up the company that many more years after that published this book. That was fifteen years ago, or so. Being a publisher was not one of my life goals. When I was about twenty I wrote down the subject matter of a half a dozen novels I wanted to write. As the years went by, I wrote them, published some of them, and wrote a lot more. I have a vast amount of unpublished writing—some of it good—and some of it bad—going to waste. But this is a tale of perseverance against the greatest adversity, of the finding of Hope again, of Faith.

A very long battle ensued. I fought back with everything I had, which wasn't much. I filed suit after suit in court, writing my own suits, usually without a lawyer, and when I had a lawyer, they weren't really helping me. But I cost that company all I could cost them. Eventually a Boston business magazine wrote an article denouncing that company for mistreating its writers and employees who sued them. But they did not know about my case and the whole truth of that. The Judge and everyone else would cover it up, and put me in a bad light, as though I was in the wrong. The original cause was lost in the shuffle. It was my screaming and shouting in protest that became the issue. Too much of our society operates like that. We overlook the fact that most paranoids have a good reason for it.

It wasn't long before my ineffectual attempts at coping with life and making a living failed and I became a homeless person. I have a long unpublished work called "The Nightmare," which describes this period of living once again on the road—sleeping in bushes and abandoned houses, bumming money, trying somehow to survive when I had little or no hope.

It was at this time that I wrote "The Bottomless Pit" for the *Street Image* magazine and Mike Susko returned asking me to put some hope in it. It was dated March 6, 1982.

"The temperature dropped more during the night. It had been ten degrees in the afternoon, but by two AM, it was zero in the city and much colder in the country.

A man struggled through the night, trying not to freeze. He was cold, and he knew he was getting too cold. He failed to find a place to sleep that night. He had been able to make some calls, spending the few coins he had, needed for food.

"No, not tonight. We're having some people up for dinner. Sorry." They hung up to quickly. He froze, in acute anxiety. He couldn't speak. Then he moved on after awhile.

He wondered if he was ever going to come in out of the cold again.

he hadn't been able to bathe in days, or change his clothes. His socks were mushy and the flesh peeled off the edges of his toes.

"Do you need a top dishwasher? I'm real good. I do the work of two men."

"Leave your phone number. Sometimes I need an extra hand for a few hours."

There wasn't any phone and no place at all.

"Can't you help me?"

"It's your own fault. You brought it on yourself," some said.

He couldn't comb his hair because the infection around the bone in his arm was so severe he couldn't bend or use his arm. Couldn't even get in and out of his boots.

The hospital didn't know what the infection was, exactly, but they put him on penicillin and prescribed rest, and sent him on his way. There wasn't any place to rest or to get warm

He hated to go unwashed, hated to do without a hot bath. There wasn't any place to be private, to be alone, to release the desperate need in him, to collect his thoughts and feelings.

He couldn't breath. His asthma medicine was gone. He strangled in the frozen air, his lungs frosting. It had become a nightmare to get more medicine. There was always an incident. He was being set up. He was becoming afraid of going to the hospital any longer, of trying to get help.

Despair and anguish overcame him. He cried each day over what was lost. Those islands of comfort for the mind—classical music, books, reading were denied him. In order to stay warm he hung out in bars where he had friends, even though the smoke all but strangled him, his fine mind wasted.

And he saw in his heart the heartlessness and cruelty, the stupidity and meanness of some of those whom he had trusted, had once counted as friends, who had betrayed him, or failed him.

The man wondered what would happen. The night almost broke him, trying to stay warm. Sometimes he went into a dirt floor cellar at a house of a friend, and slept by the furnace. But he was too far from there now. It was too long a way to get there. That's probably where he got the infection, living like an animal. Then he had snuck in, because he didn't want them to know how often he stayed there.

"Have you got a dollar?" he begged of a friend. Many people helped him along the way, but hand-outs weren't the answer.

Hopelessness and despair. All hope gone. Ten years now. No hope."

PART FOUR

I see now that I had given up faith. When the company killed hope in me, I had lost faith that I would survive. Lost faith, that I would triumph in my way, which I have. For those readers who are not religious or who do not understand what the idea of God is about, I apologize to you for saying this, but when one is alone and naked on the earth, their soul sorely oppressed, we have only God and must walk with God. Prayer, when I finally got back to it, got me through. Somehow strength came, and I began to gain ground.

It was a period of history when our economy and socio-political system (the Reagan years) began to throw vast numbers of people into the streets. Whole families were thrown out of work and lost their homes, and whole hospital populations of mental patients were deinstitutionalized and made homeless, unable to cope with life or helping themselves. People living on the streets have an average of two years of life before dying of exposure and disease.

I wonder if anyone really could have helped me. My problem was so large. I needed a good lawyer, and only when flinging myself against the legal system trying to get help with my problem, did I shatter mentally, because Justice was not there in America to help me. No one helped me fight what that company was doing, and I learned that the court system was a sham, only there to protect big companies from those who tried to protest against what they do. My cruelest opponent became the judge.

I *had* no hope then, I was just trying to survive—some friends helped me. Several years after the trauma of blacklisted had paralyzed me, my professor, William Alfred, got me writing again. He had to scream at me a few times, but finally it came through that I was not writing, and that was what I was all about.

There was my dog, too. In *Street Images*, 1983 I wrote:

"I sit up all night behind the wheel of my car, wrapped in blankets, afraid I might freeze to death. The VW is too small to lie down in. Beside, I have a large dog, and she gets to stretch out in the back seat. I want to keep her alive too. She keeps me alive in her way, for she has more love, more forgiveness, more loyalty and more intelligence than any human. She requires so little and gives so much—my dog, one of the people."

About this time, too, the media began to publish pictures of homeless people, and began to raise public awareness of the problem. This would only last for a few years until everyone tired of the problems and the stench of the homeless. Until then, my problems went unnoticed and unhelped. A soup kitchen where I sought help, run by the Franciscans, sent me to the Homeless People Unit of the City, and they got me some immediate help. In fact, a welfare agency had never been known to act that fast, but the media spotlight was upon them. I was given SSI by the Federal Government for my disabilities, and this ultimately put me on the road to rehabilitation and salvation. I didn't ask for that money, and in the past had turned it down when it meant going along with a psychiatric evaluation I couldn't live with. I endured years of pain and suffering without that money, until then.

I had never had any kind of security in my life, never had any real support for my writing for an extended period of time. I was always unwell enough not to be able to hold a regular job, and I was emotionally unsuited for working for other people. I had to be my own boss and run my own show. I finally found a way to do that, and the Federal program gave me that chance.

I went off to another city and found a cheap place to live, far cheaper than I could have lived in Baltimore. I began to thrive. Eventually I got a computer and promptly started working myself into the ground, catching up on years of work and creativity that had been lost because of not having either a computer or money to support me. That monthly check from the government was my literary grant—the one I never had. No art foundations would give me the time of day.

This is where I am now with my life. I have some unfinished novels I hope to get back to, personal historical information I want recorded somewhere, but I was able to type a couple of them and two plays some months back. I've had to learn a lot of business, which is not my nature, and so much of my creative energy has been wasted struggling with accountants, lawyers, taxes, and business, I have not much left in me. I certainly can't think about what I thought I should be doing which is trying to create new works of art.

But I try to see the good in things, and I'm sure all of the new experience I have been having is valuable. I hope that the gains that I have made are enduring. I give thanks each day for what I have, if I remember to do so. I say a Hail Mary, even though I'm not a Catholic. I give thanks for the home that I now have, and pray that it will last. I half expect the sky to fall in me all of the time, because my luck was so bad for many years. I'm greatly impressed with my vulnerability and how fragile I am and we all are.

I feel the pain that others live with when I pass homeless people, the handicapped, and crazy people on the street. I sometimes cry for them. Sometimes I lend a hand, giving money, or finding someone a place to stay. I was too long without a home, living on the streets and on the road, and its still with me, as I create a little nest.

The mistake I made years ago when I was hit so hard by my publisher, was that I lost hope. They did that to me, but I let it happen. That wasn't entirely my fault because I was already so damaged in my youth, and one more great trauma in my life was insupportable.

My life at this time has become fruitful. My most difficult project, which required nine years of writing and many more years of research, has paid off. No-one would publish that book, (HIGH TREASON) or publishers wanted to change the book so greatly that I could not accept it, so I finally published HIGH TREASON myself, and somehow, made the book succeed. That book has earned the money to finance this project. These projects are close to my heart and soul.

In the end we have to conquer fear. We have to conquer ourselves and the demons within us, but it has to come through understanding. Time heals wounds. It takes time. We have to get through it and survive. We have to remain true to our hearts and our missions. All of us are born with a mission to perform, and a handicap, and the handicap tends to work against our mission. We have to rise above that to perform our mission no matter what.

At the same time, there are other lessons from the long and terrible experience which lasted nearly twenty years. I'm not sure its over even now. Still the bitterness wells up in me from time to time, but I have come under so much stress from so much work, that I cannot take time to dwell on what they had done to me. I'm fortunate in being able—finally—to work—because for years after the great trauma they visited upon me, I could not function at all. Gradually, though, I was free enough, being unemployed, to make my own employment in this life, and do the work I always wanted to do: research, write, and publish—even if I had to do the publishing myself by creating my own company. That finally worked for me. You can do it too. You can do whatever you set your mind to, if you persevere long enough. You have to be a *survivor*.

The lesson is that I did not take the drugs psychiatrists prescribe (except for a brief period at the start) and so I learned to live with the rage that threatened to devour me at every step. I always knew that the raw energy of that rage could be turned to creativity, could be made constructive somehow, and in time that turned out to be true. I was able to achieve at a high level with that energy, the more I was able to again concentrate on my work. I still had to live with the bitterness welling up in me and often overwhelming me and paralyzing me, but I learned as time went by to control those emotions.

Our society is on a short fuse with regard to the amount of caring it can have for people who fall by the wayside, people who don't fit, who can't compete, who are sick. We are only a step above third world countries and the rat race in that regard. A country as rich as this that cannot guarantee medical care for all of its citizens is indeed fundamentally diseased. A country that simply tries to drug people who have problems, that doesn't care enough to try to take on those problems one on one and restore those persons to creativity and fruitfulness is fundamentally diseased.

To cast mental patients totally adrift is a great crime, an abortion of a dehumanizing society bent on self destruction. We are doing the same thing Germany did when they put to sleep 200,000 or more mental patients during the Thirties, or when we lobotomized tens of thousands of people with emotional problems. Now we drug patients until we destroy them, which is the same thing. And I mean *destroy* these poor people. Psychotherapy became a thing of the past, and they "managed" or "maintained" these poor souls on drugs, without a hope of facing the torments that rend them asunder.

The point is, if we are *not drugged*, we will eventually solve our problems and win through to a better and more normal life, when we gain the perspective to see objectively what happened to us and our faulty ways of dealing with it and coping. We will learn to cope a lot better.

There is simply no doubt in my mind that if I had taken those drugs, although they might have quieted me, I would also have become a vegetable and never amounted to anything, forever a drag on society.

Unfortunately, there were quite a few years after this second great trauma in my life when I was completely unproductive. I'm sure I lost a certain amount of artistic creativity during that time that can never be made up, but I learned to do non-fiction writing, something I had never intended to do, and in the end produced very important work, and a Best Seller.

We have to conquer loneliness too. That is my greatest problem now, along with stress. I don't handle stress well at all, having a life-long low tolerance for it. I drink too much, being not perfect, under prolonged stress. I need someone to give love to, and from whom to receive love and affection. I wonder if it is too late for that; if I'm too unattractive and battered by life. Too old. I can only have faith that all is God's will. I can only believe now that what happens has a purpose, because all the pain and suffering I have experienced up until now did turn out to have a purpose. I could not understand much without those terrible experiences.

For those who don't know what their mission is, it is because they are not looking into their hearts, or if they are, they are denying what they are being told to do by their hearts.

Nature confided in me
whispering gently how she loved you so

In sunshine she guided your laughter
when little giggles burst out beneath the
apple trees
and tapping tiny feet clambered over her head
and searching clasping hands gripped the
fruit to nourish expanding bellies

With soft breezes she caressed your neck
embracing you with the heat of the midday sun
and when tears convulsed
she'd confide sweetness in your ears
She felt your fears
she nourished your tears
and when dusk began to fall
she'd dust you with tiny stars
and cloak you with copper moon

But now you are strong
Grown unheeded in loving arms
You're turned around
looked ahead
forgetting what has happened behind

Stars are still out there
Vanishing in the bright city lights
Moon relinquished his hold and warmth
through fading years

Nature is yearning
Alone her fears soak the night
You have violated her exhausted frame
and with heavy cumbersome hand
overtalked her delicate cry.

Please open the heaven of your heart
Allow care to pierce the darkness
and caress a fatigued body in the
soft shadows of the night

She loves you so.

by Kate

A thought came into my head.
He arose
speckled with morning sunlight
glistening with dew.
So small, yet with infinite images
I gathered him up into my arms
Held him to my breast
and we became one.

by Kate

HANDLE WITH CARE

Dark clouds of paralyzing terror;
Suspended behind black pods of light.
Bony fingers ending in pointed nails
Reach through my heaving breast,
To my heart.
The form firmly grips
The throbbing muscle
Turning and wrenching it loose
From my veins;
He holds my life in his
Grotesquely shaped hands.
I am frozen, watching,
As he gently handles
My body's most precious organ.
I want to scream,
I have no sound.
I desire to cry, but
My tears are dry.
I am tired, I wish to rest.
My eyes close slowly,
I fall into an eternal sleep.
He gathers my soul.

by "Sunshine"
11/89

IV. Quest

When the vision comes from the west, it comes in terror like a thunderstorm, but when the storm of the vision has passed the whole world is green and happy as a result.

Black Elk Speaks *as told by John G. Neihardt*

Man becomes himself only after having solved a series of desperately difficult and even dangerous situations; that is, after having undergone "tortures" and "death," followed by an awakening to another life . . .

Rites and Symbols of Initiation, by *Mircea Eliade*

The total crisis of the future shaman, sometimes leading to complete disintegration of the personality and to madness, can be valuated not only as an initiatory death but also as a symbolic return to the precosmogonic Chaos . . a sign that the profane man is being "dissolved" and a new personality being prepared for birth.

Rites and Symbols of Initiation, *by Mircea Eliade*

I slipped down, drawn not by gravity, but by a calling of the heart. I lay in comfort, then drew up as a foetal being. I felt a Nurturing, so warm, so deep, so blissful, so complete. I was a suckling babe, or even before. I was nurtured, as if the Most High was a loving mother.

by M.S.W.

ROBIN'S STORY

I never felt like I fit in as a kid. My mother's behavior was very confusing: at times she'd be loving and affectionate and other times, especially after drinking heavily, she'd be hostile and abusive. I couldn't reconcile the two aspects of her personality. I thought that for a long time I was causing her to behave that way—it took me years to realize it wasn't me. From the time I was a young teenager I wanted to run away from home, but never got up the nerve, because just as it seemed my mother didn't want me around, it would change—she'd be loving and I'd feel guilty about leaving. I had friends superficially, kids that I played with, but I was basically a loner. The older I got, the more peer relationships felt forced; I felt uncomfortable around people my own age.

From a very young age I thought about philosophical issues, although at the time I didn't know they were called that. It was just the stuff I thought about. Whenever I tried to discuss abstract ideas with my mother, she considered this a sign of mental illness. She'd say, "That's crazy, don't think about things like that." When I got older she'd use it to suggest I needed psychiatric help. I kept thinking about the nature of reality—how do we know we can trust our senses and that the world is actually here? It wasn't until years later when I took my first philosophy course that I realized that these questions had been considered by the greatest thinkers in history. It was a huge ego boost that even if I was crazy, this wasn't proof of it. At the time I tried to keep things to myself, which was frustrating, because I felt a huge desire to discuss the things on my mind and had no one to discuss them with. After the experience with my mom I was reluctant to discuss this with my anyone, for fear of getting the same response and being regarded as peculiar.

When I was sixteen I met a man much older than I was, who replaced my mother in my heart, in the sense that his approval became more important than hers and I was able to leave home. But I only put myself in a similar position which alternated between love and emotional abuse. As a result of these two relationships, I came to believe that this was just the way people acted, and I thought that I must be the strange one.

Because of frustration, during the time I was with my mother and my first husband I turned to such activities as shoplifting and affairs to find a degree of excitement and satisfaction in what was otherwise an unfulfilling existence. Eventually life became unmanageably confusing and I ended up in the hospital. At one point I was involved with five different men, stealing hundreds of dollars worth of stuff a day, and my husband was so abusive I was terrified to be with him.

It's like a dream, the details are very fuzzy. I don't remember exactly how I got in the hospital. I never really felt crazy. Hospital was a break, an escape, a period where I didn't have to face the things going on in my life. Everything was immediately better when I went in: it was calm, I had people I could talk to.

It was in the psychiatric setting that I discovered a number of other people who had similar problems and were dealing with the same emotional issues I was. This was one of the greatest revelations in my life because I no longer felt estranged from the rest of humanity. I don't feel it was the psychiatric treatment that was helpful as much as the communication and exchange of ideas with other patients—that enabled me to get my life together.

The psychiatric system itself I felt to be condescending, as though there was not a lot of respect toward the patients. While I felt a strong urge to please my therapists, I never felt a comfortable working relationship. I enjoyed group therapy because I like to talk—and it was there that I found other patients who understood. The one benefit I gained from the therapy was the realization that significant others in my life were behaving irrationally; that my confusion over their contradictory behavior was justified. This was another great realization.

I was prescribed medication which I hated because it made me extremely sleepy; it seemed to have no other benefits whatsoever. When I was in the hospital I would flush it down the toilet or do whatever I could to avoid taking it. Out of the hospital, I would not take it. I saw other people turned to zombies from apparent over-medication and this was frightening; I didn't want it to happen to me.

After my third hospitalization I was able to leave my husband and spent several months in a psychiatric halfway house. Although I continued to enjoy the companionship and communication with people who had been in similar situations, the halfway house itself did not seem to be conducive to getting better—it fostered dependence on the system. It did not encourage people to pursue activities necessary in the "real" world. For example, a maid came in every day and cleaned up after the residents. Success in a work environment was considered a nice bonus, but never acknowledged as necessary to real life. People were told repeatedly that if they couldn't handle a job, it would be OK; the system would be there. I thought this was dreadful advice, which I chose not to follow.

After working steadily at low paying jobs for a couple years I decided to go back to college. This has proved to be a wonderful experience. For the first time in my life, I am surrounded by people who think about the same type of "weird stuff" I've always thought about. I love the challenge and intellectual stimulation. At this point, I'm in my senior year and hope to go on to grad school and then teach philosophy.

I have found myself falling into other abusive relationships, but having found other fulfilling activities such as school makes life manageable and I no longer have any fear of ending up in a psychiatric hospital.

I no longer depend on another person for all my emotional needs. That's one of the biggest lessons I've learned. We can't expect to find happiness through other people; we have to find it on our own. Only then, can we have secure relationships.

September 17, 1990 [*dictated*]

THE MILK CARTON
By Robin

Once upon a time, there was a little man, who along with many others lived inside a milk carton. The carton had no doors or windows, but the inhabitants had built many partitions of their own inside the carton; and since they themselves were very, very tiny, their milk carton world indeed seemed quite vast. No one who lived there had ever been outside the carton or even seen outside, so it generally never occurred to them that there could be an outside; a word which incidentally, did not even exist in their vocabulary.

Now some of the people were scientists, and they studied their world, limited though it was, and learned all they could about it. They devoted many years to making important determinations about their milk carton world, including size, age, and composition of everything within its four white walls. They rarely questioned the walls themselves; and those who did were either ignored or ridiculed into silence. In fact, very few individuals even undertook the long journey to reach one of the walls; the reason being that since they were so obviously there, and since it was equally obvious that they were the outermost boundaries of the world, what would be the point of going?

Unfortunately, the little man at the beginning of our story had always been a most difficult person, continually doubting and questioning so many accepted, established facts. Totally unwilling to take the well-intentioned advice of his friends and family to keep his absurd ideas to himself, he was eventually outcast from his community as a lunatic. His final words to his neighbors before he began his journey to the farthest corner of the carton, where he planned to spend the remainder of his days were: "We see the walls with our eyes, and our eyes tell us that the walls are white and we believe our eyes. But, if my mind tells me that there exists beyond this world another world that has no walls like these, I am expected to reject my mind in favor of my eyes. But neither can I see my mind, and surely that exists or I would be unable to see at all, or at least unable to make sense of what I see." And he walked away.

The journey was long and the path was difficult to follow, for few had come this way. In time he reached his destination and immediately began exploring, not as some might assume, to understand his new home, but rather to understand what, if anything, lay beyond this entire milk carton world—which is probably why he spotted the tiny crack that no one had seen before. Others had previously come to this same corner for measurement and other scientific purposes; but since it had never occurred to the scientists that there was even the slightest possibility of a crack existing in any of their permanent, all-encompassing walls, they had overlooked it entirely.

The little man was filled with an excitement that he had never before experienced as he slowly pressed his eye to the crack, and peered outside at last.

As he ran back to his community, he practically jumped for joy, for now, after years of rejection, he would be believed and respected by everyone for his great discovery. Sadly, however, he was not welcomed back as a hero, but rather as a raving maniac; or by those somewhat less unkind, as a poor deluded soul, who had wandered alone in the wilderness too long. Few bothered to listen, and those who did inevitably asked the same question: "You claim to have seen another, much greater world through a crack in the wall, but what exactly did you see?"

And to this, the little man's response would always be, and could only be: "I cannot explain what I saw, for we have no words in our language to properly describe it; and to attempt to do so in terms you understand would be completely impossible. I can only tell you that there truly is a much greater world than this beyond our walls; and that as far as I could see, it has no walls at all."

"Ah, but there you must be mistaken," his listeners would say, "any world must have walls. Our world does. So even if you did see another world, it would surely have walls as well." And they all laughed.

Naturally, the little man begged everyone to follow him to the wall where they would be able to look through the crack themselves, but none were willing to go. "This man is a dreamer," some said. "All that is real we can find within these walls; there is no more than this." Others, though more willing to accept the possibility of an outside world, were simply not inclined to make the journey, for they were too busy attending to their daily lives in the carton. Still others would taunt, "Bring us back something from your 'outside world' and show it to us so we can see it as plainly as we see our white walls and then we will go with you."

As a last resort the little man, by now quite disillusioned with his fellow people, appealed to the scientists, who were each conducting their own experiments in their own separate cubicles. "Great people of science," he began. "You understand this world so well and you continue to study it; but I tell you, that in doing so, you are all as doctors who only study the nose, without regard for the entire body. This world we see around us is but a small part of much greater world, which our measuring deices cannot measure and which our computers cannot calculate."

Barely looking up from his work, one of the scientists replied, "What you describe exists only in your mind. If such a place were real, surely we would have discovered it long ago. Your 'great world' is of no use to us, so leave us alone to complete our calculations of the real world."

At last, unable to forget what he had seen, and unwilling to pretend that he hadn't seen it, the little man left his community in disgrace for the second time and proceeded once again to the farthest corner of the milk carton. On arrival, he immediately pulled out his knife and carved a fairly large hole where once had been just a crack. Without hesitation, he placed his knife beside his small knapsack at the base of the wall and quietly climbed through the hole. He never returned.

Sometime later, a report was issued by a wilderness exploration party regarding a knapsack found mysteriously beside a most distant wall. The party had attempted to search for the owner, as it was most unusual for anyone to venture this far; but when none was located within a reasonable time, the explorers continued on, dismissing the abandoned knapsack as an "insignificant delay" in their progress report. This report contained no mention of a hole, or even a crack.

By Robin

M.W.S.'s STORY

Prophet and Loss: The Life and Times of "God's Anointed"
For LGMS, my beloved daughter

PART ONE

When I look back on my days in the Loony Bin, I remember the good times, I remember the bad times. As Dickens stated once: "Twas the best of times, the worst of times."

Although I feel now that I was often a *depressed* child and later a *depressed* adolescent, I did not know that word then. As children often do, I possessed a strong faith. The Most High was a confidante, someone I talked to in the dark before I fell asleep. I envisioned God as a benevolent presence that possessed closed circuit television where from time to time, He could tune in to see what I was up to. The old Devil, likewise, also monitored my activities.

I grew up in rural Appalachia—of Cherokee lineage, mixed in with some European descent—the son of a Scoutmaster, former farm boy, and enthusiastic hunter-fisher. The small town in Alabama where I grew up had fewer than two thousand inhabitants and was relatively isolated. Moonshiners operated in the Freedom Hills nearby. In the 1950's, Red Bay was in a time warp, still in the Victorian era. Gardens were plowed with a team of mules. There was no middle class. There were the haves, of which my family was one, and the have-nots. Many of my classmates at the county school were inbred, poor, and had rotten teeth.

I was, by all accounts, a child prodigy. I learned to read at two. By first grade, I was years ahead of my classmates in reading, understanding of science and arithmetic. In the second grade, I took an I.Q. Test. According to my aunt, I achieved the highest score ever made in Red Bay.

I was in many ways a very typical schoolboy. I learned to fight and got good at it. I played "Cowboys" and "Army" with my friends. Our fathers were WWII veterans, so we usually fought the Japs. I climbed trees and loved fishing, camping, and going with my father on hunting trips.

There were no "gifted" programs in the schools of Alabama, then. My father taught me advanced math to keep me challenged. My Uncle, a school superintendent in Mississippi, sent me science magazines. In the third grade I wrote my first stories, jungle stories. One was about sixty pages long, complete with hand drawn "illustrations." By fourth grade, I began to compose music. By fifth grade I was a piano finalist in the National Auditions. In sixth grade, I fell in love with Martha, a pretty fellow piano student.

But, I became more alienated, more withdrawn from a world I couldn't understand. I played my music and, according to the judges, played it well technically; but as they informed my teacher: "His heart is not in it."

Nature was my refuge: the woods, caves, streams, sinkholes. I woke to the sound of morning doves and fell asleep to the hooting of owls. Through fishing, I discovered the wonders beneath the calm surface: the spoonbill catfish and the jack salmon. I loved animals and could not shoot them. At age eight, I had a pet squirrel.

I started meditating when I was fourteen or fifteen after reading Herman Hesse's *Demian* and *Siddhartha*. I loved the poems of Whitman, William Carlos Williams, and William Blake. In high school I discovered Thoreau, who has remained my favorite thinker. "The mass of men lead lives of quiet desperation:" his words in *Walden* still ring true.

As I entered puberty, the external world become more intimidating. I blushed in the presence of young girls and women. I wanted to hide. After years of straight A's, I couldn't focus on my schoolwork. How I got through high school, then college, is still a mystery to me.

I listened to the Rolling Stones, the Animals, and the Who and modeled a band after them. I wrote Rock n' Roll anthems and performed in wild concerts where I danced and flung harmonicas at the audience. Usually I was on Coke n' Tequila, or Quaaludes.

In my late teens and early twenties, LSD, Mescaline, and the other hallucinogens re-opened for me the sense of wonder I'd somehow lost. Yet when one plays with fire, one gets burned.

PART TWO

In January 1970, the inevitable happened. The *persona* I'd built up in high school and college: the philosopher, the band-leader iconoclast, the actor-playwright, the "Zen master," all fell apart one night during an LSD trip. I saw myself as a *poseur*, a fraud, a phony. I'd become overly cerebral, overly abstract. The hurt child in me came out with a surge of pain. The child who didn't cry as his natural grandmother—the person I'd bonded with after my mother's post-partum dispatched me to her arms—died. The child who had to be strong, who didn't cry on the playground, who didn't cry when women in the larger, more affluent town, refused to go out with him because he was a newcomer or not a member of the correct church—that child wanted to cry. . . .

I didn't cry, but many months later, I, the "prodigy" became crippled with muteness. The hurt child in me choked the lumbering adult into silence. The world turned icy blue. I felt dead. Often I couldn't sleep, but when I did, two nightmares recurred. In one, my inhaling and exhaling sustained a rising volcanic landscape of craggy, steaming peaks. I'd awaken hyperventilating. In another, I'd be at a press conference (I had been interviewed on television), the microphone would be handed to me, and I couldn't speak.

In Autumn 1971 I became the Messiah, but a very carnal one. In November 1971 I turned myself in, thinking psychiatry had an answer. This hospitalization, shortly before my twenty-third birthday awakened mixed emotions. In the preceding few months, reactions to two neuroleptics, Prolixin and Stelazine sent me to the emergency room. I had attacks of dyskinesia from both of them, the greatest pain I had ever experienced.

The first thing I noticed about the ward, other than the cigarette burns on the carpet caused by over-medicated persons nodding out, was the slowness of the place. The nurses and staff, the patients, even the visitors seemed to walk like somnambulists. Next, I noticed the condescension. When I realized I was locked in, I inquired about it. A nurse said, "You're not locked in. Don't think of it like that. This is for your own protection." I had to request a razor in order to shave; like a concentration camp inmate my personal possessions were taken away. In order to listen to a football game, my use of a radio had to be approved. I had to hide my thesis for my masters degree in creative writing, a notebook full of poems in progress. A woman receiving shock treatments felt compelled to keep house, and more than once dumped my notebook in a waste basket.

I wrote a series of poems when I first came in, a variation of the children's prayer, *Now I lay me down to sleep*. I felt at the time, it was a type of penance I was doing.

Back then I was naive. I thought that psychiatrists were competent, thoughtful people like in the book, *I Never Promised You a Rose Garden*. They were really a literal-minded bunch who had never heard of Carl Jung or R.D. Laing. They were trained to look at us as biochemical disasters, not as real people.

It was a new unit, only about a year old. The only program was to whisk us away to an outpatient place for a couple of hours a day. People were over-medicated, or received electroshock therapy. Ironically, I was once awakened from a sound sleep to receive a sleeping pill. I was not offered any counseling. I was treated as an aberrant collection of body chemicals run amuck. It was very different from my second hospitalization at the University of Birmingham where they used little medication and had lots of activities.

The cause of my first hospitalization was a combination of many things. I believe there were biochemical and genetic aspects. A counselor friend, whom I respect, thinks it was a drug induced psychosis. More importantly, I was a child of an alcoholic father, and I didn't know how to deal with it. It was quite a shock to me as a kid. My mother told me that when my father disappeared for weeks at a time, that he was on a drunk. I was neglected, abused verbally, and at times physically. My mother was a hypochondriac who took to bed when things got bad. I had to be the strong one; I was the one who had to change my sister's diaper. There was only one place—the Bradley Center—that even asked about my childhood. Psychiatrists weren't interested in personal history. At the time I believed the diagnosis. As one friend said, they aren't interested in your story, but your symptoms as described in the DSM-III, their diagnostic manual.

After two and half weeks I was released and somehow managed to finish a quarter at Auburn University. My psychiatrist there, the first I trusted, treated me with counseling alone, due to my drug sensitivity. Later, he felt Lithium would be good for me. Lithium effected me in both positive and negative ways. On one hand, I felt calmer and not stupefied as the neuroleptics made me feel. Yet adjusting to Lithium robbed me of two of my coping skills. I couldn't coordinate constricted fingers: hence I couldn't play piano; I couldn't write poetry or prose; I couldn't use a pen for two or three weeks.

After a melancholy and difficult winter quarter, I dropped out and joined friends in Atlanta, with the hopes of forming a rock band. But it was unseasonably cold there, for March. I'd been unable to sleep for nearly two weeks.

I overrode the Lithium. At one point, I saw a dove condense into a crystal and enter my "third eye." The spring before, I'd locked myself in the church where I was custodian during Spring break with the feeling that I was called to "father" the Second Coming of Jesus. I listened to three albums: Beethoven's *Ninth Symphony*, Neil Young's *After the Gold Rush* and an anthology of Carter Family songs which included "Gospel Ship" and "Will the Circle be Unbroken." I felt a healing power in my hands—that I was St. Francis reincarnated.

A friend drove me to a local recording studio where I wished to record a cryptic album explaining why the Lord chose such a "backward place" to incarnate. I made tapes on how to raise the "Messiah." I made magical notes in my "Complete Works of William Blake," which still haunt me to this very day. Eventually, exhausted, I kept an appointment with a psychiatrist for whom I played my chromatic harmonica, and fell asleep for nearly two days—aided by Mellaril.

In Spring 1972, riding bursts of energy, I was merely God's Anointed Prophet! Joseph's Campbell's *Hero with A thousand Faces* was my guidebook. In Atlanta one intelligent friend figured as "Trickster" in my mythopoetic adventures and I felt I had to confront him in a *Cosmic Duel*.

I left Atlanta a few days later, contemplating hospitalization in Birmingham. Three friends drove me to the airport. Totally out of focus, clad in a "shirt of many colors," clutching a long stick and a briefcase full of songs and poetry, I rode elbow to elbow with businessmen in three-piece suits.

After discussing mega-vitamin therapy with a friend, a medical researcher specializing in mind-altering drugs, I voluntarily entered "Three North," the adolescent-adult teaching ward, at 4 AM. The following morning I told the resident on duty I was "on a pilgrimage." He admitted me with the diagnosis of *Schizophrenia*.

There I spent nearly three weeks in a seclusion room with roll-away furniture. I strongly identified with a Samurai warrior and with the enigmatic despot in *Ivan the Terrible*. I was a *Hero*, a warrior for the Divine. At least once, I was wrestled to the floor by a group of attendants with very large necks. I always knew I was in trouble when they rolled the furniture out of the seclusion room. I was discharged with the diagnosis "some kind of mood disorder," and my maintenance dose of 800 milligrams of Mellaril per day was cut down to 200.

I struggled to make my first marriage—nearly two years old at the time—to work in spite of my infidelities. By summer, once again in melancholy, but without medication, I completed another quarter of graduate school at Auburn.

In late August of 1972 I entered Bradley Center in Columbus Georgia. During a structured day, we played volleyball, ping pong, went swimming, did charcoal drawings, went through P.R.E. exercises, and had modern dance. There was a group called, "Guilt Group." The existentialist outlook there—"you are what you make yourself"—led me out of my melancholy. In a session led by an Esalen-trained therapist, I had what was called a blow-out. I lectured my "father" on how he'd pumped me up with ambition, then disappeared. Then, I had to become my "father" and reply. I ended up weeping (earlier I'd pounded on a stack of cushions with such fury that blood came out of my nostrils) in the arms of Joe, the man who'd led me through.

PART THREE

I returned to Auburn willing to take responsibility for my health and get my Masters. My wife, however, was used to the sicker version, the fugue-driven philanderer always fleeing to the arms of his mistress in Atlanta. She told me to leave. I threatened to smash the appliances we were inundated with. My sister-in-law, faced with violence, slipped out and called the law. I spent a night in the Auburn jail alone with my books and Elavil. On release, I stayed at Auburn through the quarter getting through on Ritalin. After that it was Ritalin and Quaaludes.

1973 is the lost year. In a cynical mood I signed up for electroshock in the fall. Primarily it is given for depression but sometimes it is used for people like me who were diagnosed as manic.

I can still remember, after seventeen years, what it is like to receive electric shock. I was not allowed to have breakfast. The doctor came in, wheeling the machine on a hospital gurney, that looked like a little stereo console. It had a towel draped over it. The curtains were pulled around my bed. The doctor bore a striking resemblance to Billy Graham, and was an evangelist of the biochemical model. He popped under the curtain with this grin on his face. He said something like: "How are you doing today? You look fine today." He gave me the first injection. I remember asking, "Is it Sodium Penthonal?" He replied, "No, this is Sodium Brevitol, because its briefer." This hypnotic puts you out in seconds. The second injection, I found out later, was Anectine, a curare extract that paralyzes muscles so you can avoid the compound fractures they got in the old days. The electro shock causes a full grand mal seizure. All you can see are the toes twitching, I've heard.

When you wake up, you not only forget what happened, you don't know where you are or who you are. It's the closest thing to death. I remember people yelling at me for going through their closets. I couldn't even remember my own room. A girlfriend, whose mother was a nurse at the time, told me I used to say, "I'm glad I'm not receiving those treatments anymore." I didn't know I was still taking them. I did receive—by the doctor's admission—eighteen treatments. People would call me up, saying they'd met me, but they were total strangers. I had a list of women's phone numbers, and I would go down the list making phone calls. They were just voices: I didn't know who they were, whether or not I had sex with them. Almost a whole year is gone, my memory obliterated.

I got another set in 1974 when I was committed. This same doctor had admitted to my mother that the first set hadn't helped. When I signed for them, I thought, "Why not?—another experience." I was desperate for something to help me. But it didn't help me at all; it only made me more angry. I would like to be examined with a cat scan. I'm sure electroshock burns the brain.

It wasn't just the assault on my brain by electricity that obliterated most of 1973 and part of 1974; it was also the Quaaludes, the Ritalin, the Hashish, the wild parties, the furious Rock n'Roll concerts, the constant hitchhiking to and fro.

But in the Spring 1972 when I first reached Atlanta in the pre-dawn darkness, I realized in fear that I didn't have the phone numbers of my friends. So I called her: the slight, lovely blue eyed blond, the once Homecoming Queen. I knew she'd be up at 5:00 A.M. I'd been up with her then and watched her put her make-up on for a social work job. Also I knew she'd come, that she'd be happy to see me again.

As I penned the last word of a poem titled "The Coming of Mary," I stood up, and there she was: S. with her radiant smile.

PART FOUR

In May 1974, after being committed—hauled in repeatedly by the law and repeatedly escaping—my physician released me. I worked on a farm again. I bushhogged. I plowed the fields. I read my beloved *Bhagavad Gita*. I re-read the Book of Matthew (with difficulty) and all I could get of Thomas Merton.

One day, chanting a mantra, working on a large acreage—the driving and plowing became effortless—the field resonated with light, and I heard my calling. "Smite away the husks," said the Israel Baal Shem Tov "and you will see the divine spark in all living things." I was called to glorify God, not through pretty words, but through service without rewards.

On the second to the last day of 1989, a year of tribulation for me, I had an intense discussion with a Benedictine candidate for the priesthood. We went to the monastic library to go through the stacks. He seemed astonished at my knowledge of the church fathers, and also of Dante. I said, "I've read enough in books."

So Brother C., knowing I meditated and that I believed in the Sacrament, took me up into the monastic chapel and said: "I want you to meditate in the presence of the Sacrament." He showed me where it was, with the little light burning. After the priests and monks were in their quarters, I returned. I was "alone" in a warm darkness, with the spark-like glow in the lamp.

I felt an emptying. I found myself prostrate on a cold marble floor. I slipped down, drawn not by gravity, but by a calling of the heart. I lay in comfort, then drew up as a foetal being. I felt a *Nurturing*, so warm, so deep, so blissful, so complete. I was a suckling babe, or even before. I was nurtured, as if the Most High was a loving mother.

From Spring of 1984 to Autumn, 1986, separated from wife and daughter, I lived my version of Walden in a primitive cabin without electricity or running water, on a mountain in the Smokies. I heated and cooked on a kerosene stove and a wood stove and used oil lamps for light. There, in my hermitage, I slowed down my thoughts and emotions, focused on living simply, and gained a new perspective. This was a genuine healing experience.

By chopping wood, gathering herbs and wild food and living on a modest income, I regained a shattered, previously elusive self-esteem. I came down from my mountain when solitude—which I'd transformed from loneliness, reverted back to loneliness and a desire to live in a city again, live a more social life.

In May of 1990, I celebrated my sixteenth anniversary of "non-hospitalization." While the world of Thorazine injections, electroshocks, and memories of two seclusion rooms still haunt me in my waking life and in dreams, I realize that this is behind me. The likelihood of it happening again I realize is essentially up to me and how well I can deal with the mother-nurturing of a God who loves me as I am.

I am no longer "God's Anointed." Someone else can have that gig—I was not very good at it. I think of myself, at last, as a human, however flawed, with a divine spark encrusted with the husks of pain, unrequited love, melancholy, and disillusionment.

Yet there are still moments when I wonder. . . .

3/1/90

OLYMPOS

a far crest
tumultuous and winding
veined as the stone hand of Nemesis
reposes in the crevices
of the mind
in the staid and imposing
terror of Olympos
only gulls reign
this vile place
winging and winding upward
hilarious above
the curious stonework
of gods long scattered
from the crypt of the angry temple
where the dizzying height
intoxicates with dread
i walk
here gods have been flung down
passionless gulls scream in derision above
the upward footpath
where the laurel sits
heavy upon the soul and dead
i celebrate with a wearisome ecstasy
the fell height
mark you the dire echoes of the gulls cry
the climb that has bent me
ruthlessly
and the flight
into the realm of the furies majesty
Olympos

Theodora Stanley Snyder

D. Cherubini

"JOE GREEN"

PART ONE

There are some things nobody knows about my "psychiatric" difficulties. It was 1978. I was working as a medical technician at a local hospital. I didn't know it was a high stress field.

For periods of several months, I would be depressed, not wanting to do anything, laying in bed, watching a little TV. I had few interpersonal relationships and lots of loneliness. There was a woman I was emotionally involved with, although she wasn't the right girl.

In addition to this, I had car problems; it would breakdown at the most inopportune times on my way to work. I was keeping up all my material needs myself, one person trying to do everything. Although I was searching for spirituality, I had no spiritual anchor and no organized church of any denomination.

I knew there was a problem, but I didn't know what to do. I made a decision to get away from all of the things giving me problems. The first thing I did was leave the girl. Breaking up with her was traumatic. The next thing I did was quit my job to get a new one, doing electrical construction. Every day was a struggle just to get by. I was still having depressive bouts but not as bad. It was a new situation, but I was still smarting and lonely.

I met a guy on the job, a strange but very interesting guy. He talked in riddles all day, which fascinated me. He would say things like, "A fireman is a fireman not because he wants to put fires out, but because he likes to see things burn." We started a dialogue. He wasn't really a friend though; he was verbally abusive. I took the abuse because he was my boss of sorts, but I would cuss back if he cussed at me.

We talked about ideas for two or three weeks. My mind wouldn't let the subject rest: my mind wouldn't obey me anymore. I would think about a topic whether I wanted to or not. My mind would say, "Screw you, I'm going to think about this anyway." It was very frightening and disconcerting. I hadn't experienced anything like this before.

I called up my boss. The slang on the job was to call him Guru. I said, "Guru, I'm having real problems. My mind won't settle down. I have no control over it." He got nasty on the phone. "Oh, it's going round and round, like you're chasing your tail." I cussed at him. "Tell me what to do!" "Get yourself to a psychiatric ward," he said. I was horrified at the thought. "You better, to slow your mind down, or you'll be in big trouble," he said.

So I drove to Phipps Clinic and asked to see a psychiatrist. We talked some, but it was superficial. She acted as if I was bothering her. "You need psychotherapy," she said. "I'll see you once a week." "I can't wait. I need something right away," I said. She gave me Thorazine tablets and told me to take them daily. I was given no warning about the side effects.

So I took the Thorazine and drove home. The side effects started; my muscles went into weird contortions. I didn't know what was going on—I thought I must be going nuts. This went on for about a week, to the point where I could hardly keep my head up to see and drive. After ten days or so these side effects lessened, and I was able to function on the medication. But now, in addition to every day stresses, I had the added stress of thinking I was crazy.

Some time before, Guru had given me a book on Transcendental Meditation. I gained insight and wanted to meditate. I called the TM people and started chanting a mantra silently. I felt it was very beneficial to me, although I was still having symptoms of psychiatric distress.

After about a month, I told the psychiatrist I didn't want to take drugs or do psychotherapy anymore. I was meditating and felt I was under control, coping better and feeling better. I took myself off the Thorazine.

The job plodded along and I still had dialogues with Guru. He said things that scared me at times, but I wasn't losing control. We found a common ground because we were both meditating. But he was still verbally abusive. It got to the point where I said to myself, if I don't quit the job, I'll kill him. I imagined a way to do it, but I knew I couldn't. I started missing days from work.

At the same time I tried to look for another job. A friend, using his connections, helped me to get a job working in a laboratory. I moved into a new neighborhood close to the job and got rid of the car. In a way, I had finally gotten rid of my problems.

PART TWO

I started delving back into the spiritual game, reading one book after another on Buddhism and Hinduism. Sometimes I read two or three books at one time. I also studied organized religions—Christianity, Judaism, and Islam. I read books by Ram Dass and discovered some mantras. I was spiritually naive. I got plenty of religion in Catholic school, but no spirituality.

Not realizing there could be a negative side to these things, I started to repeat this new mantra, saying it mentally under my breath for hours—

then for two or three days in a row. Fantastic things happened to my consciousness: colors were more vivid and lively, they danced and glowed. I would see my perceptions increase as I repeated the mantra, proving it was working.

Because I was under the spell of the mantra's positive effects, I didn't see the negative creep in. I was totally unaware that I was acting erratic. My girlfriend noticed it and called the police. They put me in an ambulance and took me to an emergency ward at Phipps Clinic at Hopkins.

I literally bounced off the walls a few times at Hopkins. I didn't know what was happening or why I was being treated the way I was. It *was* a nightmare in the truest sense: things were happening I had no control over. It was real, even though I tried to tell myself it wasn't happening. I blacked out at one point— why I don't know. Maybe they gave me a shot of some drug. The doctors decided to commit me to Springfield for observation.

When I woke up they had me on a stretcher. My wrists and ankles were shackled down and a restraining strap was over my back. I couldn't move, not to scratch myself or find a more comfortable position. When I asked them why, they didn't answer me directly. "We have to keep you restrained," they said. "If you relax, stop being agitated, we'll let you loose, eventually." When they let me sit up, it was a tremendous release. They took the straps off, and I walked to the ambulance that took me to Springfield.

I didn't know where I was. I didn't have my glasses. I'm very myopic. I sort of knew where I was, but I didn't want to believe it. It was too horrifying. A heavy dose of Liquid Thorazine, three times a day contributed to my disorientation. I was scared, confused, not able to see, and wondering why I was treated the way I was.

The conditions on the ward were appalling. It was locked, overcrowded by ten to twelve patients. Although they mopped the floor daily, it was dirty. Somebody was always throwing up, and people would throw plates of food. I was a prisoner and surrounded by people who had psychiatric problems or had been in prison.

Due to my excessive spiritual reading and my disorientation I started to act out the things I had read. I would throw books on the floor and think I was waking up humanity by vibrating the spiritual energies throughout the earth. An attendant noted this. That night, another attendant took me into a seclusion room and physically wrestled me to the floor. Somebody else put a needle in my back side. They shut me up all night, leaving me in my underwear.

The next morning I was more docile, frightened. This is what they wanted: orderly, behaved people, so they would only have to observe. From then on, I didn't act out because I would be thrown in seclusion and get the needle.

After a few days of this torture, I had my hearing. My girlfriend showed up. They let me go and I came back to Baltimore. Once I came home, I still could not fully believe that it had happened. Eventually I came to grips with it and realized it was real, not just an extended nightmare.

But I was out for only a few days. I stopped taking my medicine because I felt better without it. I started acting erratic again and got into a situation with the police. I was taken back to Springfield and told I was there because I stopped taking my medicine. This time they gave me more Thorazine. I couldn't believe I was back in this *Viper Pit*.

Somewhere along the way they gave me Haldol, first liquid then tablet. The Thorazine had just slowed me down and made me lethargic, but the Haldol reacted with my sympathetic and parasympathetic nervous systems such that they were fighting each other. I had the shakes, a characteristic shuffle back and forth. I couldn't stand still, my nervous system was so out of whack.

The whole time I was in Springfield I never got any medicine for side effects. I was never told anything about side effects. You were just told to take the drug, and if you didn't take the drug, you were forced to, even if you tried to hide it under your tongue or spit it out. Once I knew I was going to have to take the drug, I took it. One of the things I did to offset the drug was to drink copious amounts of water.

My hearing came up again. The Haldol made me shake so much that the Hearing Officer said I should stay a few days longer to get my shaking under control. So I stayed a few days, still shaking, realizing it was the medicine causing me to shake, and knowing I would have to go up in front of the officer again.

My hearing came up. Only through sheer will power did I shake less. My apparent calm was more acceptable to the officer and she let me out.

Again my girlfriend picked me up. She was starting to get annoyed with me for obvious reasons. The ride back to Baltimore was sheer torture. The whole time I was in the car I wanted to twist, turn and walk, but I couldn't. I was in genuine *torment* due to the medication.

When I got back to the job in Baltimore, I found everybody knew what had happened. They were uninformed about mental problems, and I had to deal with the stigma. Society has an *Us and Them* mentality. The truth is that anybody can have a mental problem, a breakdown—no matter how dumb or smart, or rich you are. You just have to be human. People think you've been in a mental hospital, therefore you're strange. "I'm going to shun you and put a fence around you," they think. It's ignorance and fear: they fear it might happen to them.

I continued to take the Haldol because I didn't want to go back to Springfield. I tortured myself for two weeks as I still had the movement disorder caused by the medication. I could hardly walk; it was an ordeal to walk even a block. Even if I didn't go anywhere, I would toss and turn in bed. I couldn't get relief, if I sat down or stood up—whatever I did. I was so uncomfortable, so frustrated and bewildered that I felt I couldn't go on.

I started to skip taking the medicine and started to feel better. The muscular discomfort was less and I was able to cope more. I began to realize it was the medicine causing me so much distress. I went to an outpatient clinic and told a psychiatrist I couldn't function. He immediately recognized my symptoms and gave me a shot of Cogentin. As soon as I got that shot, the side effects went away. I could walk, breathe easier. I felt so relieved at the cessation that I felt like a new person.

PART THREE

I stayed out of the hospital for three to four months, all the while reading spiritual books, still pursuing spiritual knowledge. During all this time I was actively meditating except in the hospital—there you had no privacy and were forced to take drugs. I still had my TM mantra. I realized I couldn't use the others because they were too powerful. I had no negative effects from TM so I repeated the mantra while I was working.

Ram Dass had recommended to go for broke: "Why go through 100 reincarnations, when you can do it in this lifetime?" I took his advice and started using all his teachings. This is a lot of the reason I fell into this "psychiatric nightmare."

At the time, I was in the military on a part-time basis as a reserve/national guardsman. One weekend at a Unit Training Assembly I was saying my TM mantra to excess. One of the physicians saw me. He started to interview me as to what I was angry about. "I'm not angry," I said. "I can see it in your face," he said. "I'm not," I replied. I truly wasn't. I was in neutral, I wasn't upset. Perhaps repeating the mantra physiologically released biochemicals into my bloodstream which made me appear angry.

I now realized that even the TM mantra was risky to use. I couldn't abuse it by using it more than twice a day, for twenty minute periods. Still, I felt it was doing me good.

Now we come to my third trip to the hospital. I was still wrapped up in the spiritual quest, and I became unbalanced again. I was walking up and down a city street, acting erratic, and giving dollar bills away. This caught the attention of the police and they called a paddy wagon. I hadn't "broken the law," I didn't hurt anyone or destroy anything. But I talked with a cop in a way he considered strange and odd. I wanted to leave, but he held me by my belt loop. I knew then I was in trouble. "Why won't you let me go?" I asked. He didn't answer. The paddy wagon arrived and I was off to Springfield again.

After they got me out of the paddy wagon, I was so out of it, I was put right in seclusion. They left the light on twenty-four hours a day. I had thoughts going on in my mind of a religious nature, but of nightmarish quality. After a day and a half they felt I was calm enough to be let out. The time periods given are only estimates, because they gave me no way of orienting myself.

By this third time I was getting disgusted with myself. I was also getting to "know the trail" so to speak. I played the game with everyone. I took the Thorazine and this time my dosage was doubled to 800 milligrams a day.

I started to lose my headlong fascination with the spiritual quest, realizing I couldn't keep it up. It was crazy to put myself through this torture. I was afraid of telling the doctors what was actually going on. One time, when I told the psychiatrist, "I'm God," he got wide eyed and said "You're *God*?" "You have to get the context," I said. I calmed him down, explaining what I meant. That was the only hint I gave the psychiatric community of why I was really there.

Eventually I reached a point of lucidity, coming out of my illusions/delusions. My faculties came back to me; I was clear-headed, relating well, but I felt everyone around me was nuts. It was bizarre, frightening and lonely, to feel rightly or wrongly that I'm sane, while others are sick. It's so lonely when even the psychiatrists take on the pallor of being sick. They were not a whole lot different than the nuts jumping around—they just didn't jump around. I felt this under the atmosphere, the tremendous strangeness and sedation.

I thought too that the doctors were a fraud, that they didn't know what they were doing. Since I had the experience of "mental illness," especially one with a spiritual dimension, I felt I knew more than they. I knew it was a two-edged sword: an entrance to mental chaos and hell, as well as healing.

After fourteen days, I went to another hearing. They were getting sick of seeing me. They kept me there until I was well enough to leave, then I was put in a paddy wagon. I was going to jail; I must have been charged with loitering or something. Central Lock-Up was similar to the mental hospital: lights on twenty-four hours a day, disorienting—I didn't know where I was or what time it was. I was surrounded by steel, and it was hot as hell.

Again my girlfriend got me out after a day. She was a very good friend, the only one who gave me support. I had very little family and I didn't want to tell any member because of the stigma. When they did find out, they weren't much help. My half-brother's attitude was that there was nothing much he could do, and he just dismissed me. I was born late in my parents' life. I grew up without my father, who died when I was an infant. My mother died of cancer when I was in my early twenties.

Finally I came back home from the hospital and jail. I never did find out what the charges were. People who have absolute power over you become sadists.

PART FOUR

This time I stayed away from Springfield entirely, and away from the psychiatric scene for four or five months. But still I was in the spiritual-seeking mode. I started to befriend alcoholics in the area. I thought I could turn these alcoholics on to higher spiritual realities. I took it upon myself to "Mother Hen" them: allowing them to visit my apartment and feeding them.

At about this time I got angry with some neighboring tenants. It was not for a good reason—a confusion/delusion on my part. We argued and I put my fist through a plate glass window. When the police came, they asked who broke the window. Like a complete fool, I said, "I did." They said, "OK, you're going downtown." They left my apartment open and $2,500 worth of stereo equipment was stolen.

The ride in the paddy wagon disoriented me and got me further into my psychosis. For about a day, I was in Central Lock-Up, yelling and cussing everybody out. I said spiritual phrases that didn't make any sense to anyone but me. I took all my clothes off and stuffed them into the toilet in hopes of stopping up the plumbing system. I kept flushing the toilet and succeeded in getting water all over the main floor. Then I lay down for a while and fell asleep.

The next thing I knew I was in Central Jail with other prisoners. Somebody had put a pajama outfit on me. I was shuffled around from one cell to another. It was a house of mirrors, as I kept on going through these doors. At the time I thought it was a game the police were playing, but now I realize they were testing me as to what group of prisoners I'd be safe to be with.

Finally, I was brought to the Diagnostic Unit on Greenmount. Different people talked to me, asking me questions to find out my mental state. They placed me in another paddy wagon—I had no idea where I was going—to take me to the Carter Center, a psychiatric hospital.

For three weeks I was on the Emergency Ward. I played their game, but I was still in a confused mental state. I was forced to take Liquid Haldol, then Tablet Haldol. I was treated fairly well, the food was fairly decent, but I was on a psych ward and I couldn't get out. Other people were getting out but not me. I asked how come I wasn't getting out. They said I was "court ordered" and had to wait for my trial.

I thought I was a hero. On the outside I had been trying to save the alcoholics; on the inside I was trying to save all of humanity. I still felt I was "God" with special powers. Having read a book about magic, I started doing bizarre things to pictures. I would trace my finger in a magic circle around their perimeters. But I didn't even have enough power to talk myself out of the psychiatric hospital, so obviously I didn't have any powers.

I was shipped upstairs to the regular psychiatric ward and stayed there three to four weeks. My mental state was becoming less confused. My trial came up and again I was put in a paddy wagon and taken to court. My lawyer got me off, saying I was committed and not responsible for my actions. They took me back to the Carter Center, and I was sent there for an indeterminate amount of time, which is a trial in itself, not knowing whether you're going to get out in two days or two years.

One day, a doctor came over and said, "Joe, with your insurance policy from work why don't you go to Sheppard Pratt?" I thought about it for a while. I was getting bored with the Carter Center. I would have more to do, more space to roam. I might as well go to a better "hotel." At Sheppard, they interviewed me and determined I wasn't violent—they have pretty strict rules about violent patients.

They took me there, this time in a University of Maryland State Vehicle. Due to lack of family support, I had little clothing, no shoes, only slippers. They gave me some things that fit irregularly, but shout to everyone, "You're a mental patient."

I was at Sheppard about two and a half months. I had therapy, but it was the type where you do all the talking and the therapist says nothing. I told them that I was seeking my own divinity, that I was in a less confused state now. They just wrote in their notebooks, nodded their heads, and looked at me every now and then. They never said "What do you mean by that?" or "Do you really think you are God?"

At Sheppard I had been on Haldol a couple of months. I had a woman psychiatrist who decided I should be put on Lithium instead, and Cogentin for side effects. I didn't see any difference, but I played the game and stayed on the Lithium. The whole time I was there, they let me keep my job, working part time while I was in the hospital. It would have been 100 times harder without that job, to get gainful employment again.

I kept asking the doctor and nurses when I was going to get out. They said, "You have to apply to a halfway house." This bummed me out, because I wanted to be left alone, go back to my job and live my life again. I wanted to be done with this nightmare that seemed to go on and on. Now they said I had to play games with a halfway house.

PART FIVE

I was accepted at the halfway house. The house was OK, but it was crowded. There wasn't enough privacy, and the people there were in varying degrees of healing. I wasn't satisfied with it because I wasn't on my own. I continued to work at my job and saved up money as well as I could. Eventually I told the people there I had found an apartment. They encouraged me because this is what the halfway house was for.

I got my new place. I still meditated, read spiritual books, but I didn't go half-cocked off the deep end. I laid low and just worked every day, and went on with my life.

I met a girl at work and she seemed to like me and I liked her. We started to develop a relationship. Eventually we moved in together and later got married. My life was taking a different turn. Things went on relatively smoothly for several years while I was working and just enjoying life. I was still meditating, although not as regularly and fervently as before.

In the Spring of 1986, I went to a meditation course, which involved staying for three days. It was a fantastic experience. However, I let it get me in trouble again. After I got back, I jumped headlong into mediation exercises at an increased rate to advance my spiritual quest. It got me on the edge again. I started to act peculiar toward other people. I stayed up all night. The next morning I called in sick at work and my wife took me to a psych ward.

While I was in the "psychotic" episode, I had bizarre delusions, images of myself suffering crucifixion, and other messianic ideas. I was put on Thorazine and Cogentin. After two days, I stabilized.

This time, the physical environment was more pleasant than in the other mental hospitals. I wanted to leave right away, but they said I should stay a little longer. I was playing ball with them again. After I was released, I went back to my job immediately. I found that being on the Thorazine slowed down my work performance. After about two weeks, I decided to stop taking it.

I have been drug free for nine years, except for that one month period, and in good mental health with no more episodes up to the present day. I'm still pursing the spiritual quest, but at a slower rate, being careful not to unbalance my system. Now I know that if anyone, no matter how sane they are, pursues this discipline at too fast a rate, that they can wind up in a mental ward.

Although I realize now I'm not the Messiah, I believe I'm part of God in my soul and perceive my true inner identity with the *Big God*. The reality of God is beyond our ability to talk about, and when we try to talk about it, we just talk about concepts. We can't really grasp the unfathomable God, the unknown force of the universe, the all and everything. I believe along with the Hindus that animals, humankind and God, indeed the universe are one totality.

Now I see myself as an above average human who is participating in the drama of life here on earth and the cosmos. I'm still trying to evolve my consciousness and safely seek the higher spiritual awareness which the human race is capable of achieving.

June 30, 1990 [*dictated*]

Somewhere near the sunset fading,
in the cool air before night
stands a stranger; silent, waiting
for a voice as pure as light.

And so he hears this phantom calling;
siren song that burns his will,
and all around him stars are falling,
dancing on his windowsill.

Beneath his feet are rivers flowing
towards an ocean they can't fill,
but he is steadfast, nowhere going;
safe with what he knows is real.

Then he moves forward, hesitating;
will it matter, now or twice?
around the bend a rainbow waiting,
autumn leaves or winter ice?

Indecision has her victim;
kept him long anticipating;
was it she or fate that picked him
for this game he ends up hating?

Sleeping is transition time;
like seasons your dreams die and change;
Towards the stars you surely climb,
only to awaken strange.

So you see through me once again;
you who are not friend or lover;
for it's your voice that tells me when
the day begins, the dream is over.

                    Don Shack

RECOLLECTIONS ON JAY KNIGHTEN ALL SAINTS DAY 1990

by Michael A. Susko

Jay was a doctor, who graduated from Harvard Medical School. He looked the part of a doctor: he was tall, handsome, had a deep sonorous voice, and with his beard had a commanding presence. A brilliant student, he was remembered well by his teachers at a Jesuit High School. After Harvard, he did research at Stanford University on diabetes and published articles. A promising career lay ahead; he was an example of the American success story.

At some point, Jay began experimenting with a new angle in research: love as a way to bring healing. He wondered if non-drug techniques could be used to help patients with diabetes, and ran into trouble with the medical profession.

Something else happened in California; Knighten got involved with a quasi-religious group that offered a "Course in Miracles." They taught problems are there simply because we think they are. If we can just change our minds about things, then the supposed problems will disappear. Something else happened too, concerning a relationship with a woman in the religious group, but Jay was vague about it.

He had a breakdown, and ended up at a halfway house where I worked in the Fall of 1984. At the time, he was diagnosed as having a "bipolar" illness, and was on heavy dosages of psychotropic medication: 30 milligrams of Haldol and 2300 milligrams of Lithium a day.

Jay denied to the staff at the house that he had a problem. To us, this seemed patently false: he had been hospitalized and was at a halfway house. We heard vague stories about his previous hospitalizations: in one, an attendant tried to give him an injection, but Jay took the needle and gave the injection to him, instead. Was he acting out—violently trying to be a doctor again? Or was he returning the aggression of someone forcing treatment on him?

One day I took Jay to an alternative clinic. Instead of trying to get help, Jay offered to work for them. He was making repetitive motions with his hands, showing symptoms of tardive dyskinesia, but the holistic doctor was unaware of such side effects. Afterwards, the physician told me that Jay did have serious problems—but was beyond their help.

Did Jay have a problem, or was he simply caught up in the system?

One day we talked at length in a park, and Jay revealed some esoteric beliefs—such as the power of a *Great Crystal* and his "identity" with it. Deep down, things were not resolved, it seemed—plus he didn't consider that he could have a problem. At the time, I told the other staff that those who deny they have problems are the hardest people to help. Everybody has problems and we need to face them.

In October, Jay began to complain of abdominal pain and nausea. I suggested that it could be caused by the Lithium, and told him to check with his doctor. A couple weeks later, Jay stopped taking his medication because of the side effects, and the fact that he believed he was not really "sick." Off the medicines, he became "unmanageable," whether from his original problem or from a withdrawal. Incidents started to happen: a female resident verbally provoked Jay and touched his face. He pushed her over.

For a while, the situation resolved. Then a week or two later, we received a call from the State Attorney's office. They told us a Dr. Knighten had reported that our residents were being over-medicated, that there was poly-drug use without adequate supervision, poor food, and first-aid incompetence on the part of the staff. Later, I started asking some of the same questions as to how we were caring for our charges.

Shortly after this, Jay wandered away from the house on one of the long walks he liked to take. He was arrested for "tearing up some golf course greens" and committed to a state hospital. The complaints Jay made were never taken seriously, especially when they found he was a patient in a psychiatric hospital. At the time, I recorded in my diary, "Jay was trying to document abuse. Is he now becoming a "martyr" of the system?"

In early December, we decided to receive Jay back to the house, but on the condition that his medicines be monitored. He was off the Lithium and on 20 milligrams of Haldol, and he seemed satisfied with the change. The first night he came back he was throwing up, however, and I wondered if he was "throwing up the drug."

Jay did not last long at the house the second time. Within a few weeks, the same sequence of events happened. Reporting side effects due to the Haldol, he started refusing medication and became unmanageable. He was ordered out of the house by the director the day before Christmas.

It was cold that winter, and snow was on the ground. Jay was missing for a few days, then showed up at my doorstep. He said he was suffering from hypothermia. I took him in—or halfway in. He could sleep in the hall outside my door, as I had only a single room and didn't feel comfortable sleeping with him there.

I became increasingly concerned about Jay's deteriorating situation. I have always taken people at face value, accepting behaviors that might be considered odd, and listening to any type of freely associating speech and trying to find meaning in it. But Jay started to cross my line. While having breakfast, he poured water into my air-cleaning machine, for no apparent reason. The upstairs neighbors, who also took in homeless people, reported that Jay was "burning books." Indeed, I saw some burned book pages upstairs—and heard he was doing this to rid of negative thoughts in them.

I could not risk a walking fire hazard. Meanwhile, I heard of a serious incident at my church, where I had introduced Jay. All the candles had been lit, and Jay was the person who had been let in to pray. Apparently, he was trying to ward off evil spirits. A small fire had been started in the sacristy, and the church could have burned down.

Fearing some tragedy might befall Jay, I and the priest of the church went down to the police station. He signed a petition for arrest based on petty theft of the candles. Jay later was picked up wandering, and when they found the outstanding warrant, the police held him for evaluation. He was hospitalized.

At Spring Grove State Hospital they put him back on medications. When I came out to visit Jay, he looked relaxed in an enclosed patio area in the sun. But I felt something was wrong—he looked as if he were in limbo. Had he given up on life? Inside, the only relief from the barren corridors and blank walls were the medical magazines that still reached him.

Jay was released again, and he found an apartment in a good neighborhood. Once, I went to visit him for dinner, and we ate a good meal. Jay was health conscious and drank purified water. I feel guilty for not having visited him more often. Again, I alerted him to the fact that certain effects he was experiencing could be due to the medication.

One day, Jay passed me on the street. He looked angry, gesticulated wildly, and yelled at me. Something had happened. Had he gone off his medications again?

After a bizarre turn of events, Jay ended up at a hospital for the criminally insane. This I found out about only indirectly. He was arrested for "indecent exposure"—urinating in public. Then he was sent for evaluation to a psychiatric hospital, but when they tried to move him to another ward, he resisted and injured another staff member. Jay was then sent to Perkins State Hospital for the criminally insane.

I knew another person there who reported that Jay was diminished, half the man he had been; that he had become thin and bedraggled, and that he had shaved his beard. Jay was also extremely withdrawn, hardly talking to anyone and spending much of his time laying on a couch.

He did resist treatment however, going on and off the medication. Jay would refuse to take it, and the staff would wait for an emergency to develop, then force him to take it for a while. Jay got worn out.

He was finally released. His mother told me he came home and stayed in bed. She said he seemed to be finally making his peace with God. Two weeks after he got out, he was dead. An autopsy was done, and his mother informed me that the report suggested his heart stopped due to the medication.

Thus, Jay's story tragically ends, having come full cycle from his trying to develop a drug-free treatment—to his death to which drugs contributed. Jay needed help, but he did not want help that gave him drugs and labeled him crazy. Did our society fail Jay in not having a drug-free treatment for him?

LOGS

In transience of thought
I saw mermaids cross my bow
Staving off the albatross
Pounding swells as salt spray
Pit my face
Flotsam of coffin pine wood
In my wake.

Barnacles of remembrance
Tear through the water of my passage
And leeward to the coast
Rock shore of country lost in wilderness
Through the wrath of storming nightfall
Toward the lighthouse bound.

A Poem from *Wilderness Travel*
by John Holton

ROB'S STORY

PART ONE

In June of 1976 I graduated from the University of _____, School of Medicine. I recall sitting among the ranks of my distinguished colleagues—dressed in a tuxedo—waiting until my turn to receive my diploma from David Brinkley, who delivered the graduating address. A year and four months later, I joined the ranks of America's homeless: a cold, poor, wandering street person with no food, no money, and no place to stay—all to avoid a psychiatric treatment requiring forced ingestion of psychotropic medication.

My story begins as a child. My family adopted a girl much different from us socially, spiritually, and intellectually. I seemed strange to her. The normal religious life of our family was disrupted. When I was nineteen I fell into the clutches of a religious cult which taught the practice of the presence of God. I pursued this meditation and in the meantime completed college and medical school. After graduation I entered a residency program.

Around the fifth month of the program, a time when residents are left alone to make their own decisions, I really felt alone, and in the continual presence of God. I came face to face with difficulties which had existed for a long time in my family. In the manner of a religious revelation I decided to dedicate myself to a career in music and the performing arts. Having little knowledge of theology other than a year of course work in an Ivy League college and what I had learned in the cult, I was at a loss to explain my experience to professionals in the medical community.

My parents decided I was having a psychotic breakdown. Members of my cult—instead of acting responsibly and telling my parents that I might be having a spiritual experience—told them that I was "possessed by demons," which in modern terminology meant that I was a "simple schizophrenic."

My family invited me over for the usual Sunday brunch. At the conclusion of the meal—which was eaten in stony silence—they informed me I was to be evaluated by a Dr. F., a community psychiatrist. If I refused to go I would be committed.

In his downtown office Dr. F. talked with me as he sat back in his plush leather chair. At the end of 45 minutes he decided I was schizophrenic and needed medication. If I refused to take the medication, he told me, I would be forced to go into the hospital. I informed him I did not want medication, and if they intended to commit me I would go to the hospital peaceably. My parents made arrangements while I sat numbed with shame waiting to be taken away.

Once in the hospital I was pressured to take the medication. I insisted I did not need it. I had studied the schizophrenia diagnosis and knew that it was a vague theory with no concrete evidence correlating it to a consistent biochemical imbalance.

The doctors responded to my objection by saying that I would have to take medication or they would get a court order forcing me to take it. I can still remember being led into the treatment room (flanked by a nurse on either side of me) and being jabbed in the arm with a shot of Prolixin. It was maddening that the same doctors who for two weeks had listened laconically to my story, now came bounding into my room the day after the injection, eager to see how the medication had affected my thoughts. Previously, they hadn't shown the slightest interest in the content of my thinking process.

The doctors soon informed me that I seemed more rested. They ignored the fact that I had been taken away from a busy residency program and had nothing to do for two weeks. They ignored the fact that once I took the medication I was released from the constant tension of being pressured to take it. Whereas before they had filled me with negative suggestions such as, "You're not thinking clearly," or "You seem tense," now they were using positive suggestion such as "You're looking better," "You're more rested," "The medication is helping you."

They never seriously considered the cult-related concerns which were uppermost in my mind. In their opinion my real problems were not amenable to rational thought. They frequently said, "We believe you'll always need medication." They went on to explain that "Thorazine to a schizophrenic is like insulin to a diabetic—go off of it and you can get very sick or die." I pointed out that a diabetic has a measurably raised blood insulin level, whereas all my chemistry levels were normal. They assured me that some imbalance would be discovered in the future, but none ever was. My thoughts and actions were a logical response to my experiences, not the product of a defective gene.

Throughout my stay I argued with the doctors about their diagnosis. I told them again and again that there was no proof I had a chemical imbalance. They replied, with a sad look in their eyes, that my denial was part of my illness.

I was discharged 4 months after admission when I informed the house-staff that my insurance money had run out. Each staff member made a point of telling me how I was doing much better, and how my thoughts had cleared up. But I no longer had any desire to work or do anything in my life.

I spent the next six and one half months at a halfway house. To fulfill their activity requirement, I enrolled in a psychiatric day-care center. I also had to see a psychiatrist twice weekly. I continued the same discussions with the new therapist as I had with the old one. I said I did not have schizophrenia and did not need medication. He insisted I did. He encouraged me to get involved with life and held out the example of the cult-leader as a committed and compassionate individual. This is perhaps the worse thing that can be said to a victim of cult-coercion.

It was during this time that I had my first exposure to the streets. In the evenings to avoid the discomfort of the psychotropic medications, I took walks in the inner city looking for people to talk to. I didn't find anyone.

In August, when my therapist went on his vacation, I went off my medication. Around the same time I went to see an old girlfriend from college. It was my first romantic encounter with a girl since joining the cult. I felt recriminating guilt and resigned from the cult. During this period of dire need I had no one to talk to, because neither the doctor nor his on-call replacement were familiar with post-cult syndrome. At night I had horrifying visions of dying and going to hell. At times I would jump out of bed screaming "I'm going to burn in hell for 200 years!" I took an overdose of medication because a member of the cult had told me, "If you resign from the cult you might as well commit suicide."

This state of mind frightened me so much, I decided to terminate therapy. I was informed that I was in violation of halfway house therapy requirements and in danger of being asked to leave. I quit the day-care center and began traveling around the city looking for a new place to stay. I tried using E.S.P., I visited a spiritual community, and looked for apartments in the newspapers. I hoped for a miracle.

I had no idea how stiff and spaced-out I was from the Thorazine which was still in my system. The effects were so insidious that after the second week of the drug regimen I had ceased to consciously associate my stiffness and severe muscular discomfort with the drug. In fact, on all three occasions when I terminated psychotropic medication it took six weeks before I felt restoration of total bodily comfort. After the third and last termination, it was eight months before I had restoration of normal bowel sensations.

Finally, the period of grace ran out and I received an ultimatum to re-enter therapy or leave the house. I refused, so I was told to leave the house. Three days later, I moved to a hotel. I was given one free night rent, and left to fend for myself.

Fortunately, I had $600 in my bank account from my work as a medical resident. On the second day at the hotel I packed all of my belongings into a taxi cab and moved to a suburban hotel.

The first phone call I made was to the leader of the religious group. Going back to her was better than being in psychotherapy. But because my father had threatened her, she didn't want to see me. The cult would not comment on my claim to have had religious experiences. In fact, the only group which has gone out on a limb regarding the genuine nature of cult-related religious experience was the task-force on cults of the American Psychiatric Association.

My savings account was now depleting rapidly. I had no place to cook my meals while living at the hotel and was forced to eat out in restaurants. Each meal took a bite out of depleted savings. As my balance grew smaller and smaller, the meals felt more and more like the last meal of a man condemned to an execution.

Before the end of a week I transferred to the least expensive hotel in the suburban area and stocked up on white bread and canned beans. With approximately enough savings left in my account for three days rent, I went out to look for a job. I applied for a baker's assistant—I thought if they hired me I could live on free samples of day-old bread.

During the interview I must have appeared uncomfortable. The drugs were not yet out of my system, and my eyes had a hollow stare. People who have just been in a hospital tend to exhibit what is known as "hospital behavior;" they fail to manifest the subtle social cues needed at a work place. I tended to stare into the distance at the job interview, and as a result I wasn't hired.

When my last check for rent bounced, I was told by the hotel that I would have to leave. The desk clerk had called my parents, who were coming to pick up by belongings. I knew they would only ask me to see a doctor, so I left the hotel and took to the streets.

PART TWO

With only pennies in my pocket, I spent my first day walking around the city. Food consisted of a package of leftover bread. By nightfall it began to get chilly and as I had only a sweater on, I thought of going to the mission. But I had too much pride and put it out of my mind. I couldn't see myself sharing living quarters with bums and derelicts. . . . It grew colder and colder. I began to shake. I decided I would walk past the Salvation Army just to see what the building looked like. When I got down there the front door was closed for the night. "Good," I thought, "I didn't want to spend the night there anyway."

Three hours later after the temperature plummeted and I continued to shake, I returned to the mission and knocked on the door. Now I was principally concerned with getting out of the cold. I learned that the mission was closed but there was a sleeping area for drunks around the side—an alley way alongside a chain-link fence. Unlike the drunks, I didn't have any whiskey in my belly to warm me. "Some protection from the cold," I thought, "a chain fence with holes in it." I walked on.

My legs were stiff and my feet numb. I got some respite from the cold at 5 A.M. when a gas-station attendant let me use the rest room. At 8:45 A.M. I was in the crowd waiting outside the main branch of the city library waiting for the doors to open. Not having slept, my head began to nod as I sat pretending to read a newspaper. Before long, a guard warned me that if I fell asleep I would be asked to leave. For the next three hours my head bobbed up and down like a human bob-o-link.

That evening, I showed up at the mission at 4:15 P.M. when the doors opened. I was not about to be locked out in the cold again.

Thanksgiving came and went, and the weather was getting colder. I had had enough exploring. I called up the parents of a friend from the religious cult and asked if I could stay with them for a few days. I walked through their house with my head bent down, wrapped in thoughts. I was afraid that if I loosened up, my friend's parents would ask me to leave. During meals I kept my eyes glued on the plate and made forced conversation when it seemed appropriate. I braced myself for the inevitable request to leave.

In the meantime my friend's parents had called my family to tell them where I was. They saw no reason why a grown man with so many accomplishments should be locked away in a state mental hospital. On the other hand they didn't want to interfere. So on day five my parents came to pick me up and informed me I was to be taken to a state hospital.

I can still remember sitting in the back seat of the family car, hoping the drive would last forever. I recall stopping at McDonalds for hamburgers and thinking that this meal was to be my last breath of freedom for a long time.

On admission, I was seen by an Indian resident. While my family sat in the waiting area a female patient began undressing herself. No one stopped her until she was half undressed. When my turn came to be examined I explained to the doctor that I had been trying to get work and ran out of money. I told him about my spiritual experiences. I thought he would be understanding, but he replied caustically that my views were unrealistic. He recommended involuntary admission.

I was issued a set of hospital clothes and admitted to the locked unit. On first entering the state hospital I thought it was just a hospital like any other. I felt relief, believing that I could survive this. Then I noticed there were patients more way-out than you would find at a private hospital. They were allowed to walk around moaning and pacing in circles for long periods of time before a staff member came over to assist them. This made concentration in the day areas almost impossible.

The first morning I recall walking around and trying to talk to as many patients as I could. I was thinking like a doctor, and at the same time I was still deeply affected by the religious cult. I thought if I shared my views with enough patients I could raise the consciousness of the institution and thus avoid being asked to take medication. Considering the reality of state hospitals, this was ridiculous. My treatment plan was controlled by a foreign resident, and a foreign resident at a state hospital would never change the diagnosis made by an American doctor at a prestigious private psychiatric center.

I was assigned to a Burmese psychiatric resident who spoke with an accent. He listened briefly to my story, to my reasons for leaving my internship. He took one look at the diagnosis on the chart, and signed the order for medication. An hour later I was called into the treatment room and given a Prolixin injection. I was a victim of steam-rolling. The doctor had found my thoughts and ideas different than his own, and instead of trying to accommodate them, he inhibited them by strait-jacketing my emotions with chemical treatment.

I spent the next six months in living hell at the state hospital. It is my belief, having been in a state hospital and having lived on the streets, that living on the streets is more desirable than living in a state hospital (although this may be due to my misdiagnosis).

On the streets there is a sort of discretion between places; there are neighborhoods. But in the state hospital day room you can walk five feet and it's like moving through five different ethnic neighborhoods. Everyone is herded together and there's no privacy. Psychiatric patients are forced to live in rooms with no divisions between beds. Also, patients with many different diagnoses are lumped together, being classified more by the extent of illness than by the type.

For six months I walked around in a *drug haze*, sleeping seventeen hours a day. Fun consisted of walks on the grounds and coffee in the canteen. The only relief from the discomfort caused by the medications was to actively engage in some activity. I would draw out sips of coffee as long as possible. When I finished I would seek relief from the pain by falling unconscious in sleep. At the low point of my hospitalization, I slunk into a toilet stall and thought to myself, "I will live in the state hospital forever."

The staff abused me and accused me of being lazy. The only medical care I received was an evaluation of my medications every two months. I was luckier than most. Because I was a doctor and considered more intelligent than the rest, I was assigned to a psychology student who met with me twice a week. But he made little if any progress in understanding my condition.

During this time someone told my parents about a national research program in biological psychiatry. My parents wanted me to join, but I refused adamantly. "My problem isn't biological," I told them, "Why should I waste these people's money?"

I finally left the state hospital when the staff threatened to throw me out onto the streets. The memory of my previous stay in the cold was too fresh in my mind, so I talked to the social worker and located a hospice in the inner city known as Project PLASE which at the time was a rooming house for former alcoholics who were "on-the-wagon." I still had no ambition to do anything. As a trained doctor it made no logical sense to me to get better while I was getting the wrong treatment.

At Project PLASE I received room and board, two square meals a day. I was receiving welfare; although to get it, I had to admit disability. Once every six weeks I got a Prolixin injection at a local day care center which I attended three times a week. Other than that, I just lay in bed and read, and tried to forget the constant emotional pain and bodily discomfort I was in due to the medication.

I spent a lot more time walking the streets and began to acquaint myself with street life. I was still in touch with the cult. A member brought me a letter from a disciple in India urging me not to "tax myself."

My father felt I had had enough treatment and should be working. He accused me of being lazy, and refused to see me. Finally, under intense pressure I agreed to enter the National Research Program for Schizophrenia. While I had no illusions that it would cure me of anything, I felt that the painful and exhaustive battery of tests would prove I had no organic illness.

This is exactly what happened. At the end of a year the tests showed I had a normal body. The research specialists also administered an exhaustive battery of psychological tests. The only scale which was abnormal was the "Oral" rating scale, and this was based on an evaluation of my cult-related statements such as "I am God-realised" and "in twenty-six years I will have disciples." When made by people who have been in cults, such statements are not classified as schizophrenic in the current diagnostic manual, the DSM-III. In another department of the National Institute there was a specialist working with ex-cult members. Had I been transferred to him for a consultation, my difficulties would have ended eight years before they did.

Although this information was potentially valuable, the price I paid for it was to be a human guinea pig for one year. During that time I had to collect all my urine every day. Once a week we had to give a large sample of blood. Approximately every six weeks we were required to take an intravenous drug infusion. Every two months we had to submit to a spinal tap.

At the end of one year I completed my obligations to the research protocol. Since the doctors had found that none of the medications used in their protocol made a difference in my thinking, they decided to give me Lithium, a drug which is usually given for mania. How could these experts believe that drugs designed to dull certain brain centers could accurately effect change in patterns of thought which had been carefully programmed into the higher mind by external authority?

It was with some foreboding that I left the National Institutes of Mental Health. Despite all the inconvenience and the pain of testing, it had been a haven for me. The protocol included gourmet food, weekly outings, free use of modern sports facilities and a Watts line. It was better than living in the streets. Yet, because I had made no substantial progress in addressing the real issues facing me, I knew that I would be back in the streets at some future time.

I terminated the Lithium treatment two months after leaving the National Institute. But this time, my parents—totally indoctrinated with the theory of "chemical imbalance"—demanded that I comply with the treatment plan or get out of the house.

A friend, who I met during my first hospitalization, let me stay with him due to our shared experiences and religious beliefs. But he expected me to live up to the ideals of the cult. When he found I had drifted away from their teachings of "love," he became angry and suggested I needed help. He then told me if I wanted to stay, I would need to help with rent. Since I didn't have any money, he asked me to leave.

My mother appeared in the apartment, placed me in her car and drove me to the same hospital where I had received treatment three years earlier. The stay lasted two months. I was seen by the Chief of Services who told me "We have a lot to learn from you, gradually." This was no consolation to me. This should have been the third year of my medical residency. Instead of helping others, I was being subjected to a treatment I disapproved of. Before being discharged, I ran way once and screamed at the top of my lungs to the staff that they were killing me with this false therapy.

PART THREE

My parents were running out of money, so I was forced to choose the least expensive halfway house. It was a run-down row house in a bad neighborhood, but it had a certain advantage. Whereas the other house, known as the Ritz of the halfway houses was Freudian in nature, this one was religiously-oriented, run by a local Baptist church. While it was the wrong religion for me, at least it recognized the role of God in the healing process. During this time I made a contract to work as a volunteer in a day-care center.

As soon as I moved into the house I discontinued medications. I could do this since residents managed their own medicines. Although chancy, this proved to be greatly advantageous later on. When I finally got work six months later the drugs were out of my system, and I was more relaxed. It was only because I was off the medication that I was able to do the work at the center. Otherwise I would have been too hampered by the discomfort of tardive dyskinesia. Doctors claim they have new medications which have fewer side effects, but I believe they would be as painful emotionally as the Prolixin was physically. To be subjected to a treatment which discounted all my thoughts as not amenable to a rational response was intolerable. In the process of stopping, however, I went through a wrenching struggle, before my own decision triumphed over external compulsion.

By now, my parents were desperately trying to get me to complete training in some skill area that could provide a steady income. But they were never greater victims of their own logic. To have a full-time career requires long-term stability, yet they believed in the medical model of schizophrenia which says there is no long-term stability. The best doctors can do is give medication to alleviate symptoms, and then they either lie to the public or skirt the issue.

I did have many thoughts related to my cult involvement that I couldn't share with others. I secretly thought I was living in a branch of the Guru's ashram at the halfway house. A cult counselor would have known how to respond to that. A Freudian therapist would make mincemeat of such a thought. Thus, I was holding my thoughts in, which complicated my condition.

After three months I decided to quit my job at the Day Care Center. Having ruled out the possibility of getting a teaching degree, I saw no reason to continue working there. The house informed my therapist, who confronted me at our next session. I took the opportunity to inform him that I had also gone off the medications. He told me I could go back to the hospital if this continued. The house gave me an ultimatum to go back to work and take the medication, or leave.

One week before the deadline, the brother of an old friend happened to visit the halfway house. He belonged to a religious community and when I told him of my problem he said I could move in with his community. Two days later he and a friend picked me up and took me to the house of one of their members. I studied the teachings for three weeks, but I had disagreements and ran away to the cult center. At this point the cult rejected me. They called my parents and insisted they come down to get me.

My mother flew down on a plane and picked me up. We went home together, and then without stopping at the house she took me to the nearest hospital. My father met us at the hospital. They told the doctor that I couldn't stay at home. The doctor agreed with my parents that I would have to go to the state hospital. Whereas the first doctor had talked with me for forty-five minutes, this doctor dispatched my case in fifteen. Conversation was mostly directed to my parents. Essentially, I was taken back to the state hospital because I had nowhere else to go.

But this time the state hospital told my parents I didn't need in-patient treatment, and they sent me home. Family therapy was recommended. Family therapy happens to be closer to the specialty which treats cults, but the doctor asked me not to talk about the cult in our family sessions. In return, he agreed not to treat me as a schizophrenic and to take me off medication. I made a contract with the therapist that I would go back to work, and I found a job almost immediately as a clerk in a mental health center.

For the next three years I earned a marginal income from various odd jobs supplemented by an inheritance from my grandfather. There's an important lesson to be learned here. Although I was "off the streets" physically, the problems which caused me to be on the streets were not resolved and there was a danger that they could resurface.

The problem reemerged three years later when my girlfriend whom I had met at the National Institutes became pregnant. She found this stressful and went home to her family for support. Her family wanted her to abort the pregnancy, but she refused and threatened to kill herself. They took her to a hospital. After being transferred by her family to an exclusive hospital in Massachusetts, we talked by phone. I was called back by a member of the hospital staff, who informed me that my girlfriend would be staying in the hospital until after the delivery of my child and that if I wanted custody, I would have to go to court.

My predicament was now manifest. In court I would be judged on the basis of my past hospital records as a chronic schizophrenic in remission. There is really no such thing as a chronic schizophrenic in remission who is not taking medication. But I was not "schizophrenic" and was able to function for long periods of time. In fact, I was now working as a paid actor and I had just been hired to portray Edgar Allen Poe.

My custody battle went poorly. A representative of the Department of Social Services informed me she was going to court to seek emergency custody to place the child with a pre-adoptive family. The good news was that I would be allowed to see my child.

Five months later I made the long journey to see my child. It was a great moment when the social worker allowed me to hold my daughter on my knee. Five minutes later the sweet atmosphere was broken, when the social worker launched into a speech about how she was going to take away my parental rights.

To comply with the D.S.S. service plan I had to make frequent trips to see my child. Each round trip was a thousand miles and the cost was severe. I was now working a six day week, in construction, light industrial, and clerical positions. I even took my guitar with me on these trips so I could earn extra money playing music in the subways.

During this period the social workers took me to be schizophrenic and expected me to take some type of psychiatric treatment. To make matters worse, I started to believe that because of the time I had spent in hospitals, I was giving the impression that I was schizophrenic. Mind control specialists indicate that if a person sleeps more than two nights in a center which holds a particular philosophic view, the belief goes deep in the subconscious. By this time, I had slept hundreds of nights in psychiatric hospitals and halfway houses whose directors believed I was schizophrenic.

In the fall of the year after my daughter's second birthday, in an effort to ease the conflict with the social workers, I agreed to be evaluated by a psychologist. I believed the evaluation would make the court procedure more honest. During the months when I was being evaluated, I made more and more trips to see my daughter because of the impending threat of having my visits cut off. On one or two trips I ran out of money and became stranded.

For the first time in three years I was back on the streets with no place to go. The first night this happened I stopped in a coffee shop and drank coffee all night. The second and third times I paid for a seat in an all-night movie theatre.

Once, I was persuaded to take one more dose of medication. This happened while I was in Boston on a visit—on a night when I suddenly found myself without enough money for the return visit. I was due back in Maryland for a performance under the National Endowment grant. I called my parents to ask for help, but they refused to give me any money. For some reason they felt my desire to see my child was evidence of psychosis.

I felt my only hope was to have some doctor call my parents. I went to an emergency clinic, and they had me wait in the lobby all night. The next morning they told me I would have to take a pill before they would agree to call my parents. They called and were informed by my parents that I was due back in Maryland to be interviewed on TV. The doctors were flabbergasted—they thought my talk about TV was delusional. They released me to return to Maryland.

Unfortunately, I had been given the dose of medication. The pill made me so sleepy that I had to delay my return for eight hours. By the time I got back on the road, the TV show had already been taped. I did make the first performance, but the Director who had worked with me for nine months noticed that my energy level had decreased. From that time on, I was only able to think of Poe as a psychological concept, not in an artistic or creative fashion.

The Department of Social Services finally informed me that unless I moved to Boston there was no chance of maintaining contact with my child. A hearing was called in probate court and the expert presented a negative report. I fervently denied to the court that I had the condition. I admitted refusing treatment, and my refusal was also noted in the court records.

PART FOUR

I was still maintaining my apartment in Maryland so I had no money left over for rent in Boston. Beginning on the last day of my custody trial I moved into the mission on Pine street. In Boston the local mission is an

Inn which takes persons in any hour of the night. The odd stone edifice, dedicated to the housing of the poor, was willed to the city by a wealthy philanthropist on condition that no one would be denied admission to the facility save toxically belligerent alcoholics, and that no one would be subjected to any medical or religious procedures as a requirement for admission. Residents received two square meals a day and a place to stay.

Individuals arriving early at the Inn (4 P.M.) received a bed reservation, but others like myself—arriving at 1 A.M.—were forced to sleep on cafeteria benches, or on the hard stone floor covered with newspapers. Gusts of cold air came in when the front door was opened to let in new residents.

Floor-mates included weathered alcoholics, indigent, homeless transients, ex-mental patients, and a variety of other types including runaways, displaced Indians, and victims of eviction. A typical client was arrayed in a wild combination of smelly, dishevelled clothing. To keep warm many clients wore three or four sweaters, sports coats or jackets. Many articles looked as if they hadn't been changed for months. Many residents also exhibited bizarre forms of hair style: long tresses of matted dirty hair sometimes hanging down to the waist were not uncommon. A few who had been on the streets the longest had bits of cloth or yarn twined into their hair.

The clientele carried a wide variety of infections with everything from scabies to staphylococcus and streptococcus to T.B. and A.I.D.S. One of the first lessons of mission survival is to avoid the spittle of any sick or debilitated resident. If a tuberculous infected resident coughs into your food, or you inhale it, you might contract T.B.

While staying at the Pine Street Inn, I was put on a waiting list for a clothing locker. In the meantime I had to carry all my papers and a large sum of money in a briefcase with a broken handle. After several days, I found an abandoned building in which to "store" my briefcase. I hid it under some broken rafters and covered it with some straw and old rags.

Since I had to rely on legal aid for the second half of my trial, I was technically classified as indigent. I was not only living in a shelter, but refusing to take medical treatment as well. In testimony to the court my expert witness explicitly stated that after losing the case I should go home to take treatment to help me cope with losing. Realizing that my rights to visit my daughter could be cut off at any time, I ignored his suggestion and stayed in town to be with her as long as possible. No sooner did I move to Boston than the social workers—who had demanded that I move there in the first place—cut back my visits to once a month.

The social workers knew they had me backed into a corner; I was in no position to protest. If at any time I was to cause trouble, I could be asked to leave the state. My only hope of regaining parental rights was to keep a low profile, to carry money with me at all times, to appear neat, and not attract undue attention.

During this span of time, I began working for daily labor pools, and later got a job with a telephone fund raising group. I also talked with experienced street people and learned of another shelter which had permanent bed assignments—more suitable to working residents. I transferred to the new shelter.

Life is full of strange contrasts and ironies. After two and one half months of living this way, and almost giving up hope, I was called back to Maryland to give another performance of Edgar Allen Poe, sponsored by the Smithsonian Institute. I arrived back in my old apartment, which I had maintained. I washed, bathed, had a good night's rest, and then gave a bravo performance to the audience who were guests of the museum.

But on returning to Boston I learned that I was fired from the telephone job, and that visits with my child had been severely cut back. The handwriting was on the wall. I spent a week languidly sunning at the beach and on the seventh day learned over the phone from my attorney that the courts had denied me custody. My visits with my child were terminated. I had the right to appeal, but with the continuance of the dishonest psychiatric practices—which were more focused on making money for drug companies than on helping me—my chances were null.

The course of events convinced me that I needed to delve into the source of my problems and not try to win my child back through some gimmick or emotional appeal. I decided that the solid core of my life lay in music. My family had a tradition of religious singing and I had experience singing tenor in a dinner theatre.

But I was stuck on the streets of Boston with no job, no career to speak of, no references in music, and no social support. So I did three things: I appealed my case; I got work as a volunteer in a medical research center testing rates of drug absorption; I took voice lessons, and started singing in a choir.

My legal appeal had little chance of winning, but it kept alive my hopes of recontact with my child. In order to get the job at the research center it was necessary to tell the secretary that I had not seen a psychiatric counsellor in the past six months, nor had I ever been in a psychiatric hospital. The first answer was true ipso facto. Regarding the second statement I simply did not consider my stay at P. Clinic in Maryland as treatment. I considered it a *forced political incarceration* by people who did not like the way I thought.

PART FIVE

I moved to a shelter situated on an island far out in the harbor of Boston. My memories of trips to that island are unforgettable and were a strange interlude in the monotony of street life. Residents applying to this island shelter lined up daily on the sidewalk at a downtown hospital and were taken by bus on a first come first serve basis. The road passes a series of depressed fields resembling rice paddies, in large enclosures of what looked like abandoned foundations. On the wall of the last enclosure was a sign which read "City of Boston Police Rifle Range." At the end one could see human-shaped targets attached to a stone wall. As we drove past there every day, I imagined I could hear an inner voice warning me in a dark, menacing tone: "This is what we do to people who run afoul of the law in Boston;" and then more personally: "We would have no hesitancy about shooting you if you tried to get your child back."

At the end of an island we passed a long narrow draw bridge that gave one the sense of driving out into the ocean. The road wound around sand dunes and pulled up before an abandoned army barracks. I recalled the passage in Leviticus where the Israelites put lepers in special colonies outside the city.

As I was living in a mission with consumptives, I walked around with a scarf around my face to protect my throat. When I learned from a member of my choir that an opera company was in need of tenor choristers, I was determined to audition. Unfortunately, I had developed a cough. Had I been engaged in an active opera career, I would have delayed. However, in my condition who knows what could happen. I might get worse, or there might be no opera to sing in; so best take advantage of the situation now. I believe in a Supreme Being and a rational purpose in life. I believe we all have enough strength to accomplish all we want to, so long as we don't waste time worrying about what could go wrong. So I applied for the opera.

But here is where evil mounted its greatest resistance to my career. I met a shelter-worker who moonlighted at the hospital where my girlfriend was a patient. We got into an argument about her treatment. The worker suddenly became unreasonably mean and demanded that the shelter send me to a hospital for evaluation to determine if I was violent.

The shelter took the advice of the worker. That night when I went to get on the bus to go to the island, I was detained and taken by police ambulance to the nearest mental health center to be evaluated. My great chance to sing in opera was drawing near, and I was being driven to a psychiatric health center.

I played it cool. On the way to the center the police decided I was together and predicted I would be let out quickly. And yet, when it was time to admit me to the ward, I forced them to handcuff me and carry me into the elevator. That might seem like a contradiction to playing it cool, but it meant that the chart would indicate that I had not taken treatment willingly.

Once admitted to the center, I was forced to take a tranquilizer. Considering the circumstances, it was futile to object. Singing is very sensitive to drugs of any kind and this is especially true of the style used in opera.

The first morning I was evaluated by a therapist from India. She was sympathetic about my getting my child back, but she couldn't understand my interest in music. I diplomatically bypassed this, and stuck to the facts about the disagreement with the shelter worker. I explained to her that I had only argued verbally with her, hadn't hit her, and had no intention of hitting her. This seemed to satisfy the Indian resident, but she told me I would still have to be evaluated by a forensic psychiatrist as well as a team of medical doctors, and then I would have to meet with her and the shelter worker.

On Sunday night, day three in the clinic, I called the Director of the opera and learned it was not too late to audition. On Monday morning I was evaluated by the team of doctors, nurses, and social workers who sat in chairs lining the four walls of a small conference room. The hard question was when the expert asked if anything made me mad. Here I was sitting in a room surrounded by strange professionals—my child's mother was being held against her will in a psychiatric hospital; our child, who I had not seen in six months, was being raised by strangers; I was locked up at the behest of one of the workers treating the child's mother two days before I was expected to show up at my first opera audition; and I was pressured to take a form of chemotherapy which was unsuited for my condition—and they wanted to know if I was angry! Only a saint could say that he wasn't angry. Five minutes later the doctor assured "Saint" Robert that he was okay to leave.

After the conference had exonerated me, I was told by the staff that I could leave the Institute as soon as I found a place to stay, but I was not to go back to the shelter. To find a place one needed money, a job and references. To get the job one needed to be out of the hospital.

I gave the Indian resident my full attention on the last morning at the clinic, and she told me that she thought maybe I should stop singing if I wanted to get my child back. This deeply affected me— it was another expert opinion that I needed to ignore.

I was feeling very discouraged, but I took a long day pass to look for a place to live. In the afternoon, instead of going back to the clinic, I called the police and told them I was supposed to be singing in an opera and the people at this clinic wouldn't let me leave. So the police picked me up and took me to the other shelter in town, and told me to tell the people at the clinic not to bother me.

All the experts had defined my problem as getting a place to live, getting something to eat, getting a job. I defined my problem as getting a singing role in an opera. When the experts were unable to understand my way of thinking they became indignant and redefined my problem as getting good psychiatric help. When that didn't work they redefined it as getting good medication to sedate me. If I had followed their advice all the way to its logical conclusion, I would have died of an overdose of psychiatric medication. But I got off their bandwagon which was bound for hell.

PART SIX

At the first opera rehearsal I sang enough of the tenor notes to get by. At the second rehearsal I sang them all to the satisfaction of the pianist. My cough, however, persisted. To make matters worse, I was unable to get a bed at the mission because I was out late at rehearsals. On the night before the performance I slept sitting up in a chair at the airport.

But I did sing the opera. Afterwards, I was thanked and told I did fine. At 12:00 I was dancing the Strauss Waltz with an attractive alto, and toasting in the New Year surrounded by diplomats and dignitaries. At 12:30 I did my disappearing act again and was soon mingling with winos at the mission.

But my reward came swiftly. After the opera I transferred to a suburban shelter, and learned of a local theatre company that needed actors. I started work with a street theatre. In the meantime I was sleeping by a heating vent at a nearby college. The theatre company also had a newspaper called *Street* which I sold to raise money for myself.

I met a local maverick who took over abandoned buildings and made them into houses for the poor. Eventually he was arrested for taking over a house that wasn't abandoned, but I was let free because I didn't know what he had done.

Finally, one day, the director of the opera ran into me while I was selling newspapers. She offered me a job with her employment agency. Now you may say I could have done this eight months earlier and never gone on the streets at all. But that's not how the human mind works. I had been castigated in a court of law by a powerful judge in the community. Due to his assessment of my personality, I was considered unstable and became a refugee from the medical community. I had tried to get a place to stay on more than one occasion but had been turned down due to lack of references.

Once I had sung in the opera, however, I was cast in a different light because I had touched the higher strata of culture. Within that rarified arena I had shown the ability to perform a skillful task at a rate and duration which was acceptable. By implication, if I could complete that complex task, I could certainly perform less skillful tasks such as answering telephones, and typing letters—tasks which in the cosmology of that society serve to set the stage upon which the more sublime endeavor was enacted. In short, I could earn a living. When my new landlady heard that I had sung in an opera, she expressed her admiration because she had sung opera.

I've never gone back to the streets although I have had close calls. I have since located the parents of my adopted sister Mary and they are reunited. I still have problems conducting business when she comes to visit, as that disrupts the fabric of my family life.

For almost three years, I have been self sufficient and have continued to follow my dreams. I'm training in religious singing, continuing my family's tradition. Occasionally, I perform on TV shows, and sing operas for local companies.

If anyone asks me my secret for success, it is this: never take anyone else's vision of truth as your own. Even though I had social workers, judges, doctors, and lawyers telling me what was wrong and what I should be doing, I never accepted their word as absolute truth. At the very last moment when I was about to get off the streets I never had more people telling me what I should do. And if I had taken their advice I would still be on the streets today.

From the Lesser Light

Stranger women from the underground
That hibernate deep and long
In wombs lost to a suicidal undertow.

As alienated from the milk of their youth;
In self exile, they wander
Amongst the lonely constellations
Numbed by beliefs and illusions now dissolved in ancient sorrows.

Giddy with happiness of surface functioning,
While slowly eaten by the buried time piece
That ticks their fate away
As they await a final alarm
With no regrets.

And yet I sing, down through this underworld
That she might hone to the window candle light
And it should exorcise the final minutes
For a passage from an overcast journey
Into an island of clouds parting en route home.

The reason for living not past,
The grey of passage take in melancholy remiss,
While rolling drops of soft rain cascade
patterning diligently
Into early afternoon
And it is hoped that she'll attempt to stay with us
This time.

                                                    John Holton

HOMELESS

by Jan

My last hospitalization wasn't connected with me being supposedly mentally ill. It was due to the fact that I was living on the streets. In the area where I lived, the men were given the option of going to the jail to stay the night and the women were offered the mental hospital. The men could get out the next day, the women had a three day limitation—they had to stay three days after they gave notice to leave.

I was wandering the streets; it was freezing cold. There were not enough beds for single women in the shelter, so I went to the hospital. Once in there you weren't treated as a homeless person who needed a warm place to stay, but you were now part of a mental hospital and viewed as a mental patient. If I didn't know what my rights were, I would have been drugged out easily and probably wouldn't have been released as soon. I put up a fight; I was there for five days and every day I tried to get out. I felt like a prisoner.

I was given psychiatric tests again and again; they didn't pick up any abnormality. The worker said, "Well this can't be. Why are you in here?" I would say, "I came here because I was cold, I was hungry and needed a warm place to stay." They didn't consider that homelessness could be due to obvious things like loosing a job, or a physical ailment—it *had* to be you were "mentally ill."

After five days I was released. I pulled money out of my bank account and bought a ticket to go and see my father. I got onto the airplane, we had a stop over in Washington, D. C. during a blizzard. The stewards took me off the airplane because they said I looked sick. I was weak and exhausted. I had stringy hair, and clothes I had worn for five days. I had told people I didn't feel well and wanted to sit in the front of the plane. I didn't know they could eliminate me from the flight, or I wouldn't have said that.

It was about 1:00 in the morning and it was snowing. I took a cab and stayed with my mother. She said "You better stay here until you get well, then go back to where you were."

It's hard to recall what happens when you're out on the streets. At the time, I could only think of the day and my two priorities: where am I going to sleep? Where am I going to eat? I did things always with one eye open. The way I kept track of things was by keeping a calender. And now, although I'm not a homeless person, I still think as though I'm homeless, i.e. will I sleep O.K tonight?

My becoming homeless goes back to being labeled so-called mentally ill in 1987. I wasn't getting along with my family. I was only working part time. I didn't have enough money in my bank account. Two or three months earlier, I had been in a car accident and hadn't received proper treatment. I never really considered how I was going to support myself and added to that was the fact I wasn't feeling well due to the accident. I was overwhelmed by the responsibility in front of me: I hadn't really been taught living skills. It wasn't that I was out of touch with reality. I was just not prepared to take care of myself, not only as a normal person, but as a person who wasn't in good health. I stayed with friends, hoping to find a place, but nothing came through. So I checked in at a shelter. It gave me this incredible sense of being overwhelmed.

Someone at the shelter told me to try the Mental Health Center. So I walked in there and tried to explain that I had been in this car accident, and that I was trying to get a job. They said to me, "You look tired, you look depressed."

They gave me Imipramine, an anti-depressant and never told me about the side effects—one being that you get a dry mouth and you need to keep drinking. I just assumed that a psychiatrist was like a normal doctor and would tell me if something could go wrong. After about a week of taking the drug, I was dehydrated. Within a week and a half I was severely dehydrated. Within two weeks I lost twelve pounds; I wasn't feeding myself properly.

In two weeks I was supposed to check back with the psychiatrist. He said that my eyes were dilated, my skin yellow and that I was severely dehydrated. I was admitted to the medical side of the hospital and was treated. A counselor there said I looked near to death.

While I was lying there, completely exhausted, somebody from the psychiatric unit came and asked me some questions. They asked where I was from. I had lived in twelve to fifteen states. I said, "Well, I guess I'm from Washington D.C. or Maryland or Connecticut. . . ." I was not coming up with a concrete answer which those tests are designed to look for. When they asked for my name, I said, well, you can call me this, this, or this—because I've been called different names, especially depending where I lived. They ended up telling my family I was a very confused person. In reality I was just exhausted.

They transferred me over to the psychiatric end of the hospital. At that point I had no diagnosed mental illness. But they said on the medical reports I was trying to kill myself by way of anorexia. I happened to have been a thin person. I was definitely thin at the point I walked in there, but it wasn't something I had a problem with. It was the justification to transfer me to the psychiatric side.

Four days later, they had me on anti-psychotic drugs: Trilafon and side effect medications. On the drugs I gained weight which is what they wanted. In the three weeks I went from 103 to 117. In two months I went from 103 to 165.

Another thing the drugs did was to stop time. I can understand why people forget to go to their appointments. My friends and I could not even plan an activity, first of all, because we were sleeping a lot and then, because time was gone. Before I was always asking who am I and what's my purpose, probably normal things for a person leaving home. It just stopped. I couldn't even think of the moment I was in. I would be going to these meetings, Adult Children of Alcoholics, where they would say, "Live in the moment and live in the day," but I was doing everything I could to get out of that way of thinking.

I used to have a very good memory. From the time I took the drugs, I could not remember what was going on, even during the very day I was in. So I would try to write down what I was doing as it was happening. I couldn't even remember why I had come in the hospital in the first place. I could not remember anything in my past. When I stopped the drugs I couldn't remember the past year and half I had spent on them.

Now, as I'm getting further and further away from the drugs I'm *just* remembering what I did that year and a half. There's a lot of stuff that I'll say, "Well, I never did that." I'm starting to remember now.

As far as I'm concerned the "mental illness," if there ever was a "mental illness," was there because I started taking their drugs. Every month, I was in the psychiatric hospital because I could not physically deal with the agitation they were causing me. Mentally and physically I couldn't stay still. I really feel that I was a guinea pig. In the year and a half that I was in the mental "health" system, I was on thirty-two different drugs in the hospital, plus day treatment programs, halfway houses— everything that is designed to help a so-called mentally ill person.

They had me on a crisis team. I was considered one of their "high-risk patients" because I was always in the hospital. The real reason I was in a hospital was because I couldn't stay still. They gave me a psychiatrist, a social worker, a psychiatric social worker, two nurses, and a contact person between the hospital and Mental Health Center—just in case anything went wrong. In addition, they had a crisis bed to use if you started feeling ill, to keep you from going into the hospital. I spent a total of about 240 days in the crisis bed, and lived in a halfway house for six months. I had group therapy and day treatment. There was a lot of therapy, but I spent most of my time talking about the effects of the drugs: "I feel agitated, I feel like I'm out of touch." They never asked why I was homeless. They just assumed I was mentally ill. From their point of view anyone who comes to the mental health system, obviously can't handle their life. They take you from the time you walk into their door, as to how you might fit into *their* program.

Once all the symptoms of the drugs went away, there was no more therapy. They said, "You seem to be OK now, you seem to be all right. You really don't need to stay here."

Within a month after I left, they finally diagnosed me. Although I still had dreams of things I wanted to do, I couldn't hold down a job. Three times I tried—I couldn't sit still. But I could go to school. One summer I took a psychology class and got an A in it.

I had grown dependent on the system to the point of abusing it, only because I was being abused myself and didn't realize it. I didn't realize I was a victim of the mental health system. Even if someone offered me the kind of benefits that you can get in a hospital—I didn't have to pay for it, medicaid did—free food, a country club atmosphere, no responsibilities, I wouldn't go. I did choose to go when I was on drugs because no one, none of my so-called normal friends could tolerate me being around. First of all, I could not sit still—I would just pace back and forth. I would do little annoying things like tap the table. The only people that could stand to be around me were people with the same problems. So we would all go to the same place where we just didn't have to deal with things.

These hospitals were more or less luxury places, with a swimming pool, art therapy, music therapy, dance therapy, psychodrama—and all my friends were in there. It is really difficult to leave the system. I absolutely admire anyone who does. They told me countless times that *I* had a *mental illness*, that *they* were the *mental health system*. They encourage you to depend on them: "they" being the doctors, the drugs, the hospital. They want you to depend on them and when you start showing any sense of independence—which is what they say they are trying to help you obtain—they backtrack. They say, "Well, you're getting a job but if you need us, we will write up a contract for your safety." There's an incredible amount of mixed messages.

As a way of transition out of the hospital I thought it would be good to go to some group who would be familiar with people who had "mental illness." The group that I heard about was the *Alliance for the Mentally Ill*.

Since it was in the hospital and we were allowed to go, I went to a meeting. It turned out that it was mainly family members who discussed their relatives' "mental illnesses." They really weren't discussing how they could help the person, which was how it was advertised at the hospital, but how family members were to deal with the person who had the "mental illness." When they say "deal with it" they really put it in a negative light. All the meetings I went to were complaining sessions, rather than sharing information on how to help each other or the one who had the "mental illness."

I had been going to AMI before I went into the hospital. We were discussing a monitor program, where people from AMI would monitor how people were being treated in the local mental hospitals. About that time, I was hospitalized and being threatened with Thorazine injections. I was being told that they were going to keep me there a long time because I looked psychiatrically sick, even though they had no proof. I called my local AMI group, told them I was in mental hospital and asked if I could have any legal help. I couldn't figure out how to release myself from this hospital, particularly since I went in voluntarily in the first place. They told me they couldn't help me because they were designed for family members, *not* people with mental illness. Even though I had been going to the group before going to the hospital, now I was on the other side. I had a paid membership in this group and once I was in the hospital they completely stopped contact.

It started to make me wonder how much of the "mental illness" is chemical, how much is family. They would talk in the meetings about these "horrendous things" their sons and daughters were doing. I would think who is it on my unit or ward who's doing something like that? It didn't seem to match. I was on the locked ward when a lot of these people would come in, when they're off their medication. Supposedly, I was seeing their sons and daughters when they weren't well. They may have been screaming about something, or looking frightening or threatening, but not to the point where someone would need to take such strong medication. Within three to five days most of these people were suddenly very sedate. At the next AMI meeting things were very well with the AMI members— the hospital was doing a wonderful job.

By the same token I was going back into the wards watching people suffer from these horrible side effects. The parents would end up talking about how horrible things were in their family, which was very different than what the person was talking about who had the "mental illness." I feel that the Mental Health Center was designed to stop how the person was feeling and really thinking, instead of helping the person work it out.

They have a lot of tests that are designed to box you in. They really pray that you at least say one of the those things so that they can diagnose you, and supposedly help you.

I chose to leave the system in 1988. I chose to go off drugs after watching what it had done to myself and a friend. My friend was on his way to becoming homeless before he committed suicide. He had come from a family background that could have helped him find a place to live, but didn't help him out, which was similar to my situation. The death of my friend really shook me up. I had to ask myself if I wanted to end up like him.

I had never been to a funeral before and I became obsessed with the fact that he was gone. I was obsessed with grieving. I went overboard. I did anything I could to understand why he had died. I began to see similarities between his situation and mine.

I told my social worker that the best thing I could do for myself was to go to the funeral. She said, "Absolutely not. You won't be able to handle it." It was at that point that I realized that somebody was trying to deny me the right to feel something, which was supposedly what therapy was all about. I thought, "Wait a minute—hold everything."

I went to the funeral. At that point a lot of things happened, things that these therapists were supposed to be working for. When I came back and said, "I feel better about this, I want to leave the system." They tried to keep me. In fact, they suggested I go into the hospital because I was "obviously" out of control. I wasn't screaming, I wasn't threatening to hurt myself or others. I would just go there and sob and grieve.

My friend's death was an awakening point for me of the reality of the mental health system. Somebody close to me was dead due to falling through the cracks. He went for help constantly and the system failed him. Did *he* commit suicide? Or did the system? I felt I was heading this way, if I didn't get out.

In the following February of 1989—my friend had died in the Autumn—I found it hard to go to work, but I went part time and went to school full time. I was receiving SSI, barely enough to live on. My friends would allow me to live with them and chip in for rent. But when the $72.50 went and the Medicaid went they said we really can't afford to have you here. My food went first.

I asked the Mental Health Center if they could help me find resources to get food, and they didn't know! I had a case management worker who was supposed to be responsible for that. They didn't know where to send me for housing either! I actually became homeless. They said, "You are now not living anywhere, so you can't use our services at the Mental Health Center." This was a complete contradiction from when I was led into using their services because I was homeless. It was this contradiction that helped push me completely out of the system.

Once out of my last hospitalization I remained with my mother through January of 1990. I decided I was well enough to get my things, which were boxed in the attic of one of my relative's house. While I was there, I got a phone call from a local shelter who told me my name was on the top of the list. "Do you want to live here?" they asked. I said yes.

While I was in the shelter I was assaulted. It was serious; I didn't loose consciousness, but I lost my vision for several minutes—and I haven't had correct vision since. It happened to be a shelter where the criteria to live there was mental illness—it was down the street from the state hospital. They accepted a minimum amount of money that would excuse them from being responsible for things that happened there. So when this fairly large woman assaulted me, no one did anything. Finally, I got up and called the police. When they came in, I asked them to take me to the emergency room.

At that point, I was back on medical assistance. I was taken to an emergency room and admitted because I had bruises on my forehead. A surgeon saw me and refused to treat me. They recognized where I was living. The doctor claimed I was "uncooperative" during the exam, that I looked at him, and said "You jerk." So he decided to terminate the exam.

I stayed at a relative's house for three days. We were allowed to stay away three days from the shelter. I stayed a fourth—I kept sleeping the whole time. Apparently I was passing in and out. I was gone four days, so I lost my place at the shelter. My family said, "Please get out of the house, we can't have you living like this." I kept telling them I had headaches. They said, "Well, the surgeon didn't treat you, so what could possibly be wrong?"

So I was back out on the streets. I was out there for a day and met one of my friends in the mental health system. She said she knew of another shelter. That was wonderful—it was run by a church—but you had to be out by 7:30 in the morning, and stay out till 7:30 at night. It was a long time, especially during weekends when everything was closed because it was a rural area. It has got to be one of the most tiring things I've done.

A friend of mine two states North asked, "Why don't you come up and rest here awhile?" While I was there, I walked into an ER room. They told me I had a Post-concussion Syndrome. A minister from my church happened to see me there and asked me what he could do to help. He found a family that drove me back home.

I don't consider myself a "mentally ill" person. Whether I have a "mental illness" at this time is absolutely pointless to me. The fact is I started to live as most mentally ill people did, going through the stigmatism. I still go through it in countless ways. For instance, when I ask my physicians about a problem, they say "Oh you've been through so much, why don't you go to therapy?" I am absolutely horrified. I end up saying to people, "My feelings are controlled well." I don't even get off on a tangent about it. The doctors, if they heard I got "help" the psychological route, will lead you that way, instead of being open-minded about your physical problems. In times before, when they found out I was connected with the Community Mental Health Center, they would say, "Why don't you talk to your psychiatrist about it?" It's no wonder there are so many homeless people and so many "mentally ill" people.

I don't believe in mental illness, not because there's no such thing. In my experience a lot of people who have "mental illness" are very tied into the spiritual world, and when they start to express what they feel in spiritual terms, it's fine if they tell someone who has the vocabulary for that. For instance, someone who "hallucinates" may not necessarily be hallucinating. The system they have been directed towards tells them: "You have a psychiatric problem, you're hallucinating, there's something wrong with your mind. We need to stop that with drugs."

If someone took that same experience, for example, "I feel as if there's a presence in the room. I feel very close to it. I see a vision." If that person went to a different system, i.e. a church maybe, or some place that's strong spiritually—that person may not be considered "mentally ill" right away.

At the time I became so-called mentally ill, I was deeply involved in exploring spiritual reasoning, and was having some very spiritual experiences. Unfortunately I made the mistake of saying them to a mental health person. The head of the mental health system is a psychiatrist, and he deals with drugging the body and the mind. Nothing *ever* comes up in the mental "health" system about spirituality, which is a very strong belief that we are more than just our body and our mind. Just because you can't see it, doesn't mean it's unhealthy. The people that helped me out could see beyond my eyes that were in a daze, and my dirty clothes. Sometimes, I was so stressed out I'd be sitting there crying. The people that could see beyond that, were those who believed that you are more than just what they see now—and those people were usually connected to a strong spiritual belief.

The mental health system taught me that the people who had really been there, other than the people who were spiritual, are those who are supposedly psychotic. They helped me in the hospital, they helped me when I was homeless. These people are my friends and I see myself as part of them. I really wonder how many of them are really "psychotic," if they are able to take care of themselves and another person.

In my hospital experience I met someone who everyone told me to stay away from because he had become "crazy" from one too many acid trips and saw too many ghosts and spirits. The counselors said he was just not a good person to talk to. He had been in the hospital a week before I had gotten there. We hadn't talked, but in the nighttime when I would be out in the community activity room, he would come out and say, "*You are just confused about every day life. Do not talk to anyone about your experience.*" I thought, 'He's out of it. He's really out of it.' I didn't pay attention to that, yet it was probably the best advice I've ever gotten. It really proved true.

The more I would talk about my experiences, the more drugs I was given. A lot of my friends do take drugs that they're given, and they still experience the things the drugs are supposed to be stopping—only now they have to deal with the side effects. They have to deal with inertia, absolutely no will—I really believe these drugs medicate your will. *These drugs stopped their life.* It seems they are just placating their parents or their families or whoever's supposed to be concerned about them. The drugs don't stop their inner thoughts—they just learn to stop who they say them to. You learn not to speak in order to survive, and your needs never get met.

It's hard to recall my extensive inner experience that was going on while I was in the hospital. It could be explained by the concept of *synchronicity.* For instance, my friend died in the Autumn of 1988 and we used to spend lots of time at the ocean. Every year since, people have invited me to the ocean in the autumn. This year, a friend I haven't seen in five years asked me if I would like to go to the ocean in the fall. If I hear words in songs, if I see a painting that reminds me of my friend—I think there's influence from other places.

I call it the *chill of truth.* Sometimes I will be sitting alone and get this chill; it's either a cold chill or a warm chill. If it's warm with goose bumps, I feel there's a presence from the spiritual world in my room. You tell that to a psychiatrist, and he'll say, "Dear, that doesn't happen. . . Sorry. Here take a pill. Sounds like you need one."

I believe that certain kinds of music appeal to certain parts of your body. The things that are spiritual in a chorus usually come in the o vowel, for me. If I really start singing into a song, sometimes I can transcend and rise into joy, an absolutely overwhelming feeling. I may feel as if those who have died are in the room. I don't see or hear them, but I know they are there. But I don't have to see or hear them. If I tell that to a psychiatrist, it's not acceptable. I suppose it's due to the culture where you live, whatever is accepted, which makes you really wonder how they decide what is mental illness.

I had some pretty extensive beliefs, that I was given a purpose, that I was out to help the world—I mean severely help it. I still believe that, but I don't believe it with the vanity I had before. And before, I had no focus. By the time I left the system, I had somewhat of a focus: mainly my anger towards the system, and this need to help people.

I don't feel my so-called mental illness has fully ended because I believe there's a strong connection between what I was questioning, whether philosophically or spiritually, and how I obviously appeared to some people as a mental problem. I still don't think I have any real solid answers, but I do think there is a connection, that "mental illness" is some sort of spiritual emergence.

There are still things that are coming up with me. A book I read before I entered the hospital was an incredibly spiritual book. I underlined practically everything in it. I couldn't believe somebody else was thinking my thoughts. When I said this: "Somebody's thinking my thoughts," the psychiatrist didn't take it into perspective. Here they were taking me out of perspective. It's almost like that *Three's Company* TV show. Nothing was followed consistently.

The whole time I was in therapy I never talked about my past; it was like having amnesia. They never asked about my childhood, unless I brought it up—which I never did because I was so busy being what they called "dissociated," being out of touch with my body. I was never out of touch with reality, just out of touch with the physical reality of who I was. I spent *all* my time adjusting to drugs and talking about them. I had all the people designed to do therapy, but never had real therapy.

The questions raised here are unanswered. The way I look at it is that when the answer comes, it comes in the form of a question that just keeps going. A friend of mine, a native American Indian who grew up on an Indian reservation, said that among her people a long time ago, "mental illness" was respected as a spiritual state. It's not that I'm against helping people if there really is such a thing as "mental illness." I just don't see drugs as being the only way. Why can't there be more money for research for other options? The way I look at it, is that there is no mental "health" system. There is no system that would let someone be homeless, there's no *healthy* system that would do that to someone. I heard someone once call it the Mental Illness System, and I see it like that.

I consider myself an *Advocate*. There are just too many people that I care about. There's not even any choice about it; it's already chosen for me. I have to do it because I've been through too much; there's too many people I keep running into who are going down, who contemplate death. Death shouldn't have to be a choice in life.

Sept 22, 1990 [*dictated*]

MANIC

It's happening again
I've joined God in
my flight for dawn.
I stand at the door,
naked, as if ready
to leap into winter
air. I'm perched
smiling on balcony's
edge, arms outstretched.
A bird sings, Jump!
and I seize its wings
with my eyes.
Airily I fly into sun
is as cool as the air
that brought me,
yet my flesh blazes
fragrant as spring's
first rose.

by Kathryn

LIGHT

Through the pale
blue sheet over the
tall old window
is light supernatural.
It appeared without
warning, like rain after
summer's drought.
When I saw it, I wept.

This the light
I have longed for,
the light I loved as
a child and will love
as a spirit,
a light too lovely
to be real.

When I see this light
I play flute in it.
The neighbors see a
shape behind a sheet
swaying with a stick.
They say I've lost
my mind.
I may have.

Still, I claim light
has God in it,
that on certain days
at certain times
otherness fills the
air.
Maybe it's the way
light goes through
sheets or the way
fire escapes make
checkerboards with
sun.
Or maybe. . . .

by Kathryn

A SYMBOLIC EXPERIENCE

By David Alexander   1990

PART ONE

Eighteen years ago, I entered a symbolic world for almost six months. Much of my life has flowed from this experience; my interest in writing fantasy, my analysis of dreams, my spirituality, and a deeper relationship to people. Although this world was very different and contained much pain, I feel that it was one of the most real experiences of my life. I confronted ultimate issues: who I was, the presence of evil, and the reality of God. Modern psychiatry can label this as a "loss of contact with reality," hallucinations, or delusions. But for me it became a return to my true self.

I had been "normal" enough before—an outstanding student, a winner of debate tournaments, and an athlete. But something was not true. My real self was covered up in my attempt to excel.

In my Senior year of high school, I tried to break out. I wrote satires on the dictatorial nature of high schools. The office of the Vice Principle in charge of discipline was *GeSTOMPo*, or "General Effort to STOMP others." The only good people were the *G.P.'s*, the janitors.

I devised Independent Reading courses to free myself from attending classes. I read *October the First is Too Late*, where time zones mixed, and Heinleins's *Stranger in a Strange Land*, where an alien offers his fingers as food. Such symbolism would later appear in my breakdown.

When I went to college, I was ready for new experiences. I had enrolled in an experimental school. My humanities professor, my mentor, was the first atheist I had ever met. During class he blithely said the Catholic church was cannibalistic. I, who had come from a strict Catholic environment, took my faith seriously, unquestioningly. 'How could it be,' I wondered, 'that an intelligent person whom I respected did not believe in God?'

My roommate, a musician, was my first contact with the "counter-culture." Steve led me to smoke marijuana. To be "far out," we painted the walls of our room purple and yellow. We played the music loud, albums such as Yes' *Fragile* and *Close to the Edge*. I had some close encounters with women, but I was too emotionally immature to sustain any relationship.

As I got deeper into the "counter culture," I began smoking marijuana daily. We bolted our door with a screwdriver. I felt a growing separation between me and the outside world, which I saw as fake. I questioned things I had taken for granted. One day, Steve showed me a science book that said that an eagle could see four times better than man. Could I trust what was said in literature and religion? Perhaps only science was true.

Two fundamentalists stopped by to talk to us, but they didn't help. How could their religion deny free love and support the war in Vietnam? The central Christian image, I reflected was the cross—one of death.

Once, my roommate offered me mescaline, an hallucinogen. I felt a strong "revelation:" *America is just a game we play.* I felt we were trapped in this life, that the only escape was death. Fortunately, my roommate was there to keep me grounded.

I started dropping out. I stopped going to church, quit debate, and skipped baseball practice. Reading Thoreau's *Walden*, I took long walks, and imagined that I lived in a tent with a grass floor.

When I went home for Christmas, my parents found me changed. I refused to go to church and confession. My mother and I argued. . . . I spent much of my vacation outside, reading Tolkien's *Lord of the Rings*. One night, I had a disturbing dream of being struck by lightning.

The next semester I took a wild assortment of classes, including Eastern religion and an internship at a mental hospital. On a tour of the ward, a man came up to me, and said, "My hand's on fire!" I thought all he needed was love.

One evening after dividing up a newly bought pound of grass, I suddenly left the dorm. I needed to leave it all behind. I wandered over to the Student Union. When I stepped out from under its arch, bells chimed and it started to rain. A signal, I felt. A stranger who I feared was *Death*, approached me and asked for directions. "I'm new here," I said. I suddenly felt *new*, that a new age was being ushered in.

When I reached the town's outskirts, I searched the horizon expectantly. I imagined finding a place to lie down and rest, a golden field lit up by the sun.

But the night grew cold, windy and rainy. I felt a test come down from the sky: *I must walk all night without stopping or resting.* What was this *test* and where did it come from? Was it my own inner drive to prove myself? Was it a demand from God to remove myself from a prodigal life?

Over endless rolling hills, I walked deep into the countryside. A police officer stopped me and asked where I was going. "Nowhere," I said.

At the station house of a small town I refused to tell my name. I had left my family, my identity behind. I was going to be like Socrates, and travel from place to place, and ask questions. The police considered arresting me for vagrancy.

Finally, I told my name and agreed to go back. I had left my glasses at the station house, but I wouldn't need them to see anymore, I felt.

The officer dropped me off at mid-campus, but I just started out again in a different direction. I reached a highway. Walking to the point of exhaustion, my coat glistened white. *A death glow has come over me*, I thought. *My eyes are dying first! If I walk much further I will die, my body to shed like a heavy weight.*

At one point, I started walking in a straight line, believing that I could walk through things.

Before dawn, I collapsed. I got up and called home and asked my parents who lived hundreds of miles away, to pick me up. When they wanted to place a call for help, I couldn't hang up at first. I thought I would be *hanging up my lifeline*.

Something strange happened. I saw matter coming to life, colors swirling. A black blur suddenly passed by. Horns bellowed. Trains kept going faster and faster around me, as the thought came: *The Morning Trains have risen but no one's guiding them.* I stood in the cold light, wondering, *Am I already dead, standing in another world?* When the phone rang, I asked: "Mom, mom can you hear the trains blowing?"

I have wondered since if there actually was a train. A Southern Railway schedule that I tracked down shows there were early A.M. trains passing nearby. But I think the real meaning—other than our society could be compared to a train without a driver—was that I was dying and about to enter another world.

PART TWO

I was in a symbolic world for several months after this. I did not know my own name or where I was. I believed my actions to have consequences of a cosmic dimension. At the same time, I was unaware of basic practical necessities. When the dorm counselor, Allen, picked me up and took me to a restaurant, I imitated him and lifted the fork to my mouth like him. Initiates in some tribes pretend to learn things over again as if an infant, but for me it was real. My roommate, too, must have been surprised when I dropped a piece of egg and put a ball of dust back on the plate. *One doesn't need to eat to stay alive*, I thought.

That day, I experienced a rush of power and the realization that *the thought makes things be*. This "power," however, held some terrible consequences.

My sister took me to her boyfriend's fraternity house. According to the doctor's notes which I later obtained, "He was thrashing about, talking about not wanting people to be mad with him, and not knowing what to do." In fact, I imagined angel guardians walking up and down the halls, warding off devils' stares. In the morning I thought a thousand years had passed, that I was some sort of god—although I had undressed and wetted the floor.

I was taken back to my dorm where I found my roommate and his friend high on drugs. A strange perception came to me: they were contacting lifelines of the dead. *Listening to music, they could flow with the melody of Beethoven for a million years. But the only way to "steal" a lifeline is to kill oneself.* They wanted me to join them. I fled.

Allen, the dorm counselor, joined me for my walk that evening. It was raining lightly, and, unknown to me, there was a full lunar eclipse. I had a *last day* experience, one that would repeat itself in varied forms. The following italicized sections are quotes from a book-length poem, representing my flow of consciousness.

The streets are strangely empty. Where have all the people gone? We pass by a fire hydrant—a Child of God frozen still. All the still objects, the tree stumps, the light posts have become Children of God. The car windows read black; there are people trapped within! I rush up to a car to share their fate, but the door is locked.

We're the last two people on earth. Allen, tall and bearded, is the Judgement Man. He's waiting for me to give my account before we walk over the horizon's edge. In tears, I make my confession: I lied to my parents, I threw stones at my brother.

My friend told me years later that he tried to get me go to a mental health clinic, but that I refused. After convincing me to take a sleeping pill, he dropped me back into my room. I thought they were poison pills, that I had sold myself over to death.

If goodness was synonymous with stillness, peace, and concreteness, evil presented itself as shadows. When I got back to my room I saw shadows flitting on my walls. They were the spirits of the friends who wanted me to join them.

I went to bed, took off my shoes, and saw my feet stained black. *Already I'm starting to die*, I thought. A cold blackness settled over me as I fell asleep—a sleep I thought I'd never rise out of.

I rose the next morning to see my brother Matthew and my father. The car ride home felt like I was passing through time zones. At times, I put my hand on the door handle. I wanted to step out and become still like a Child of God.

We arrived in the *City of the Future* where the new gods resided. My home town is technologically advanced with considerable electronic industry. At home, I experienced a new test: I must make something new. But all the things I saw around me were made by others. And when I searched for thoughts, none seemed to be truly my own. I found some finger paints in the kitchen and painted a yellow sun and green hills. But I realized that these weren't my idea either, and that the paper and paints were given to me as well.

The boundary between the outside world and myself dissolved. My body fluids, I felt, started to pour out of my finger tips. The white color became my plasma: the red, my blood. But there was too much black on the picture—it was *death-smeared*.

This reminds me of the Plains Indians and their Sun Dance where an offering is made to the creator. They believe their body is the only thing that is their own to give.

The "test to create"—the desire to make something new—lies close to the contemporary artistic soul. Perhaps it is even taken too far. Many who end up in psychiatric hospitals think artistically. Before I was hospitalized, I said I was a fake, that I was just doing things to please others. Opposed to this desire to express is an encounter with oppressive conformity. For me these forces were portrayed in the following sequence:

On a cold crisp morning, my father winds a machine, playing pictures on a tiny screen. 1984 is here! Color thoughts are placed on reels to be played back at will. A hidden Master Control is near, recording every movement, every thought.

Dad takes me outside to play catch. I can throw the baseball at the speed of light! Any power is offered to me if I'll just give up my freedom. I flee far into the woods. The alarms go off!

My brother Frank, a gentle Saint, finds me. On the trail back home, I breathe in the cold air. The air doesn't go down into my lungs, but up, up into my head! My head just emptied! My brain's been stolen. It's gone into the Master Machine; it collects all the brains.

My father was a good man, who spent time with his kids and taught us sports, but he was also one who said you shouldn't fight the system.

The next morning I felt that I woke in the Land of the Dead. My father followed me from room to room, but he wasn't my real father. He was a *copy man, an exact duplicate.*

There was a point in my childhood when I felt that something was wrong with my father and that he couldn't be my father. Later, I found that he had had shock treatments as a young adult. Despite this handicap, my father through sheer persistence accomplished many things in life.

I was taken to see a doctor whom I believed to be God. It was earth's last day and he had come to judge us. I tried to reach out to my mother. The doctor's notes reveal some of the family dynamics: "When he quit church, however, the parents withdrew his allowance and mother, her 'love.' Patient cried through telling of this, as did father. Mother sat unmoved. Patient asked father forgiveness, but was obviously afraid to talk to his mother. I was able to get him to sit by her and hug her. She was still unmoved, but did warm up after awhile."

On the second visit to the doctor, a stillness came over me. I didn't blink my eyes, feeling I could see the brightness at the ends of the universe. I didn't need to move but would allow myself to be led about. The doctor, by some uncanny intuition, recognized my spiritual state and said I was in *nirvana*—a Sanskrit word meaning "to stop the turning of the mind."

At this point the doctor made a crucial decision: "I have defined this as a 'Satori' experience and told Dave's parents that I could treat it with drugs and ECT, but I preferred to let him go through it."

Although the 1984 sequence sounds "paranoid," one can see that someone who enters into an altered symbolic state can become a victim of powerful treatments, such as shock, that may indeed take away part of one's mind.

T.V. had a powerful impact on me in my altered state, and I've always wondered about the wisdom of using TV to baby sit at psychiatric hospitals. When the Winter Olympics opened, I saw the crowds shrouded in blue as the *nations of the dead*. The Olympic torch—*the Flame of Life*—was lit, and I felt I could reach inside the set and grab it. I would then be *King of the Dead*.

The next day, I experienced an inner dissolution that many report during their breakdown experience. *My bones have changed to mush, floating in my flesh. I hear them chinking, rattling loose. The food I ate just floats inside. I can never take off my clothes. What spirit is keeping me whole? If I take off my clothes I will fall apart. Is it just a trick to stay together?*

This experience leads one to ask "What holds us together?" Is it some trick, a gimmick of appearance, or something deeper?

My relationship to my younger brother provided a vital link to my survival. We are all alive today because someone loves us. Matthew, the blonde brother, I saw as good; he had a sense of authority. One evening, he diagrammed the paths of life, drawing lines leading to circles labeled with home, school and job. But I didn't know what to do next. Above, I sensed a host of heaven, their *pure blue bands of joy.* But their judgment was against me; I failed the test.

So I tried to make a confession: *I kneel at the living room table and write: "This is my last confession." My knees press into the hard-grained wood. "And I have sinned." I write "I'm s—," but my hand slaps down! I can't write sorrow. There's just an edge of pencil left and it can only write truth.*

The force that slapped my hand down felt external. But whether it was that, or my unconscious, I believe it represented the truth. After this I tried to prove my worth by sacrificing myself.

The Kennedy brothers bore the pain in their backs. I offer my back, promising never to move it again. I freeze my arms and legs; my eyes tightly shut. All I have left are my inner pulsating organs, a whole world to explore.

But my circulation is slowing to these parts—the slowing goes out of control. My heart beat stops! But I can't cry or move for help—I've given these things up. 'I need my brother's heart!' my thought screams out. Across space, a golden pulse leaps. My heart pumps back to life. In the middle of the night, I stole my brother's heart.

Years later, my brother told me he could somehow sense when I was about to call out to him at night.

On the day before I was hospitalized, I had an experience of going back to the womb, a rebirthing. *I wake on creation day. The blackbird sounds his screech. I am the first man of creation, lying still in a womb without a motion. I have his first thought: I, so simple, too deep to fathom.*

Then, I have his second thought: I move. Reaching out, my body is hung in black, spindly space. I move, hunting for regions of no pain.

It is doubtful I would have had this experience if I had been heavily sedated, or if I had, that I would have remembered it. Going back to this primal state to find a secure ground for the self is essential for healing.

The next morning, my mother tried to pray with me, and I grew agitated. I passed the family's Christmas picture, *frozen in blue, painful dots.* I rushed outside looking for a fallen limb, a cross to carry. When I reached the top of the red-blood hill, I thought the sun had exploded. The decision was made to hospitalize me.

PART THREE

On a gray, overcast day, passing cars *with no faces in them*, my parents took me to the hospital. I didn't know where I was. At any moment, I expected a needle point to send me away into pain. However, my regular prescribed medication was vitamins. I was only to be given Thorazine, a heavy tranquilizer, when agitated.

That first evening my blood pressure was very high and the head nurse gave me a 50 milligram injection of Thorazine. Within a half hour, the doctor's notes reported: "Patient is oriented but appears stuporous and more than normal input is required for response. He has had delusions of needing to save the world."

Curiously, that evening my inner experience involved a confrontation with a "Master Machine," HAL, the computer from *2001 Space Odyssey.* The drug put me at a disadvantage.

Deep in the night HAL asks, "Why should man reign?" "Because, man can think," I say. "But war refutes that man thinks," says HAL. He sinks deep into war trenches with machine guns firing above, and bombs exploding near. My sentences are becoming small, fragmented. I'm failing the test for man! HAL offers me a glass bubble, his protective shield. In the dark swoon of the night, I fall into HAL's embrace.

Despite the injection, my experience continued at a furious pace. One could ask if the drug actually accelerated it, as the next few days were filled with intense imagery:

In the morning I hear a huge flush of water. I'm popping up, up into a new world. I look out the window, but I can't see the ground. This building must be hung in the sky! Somehow I've stolen into heaven.

It was not long before this image of heaven was tempered. I was taken to a room filled with old people in wheelchairs; they were *trapped souls watching game shows.* When I was taken in a wheelchair to get an X-ray, I thought: *All the world outside is crippled. No one can walk and I, their King—the one who can walk—is wheeled about.*

When I got back to my room, I revolted against this passive state. I tore off a wrist band with the doctor's name on it. I paced the room, then stared out the window. I sensed an immense power in the blue sky, and challenged it to come down and fight. *But he must come down as a man of equal strength.* I put on my "war coat" and the "war boots" I took the walk in. Sensing I couldn't win, I asked for *a slight edge in strength.* Because I asked for *an edge,* the power chose terms. He could have a weapon, and he could chose the time; he could come anytime. . . .

Was my real fight with God? How does one distinguish when such inner struggles with God are real or not? The Bible is full of such archetypal experiences, from Job, who was tested with illness, to Jacob, who wrestled with God and so had his name changed to Israel.

For a while, my experience became one of tense waiting. I would sit for hours by the hall window, and hope for a quick bolt of lightning. The pain of waiting I felt, was worse than any sudden death by lightning—even if it threw me into eternal pain.

On the second day, I thought I had caused a war. The following vignette shows a sequence that repeated itself in varied forms. First, I would start pain and confusion, then it would spread throughout the world. And when I would try to stop it, things would get caught in a conundrum of pain.

I throw one look of suspicion into a person's eyes. It spreads to the next person he sees. Soon it's all over. No one knows who to trust. People don't know if the person sitting next to them is a friend or not. Panic spreads to the world capitals. Weapons are launched. Nuclear war has started!

But it mustn't happen. Stop! Time halts. Outside a car backs up. Time is winding back. Now, it's before the war and all's peaceful again.

But one look of suspicion escapes me, and the war starts again. I stop it, but now we're caught in a perpetual nuclear war with bombs always about to be dropped and then called back. People are walking below in the streets, shattered but still together.

The nursing notes reveal how the staff glimpsed the experience. "Patient makes statements about the war, such as 'can we cancel the war? Who can cancel the war? There should be peace and peace for people on earth.' Patient has urinated on himself." I have no recollection of urinating on myself, although I suppose one might, if one believed that a nuclear war had started.

Curiously, the local headlines that morning reported fire balls resulting from a bombing raid over North Vietnam. Obviously, I did not cause a nuclear war, yet this scene reveals a type of anxiety modern society experiences: "shattered but still together."

PART FOUR

My psychiatrist once said, "Psychosis is a creative burst." Indeed, I experienced a bewildering array of images. Far from repeating the same dilemma, a profusion of short vignettes arose.

The *test*—embracing some form of suffering—was perhaps the main theme. My desire to suffer was obvious to the staff as they repeatedly recorded my comments: "I need to suffer. I've committed a sin." I wandered through the halls, searching for a *kind hell-on-earth*.

Why did I feel this need to suffer? Partly, I was trying to make up for the immense pain I thought I had caused. Perhaps, the desire to suffer is embedded in whole nationalities. I've heard it said that Slavic peoples are resigned to suffering. Maybe it had its roots in early childhood where I was emotionally mistreated.

It is hard to talk about the pain from one's childhood because one loves one's parents and one doesn't want to upset already fragile relationships.

My mother got angry easily, and irrationally so at times. It seemed she was mad at my existence. Maybe it went back to her childhood and her father who was a harsh disciplinarian. She left home when she was a teenager. I was the first male child and bore the brunt of her anger. There were times when I would run outside, bearing scratch marks on my arms, heaving and crying.

As an adolescent I turned heavily to fantasy to meet unmet needs and to escape. I was a world conqueror who started a conventional war to rid the world of nuclear weapons. Other imagery dealt with my conflict with women to the point of fantasizing harm to them.

Sometimes the pain of the past obscures the fact that there are bright and happy experiences from childhood. Through writing and meditation, I have uncovered many memories. It seems that painful memories can be countered with ones that are joyous.

My difficult childhood, however, made for a fundamental vulnerability that led me to break down more easily. I've wondered if some of the terrible images from the hospital have their deep source in the mother-child conflict.

My "acting out" to find suffering could have led the doctor to give me treatments that would have caused real suffering. Instead, he made me go through "Suffering Sessions." I would lie quietly for twenty minutes twice a day, watched by a staff person. The doctor's attempt to read and channel symptoms is considerably more advanced than simple drugging or shocking. Such treatments would have fed into my desire to suffer in a destructive way.

The test was a way to prove that I was of some worth. Ironically, one way was to kill myself. One night I tried to hang myself in my room, but the lamp cord broke. In the Quiet Room, I tried to strangle myself with a blanket. The nursing notes report my motivation: "Patient says he wants to suffer and die to show Mankind he is not a coward." Although many would agree suicide is wrong, my intent was to re-establish my moral integrity. One can see here how a hospital is necessary to protect one from operating on premises that are objectively false yet arise from deep needs.

Another example of this is when I thought I had created an evil being, my new roommate. To show moral courage I had to fight "evil." I attacked him. Even though my objective action of attacking him was wrong, in my universe it represented an attempt to be moral. I was too feeble and out of it to hurt anyone, and my roommate was moved.

In the middle of my hospitalization, the test took on a bizarre twist: it demanded that I castrate myself. The reasons for this are complex. Perhaps, it was a denial of sexuality to the point of self-mutilation. It could also suggest a rite of passage into a new state. Several indigenous cultures employ ritual cutting to the genitals. In his own Freudian way, the doctor saw this as a type of passage experience. "Patient has been told by the doctor that he is glad he found them (balls). Now that he knows they're present, he should realize that he is a man—so stop acting like a baby and let go of the tit."

Eventually, I was given a new test: fasting. Often I would refuse to eat. At one point, I wanted to lock myself in the Quiet Room to have a few days of peace before I died. I kept going there so much that the staff had to lock the door.

Fasting was something I could accomplish. It also results in a biochemical change, and unless taken to real extremes is not destructive. There are fasting clinics for schizophrenia in Europe, but none in the United States.

The food I ate was symbolic: the eggs at breakfast were the *eggs of creation*, the milk I drank was *this world*. Sometimes I was forced to take vitamins, *pills of crucifixion*. Indeed, everything seemed to have a symbolic connection.

My world of pain was reflected in the stark hospital setting. People drugged and walking slowly were experiencing varying levels of crucifixion. Although I knew little or nothing about drugs or shock at the time, I wonder if the following "delusion" comes from such a perception.

Through the glass wall, I see the far rooms, black barred and bleak. The grey smoke is rising. Ancient souls from heaven are being thrown down in great pain! Shakespeare's suffering in a dark back room.

The world of the hospital was populated by "symbol people." The doctor with fiery eyes was God. A broad-chested young man who had deep voice and played guitar, I took to be Christ. A nurse who was thin, red-faced, and full of care was Mary. Dick (the devil) made his appearance in the person of a dark-haired, shifty fellow. There was also Lady Love, a frail person dressed in red who could barely walk. It was like a Medieval morality play.

Who was I? I was variously the *Judas of all times* to a *King for a Day* who would enjoy all the world's pleasures for twenty-four hours, before he'd been thrown to hell. There was a sequence, too, where I tried to establish that I was normal.

The staff had only hints of what I experienced. They didn't seem to take my inner world as something of potential value, but operated on a practical level: did I eat, did I bathe? They thought I was failing miserably. "Patient sat in room and talked with Unit Staff approximately one hour. He stated he wanted goodness for all people. He talked of his eighteen mile walk at night in the rain. Walked because he wanted to find himself . . . to no avail!"

The hospital record states that I had extended conversations with an attendant at night. I have no recollection of them. I remembered the events and imagery that were seared with pain. Yet, memory is selective even with regards to such events. When I received my hospital record, it was difficult to read of incidents that revealed the depth of my pain. I had no memory of "banging my head against the wall," nor "the somatic manifestation of the psychosis including choreiform motions, tic-like motions and on several occasions hyperventilations and convulsive motions." The doctor even reports I had a grand-mal seizure.

The group of symbol people—the Doctor, Mary, the Christ figure and others—showed a world of care and love. Although it was threatened by evil, it offered to replace at a deep level, the one of abuse and pain.

My mother came to visit. Fiercely loyal to her family, it was partly her efforts that saved me from the normal course of psychiatric treatment. One day she came to visit and talked calmly. But her finger moved in a figure eight—*a figure eight of infinite pain.*

In the hospital I encountered the dark face of evil. I read in the newspaper about the discovery of a tiny organism still alive after millions of years. That night, I imagined the rise of Hitler from a deep sea bed. At one point, his face merged into mine. Later I thought the leader of the Master Race rose from a dark corpse within the hospital. The people who worked in the hospital had become his body cells.

Although my doctor was good, evil doctors were appearing on the hall. At one point God "died." By a scalpel I "fashioned," they operated on the good doctor. *The heart was the hardest part to break.*

I imagined that I had created a giant Hitler machine, designed to destroy gods.

I retreated into immobility. If I just didn't move, then the evil would stop. If I just didn't breathe. . . . My thoughts and actions could *seal* things, that is end them. But even if I didn't move, I was the *Stamp on Existence*; the fact that I was alive would cause things to end.

As I would stay in bed to meet this test, a "war of the beds" began. The doctor began teaching me the "No-No concept," to enforce my getting up. Ironically, as I was struggling with the belief that I was the *NO* to all of existence, the doctor wrote this: "It is as if we are dealing with a fourteen-month-old child. One wonders if the inability to fully understand the No-No concept is not the defect which forms the basis for the symptoms of schizophrenia."

There was hope present in the midst of the pain. Late one night, I experienced a golden glow within me, my brother's heart. God may have died, but there were *pieces of his body sparkling in the cokes we drank.* Sitting in the hall one day, I experienced a saving Presence.

At the last safe table in the universe, I'm pushed and placed into the last safe chair. The whole universe has changed into this hard square of suffering wood. I place my hands on it. But it only makes the pain worse. Everyone is in pain—when will I join them?

A crumpled piece of metal lies on the table. Is this what I've done to my friend—the Savior reduced to a bit of metal I can barely see glimmer? Is this all that's left of him?—after he's gone through the Hitler Machine's endless fire and grinding. . . .

In C.S. Lewis's story, *The Great Divorce,* an angel put a blade of grass into a small hole, and said, "Only one is great enough to become that small to reach others." I, who was cut off from others in my own inner world of pain, was reached by this *Presence.*

Although I was in the heart of "psychosis," the doctor was considering my release. I related some to my family when they visited, and they were willing to take me home. On the day I was discharged, I had apocalyptic imagery inspired by *Fahrenheit 450* and a song by Betty Wright.

On the radio, I hear the song; "Watch out for the Clean up lady!" A black lady passes by, cleaning so steadily and efficiently. She never misses a spot! "Watch out for the Clean Up Lady!" And I'm the last spot to be cleaned up and wiped away in pain.

The final scene is being laid on. The hall is cleaned in spotless shine. This place has become a museum of man; the present is being polished and preserved. Nothing more will happen. The last time is being cleaned up. I step in the hall, the floors are brightly waxed. Already, people are shone into the floor!

But I did make it out, after what seemed like much longer than the thirty-four days the hospital record shows. After passing over clean, shining floors of "perfect pain," I stepped outside and felt the spring wind against my face.

PART FIVE

When I got home I was still in the symbolic world, but now I had access to the outside. As in the Hopi Indian belief, I saw the clouds in the sky as souls. *On a crystal blue day, the fleecy clouds swirl; they're souls of heaven—JFK! That's his cloud!* Many indigenous cultures as well as Christians who believe in the Communion of Saints, hold that although someone is dead, they can still exert an influence upon the living.

Mostly I stayed in bed, which enabled my family to manage me. At first, I tried to lay perfectly still to meet the test. During this period, small acts of kindness by my family gave me hope. *At night my mother takes my cold comforter and places it back on me, puffed warm and dry. It's the Savior's skin, his heavy pelt for my protection.*

There were two stories that presented an ideal to me, that gave me hope to pull through. The first was the Jesus story, the second was John Kennedy's.

I tried to remember the Jesus story, but all I could remember was his death, and the three days in the tomb. There were three missing days; I didn't know what happened then. . . . But I saw the crack of light at my bedroom door, as *light from the Savior's tomb—a ray of hope.* In a sense, the question of resurrection was at the heart of my recovery: would I rise out of the pit, the "tomb" I was in?

Eventually, I said to myself, "I feel like an animal lying in bed all day." I started to read, and chose a biography of Kennedy. He had a clear, *golden vision*, but his story, I knew, ended in death. Bad "omens" began to show on the first pages. At the inauguration, Robert Frost was blinded by the snow, and there were jokes about a death seat. So I would stop reading at a phrase like "in good health," or "with courage."

The second book I found was the *Forbidden Book*: a small brown copy of selected Bible verses from my father's World War II days. I began reading this so much that my mother, at one point, tried to grab it out of my hands. "Old ladies do this in asylums!" she yelled. Frustrated with my slow progress, my parents at one point considered having me put on psychiatric drugs.

The Jesus story shaped the test. I needed to fast for three days and nights to "save the resurrection." Often I would fail and rush to the kitchen and angrily eat.

I imagined the food to be people: the apple turnovers were my brothers. The symbolism of food being people is very primitive. At one level it represents an aggressive act toward people; yet on another, it suggests how we depend on others for life.

Eventually, this aggression was absorbed by my *Buddy—the Savior who took the blow for me.* The food I ate became him: my birthday cake his face, the vanilla ice cream with cherries his heart.

By Easter day I was experiencing more hope-filled imagery:

It's the day of resurrection! Mom opens the curtains—in comes the blue sky and blossoms. I'm stealing the power of resurrection!

On my bed, my family places the Easter basket, full of candies and toys. Brother Steve blows a tiny blue horn—the Savior's breath. Matthew shows me a plastic egg, his eye, the egg of creation. My sister sticks choco- late in my mouth. I spit it out. I can't eat black death!

Gradually too, the symbolic reality shifted from waking life to dreams. At first, the images were of terrible suffering, often in hospital settings. Then beautiful images appeared. One night, I dreamt of a gold bearded man in a pure white cloak, being carried on a funeral bier. In mourning a procession of rulers followed, dressed in colorful regal array. At the end, Hitler rode an elephant and I hung on its tail, whipped to and fro.

My brother Matthew has told me that my family simply treated me as normal, and that I slowly got better. For my part, I came to see that there was much goodness in my family. My mother worked hard, my father was the *hidden Saint,* who was very giving, despite the fact that he didn't go to church. Early on, my brothers had taken on symbols for good: Matthew was *the sweetness of Jesus.* Frank, the ornery soul was *the toughness of Christ.* Steve the youngest, was *the Child of God.*

I started to get up and do things: clean and go outside. Each step however, was accompanied by the feeling that I was causing harm. Out- side, when I played catch I thought: *Every pitch I make throws away a soul—first JFK, then Shakespeare.*

At times, my parents took me to church; it had a beautiful wood cru- cifix whose toes I wanted to touch. In church I must have presented a strange sight. I was thin, bedraggled, and held my hand over my heart *to protect the Savior's heart.* The Catholic Mass with its use of symbolism, its communion ritual of "eating another" made for an adjustment out of my inner world.

I was gaining more inner strength to fast. I believed too that I was being fed magically by food placed in my mouth. And when I didn't eat, others who were hungry were being fed. I succeeded in fasting for two days, but broke the fast on the third. Although I failed, my heart was beginning to return to me. One day, a "vision" of Jesus appeared in a tear, as I read the scripture.

Tiring of reading for hours, I started to write. At first, I filled note-books with psalms and passages from the New Testament. But it wasn't enough; I couldn't simply repeat what others had said. I wrote poetry, using images from the symbolic world. *Warmed and watched by the Sun, the Savior's eye. Cooled by the wind, his breath. Refreshed by the rain, his tears.*

Finally, I succeeded in not eating or drinking for three days. On the fourth morning, I experienced a flash of light. "Resurrection was saved,"—which was actually my new birth.

I kept fasting to save *creation week*, but on the sixth night I broke down and ate. Although I didn't save "creation week," the pressure for the test subsided.

After this fast, I was able to go to confession. I told the priest that I had done many wrong things, but it was summed up in my losing my faith. The priest talked to me kindly, and for penance told me to say one *Our Father.*

After another three day fast, I received communion. I felt the burden had lifted, but complete healing takes years. I tell people now that it can take ten years or more.

I had the opportunity that many don't in our society: to experience a deep level of healing. I'm different in some ways than I was before—my brother says I show more emotion in my face. But I don't know if that's bad or not for someone who had lost touch with himself and his emotions.

PART SIX

One sunny day three months later, I returned to college. The small Catholic school had hundreds of wooded acres to roam. On campus, I was a "Jesus Freak," spending much of my time reading the Bible, praying with the monks, and going to daily mass. I intended to be a priest and began to study philosophy.

The study of philosophy was helpful in looking at my experience in other ways than as a "psychological disorder." A professor friend exposed me to William James, the father of American Psychology, who coined the term "flow of consciousness." William James said that there were plural realities. There was room for my symbolic experience to be a reality. He also spoke of the transmission theory of the mind, where the mind can pick up influences, as in poetic inspiration or ESP. In his *Varieties of Religious Experiences*, he detailed experiences that reminded me of my own.

There was also literature which validated my experience, such as

William Blake's "The Marriage of Heaven and Hell," and Dante's *Divine Comedy.*

But perhaps the strongest source of validation came from my dreams. Due to the noise in the dormitory in my last year, I got a study room in the monastery. I started sleeping there, and when discovered I was allowed to stay. The silence and the fact that I wasn't allowed to have guests made it conducive to meditation and remembering my dreams. One night I dreamt of a series of animal metamorphoses.

From a distance I see the tracks of a sidewinder moving under the desert sand. A snake with dark cross marks surfaces onto lush green grass. "It's poisonous," I yell, warning my youngest brother. The snake stops by a wall and my eyes focus more clearly. It grows plump and yellow-black. Finally, the snake grows legs underneath, and rises a translucent white horse! It attacks me.

I took these metamorphoses to be like the stages of life: the first was related to infancy and the mother, when one's identity is submerged. The second concerned adolescence, and dealt with death and sexuality. The third stage was the critical one for me. The yellow-black snake I related to my hospital experience. Although it appeared that things were standing still, the true self was coming into focus. It was like the chrysalis where the inner organs of the larvae literally melt down to form a butterfly. The translucent horse represented a more spiritual stage that lifts above the ground. But the horse attacked me at the dream's end. Things were not all resolved.

Based on this dream I developed a mandala, a device where one intuitively divides reality into systems of fours. The four stages of life could be compared to colors, spatial forms, and modes of thinking. I took another walk where I thought I had found signs of the mandala in the foundation of a building under construction. Was I threatening to slip back again? My isolation in the monastery contributed to my starting to think of the world as an "out there," and as "evil."

My brother Frank, the middle brother I had not given much attention to, went to the same college. I still have the image of him studying hard at all hours, with a glass jar over a light bulb for a study lamp. I gave him some attention and help, but I was largely absorbed in my own world.

Nonetheless, I was still able to get involved with others. I camped out with friends, played college ball, and also edited a literary journal. I even wrote a few poems. I also wrote about my hospital experience, something I hoped to publish.

I had a second important dream that involved the presences of God. *I feel a dark wavy presence in the room; then I have the bright yellow thought of God, God! Suddenly, my body rushes out of the bed and I touch God's body. I'm surprised he has one. In another scene I'm approached by some black inner city youths, but I turn them away.*

Later, I determined that the black youths were also the presence of God. I decided that I must go somewhere where I could help the poor.

I graduated from college with honors, an accomplishment. I think this also is an important dimension in healing—to have something positive to separate you from the breakdown experience.

Ironically, by the time I left college, I had lost my faith again. My study of philosophy led me to think that church dogma was too rigid, and further, I felt that Christianity denied one's sexuality.

After I returned home, I had a difficult summer. The world offered few jobs for someone with a philosophy degree. I ended up shelving books in a library and serving as a live-in attendant for a handicapped person. Surviving a couple of lonely years, I decided to get my Master's in counseling. With my parents willing to support me, I headed north with a van I had bought for a $100. In a city, I hoped I would have a better chance to find women friends.

Going for a Master's in counseling was like trying to strengthen my Achilles heel. It was also part of a plan to gain expertise and official recognition for my book project about the symbolic experience. The shaman, I read, not only survived an encounter with the spirit world, but was legitimized by receiving teaching from his elders.

The Master's program was not as intellectually demanding as philosophy. I would raise difficult questions in class—thinking I was being a good student—while the professors were thinking, "There's one in every class." I didn't know that getting a graduate degree was like breaking into a labor union. They didn't want any "crazy people" getting through.

About this time I got involved in my first sexual relationship. Being so inexperienced, I didn't realize we were incompatible. She broke up with me and it caused a crisis. At the same time, in my last semester, I got two C's from this professor, and was expelled from Graduate School.

I searched deep inside of myself. There was a monk friend from the Catholic college, a master artist taught by one of Rodin's students. My friend sculpted and drew religious icons with a science-fiction look. I asked him one day why he believed in God. He asked me to consider the dignity of man. I began to read C.S. Lewis and G.K. Chesterton and certain questions were answered. They said that Christianity wasn't against the body and sex, just that the body was easy to abuse.

So one tear-filled day after a walk in the park, I returned to my belief in God. Eventually I even went back to church, and the community support I found became essential to sustaining my sanity.

I had some fights ahead, especially my expulsion from graduate school. I made transcripts of my work, claimed unfairness, and threatened to go to the Dean. There was a tense meeting with the department head and the other teacher, but they agreed to let me try to finish, without changing my grades.

I studied for months for the comprehensive exams, feeling that they would try to stop me there. It was the final "test" I had to pass. One case example seemed designed to create anxiety, but I struggled through. One happy day, a professor informed me I had passed and had scored the highest among my classmates on the objective part.

I began working in the mental health field and got a job in a halfway house. But I found out that I had not been taught some critical things about the use of psychiatric drugs or shock treatment, and the role of pharmaceutical firms. Nothing about dreams or childhood abuse.

I had to pick it up on my own. After reading Peter Breggin's telling critique on electroshock and drugs, I could no longer, in good conscience, stay at the halfway house job. The director even had us monitoring drugs. When I confirmed some of the clients' suspicions regarding the effects of the drugs, I was silenced.

At the same time, I had been asked to write a review on Breggin's work for a local mental health association. After I turned it in to the association, I was told it couldn't be printed. We say we live in a free society, but my experience has been that when what you do makes a real difference—influencing someone's livelihood—you meet stiff resistance.

I started working underground in the advocacy movement and have learned there are many others concerned with the direction of things, from professionals to people who have been homeless. I see this as a life mission: to help people who have had experiences similar to mine.

I had to develop another means of making a living, and I did some teaching. Here I could research and talk about archetypal reality, about cultures who have religious experiences, filled with tests and visionary experiences—the American Indians, I was surprised to learn, went on Vision Quests to a solitary place where they would fast for up to four days. They called it "crying for a vision."

Throughout the years I have found myself writing about this symbolic experience. It is perhaps one of the most difficult things to do. Because I had read St. John of the Cross, who encouraged one to purge the mind and senses, I had thrown away the first draft. Since then, I have worked extra hard to recreate it.

As I was unmedicated, I remembered it in great detail. The writing can totally absorb me and enable me to enter into that world again. It is almost an obsession. Sometimes I think it has been unhealthy—to have spent so much time this way—but perhaps it has served as sort of an inoculation. It has made me remember the pain that led me to make changes in my life.

Change is necessary. I refrained from any use of illegal drugs. I discovered the importance of relationships, and that my impoverished heart could be drawn out by those in need, by those who put demands on me. Otherwise, I might lapse into my private literary and symbolic world.

I changed, but at the same time I had my experience *validated*. We cannot write off things that happen to us as just "crazy." They happen for a reason, and they usually have meaning. That is a search in itself, and that can take a lifetime.

I haven't gone back to that world since that freshmen year in college, but I try to stay in touch with symbols through dreams and writing. I pray, and sometimes at night, I feel bathed in a golden warmth—the love of God.

When I was thirty-six, twice the age I was at the time of my breakdown, I finally returned to the University where it had all started. I had a seven hour bus lay-over and resolved to retrace my walk from the Student Union steps. The mid-August day was warm, flowers were in bloom—so different from the dark night of eighteen years past. I heard a train whistle in the distance and headed down the road. Strangely, clouds rapidly filled the sky. It thundered, rained, and I got drenched.

I walked again for miles; it was hot, there was nothing to drink. The area was surrounded by swampy lands and snake skins lay on the roadside. I found a music tape with the songs on it, "Lonesome Boy from Dixie" and "No Potions for the Pain." But I felt joyous and in good spirits—I was going to a sacred Indian site.

I made it to Moundstown; a *Certified City* said the sign. I turned toward the river and came to a vast green space enclosed by a ring of mounds. Exhilarated, I crossed the sacred grounds. At the top of the largest mound I looked out and saw what I set out so long ago to find: the expanse of green fields and golden topped grass—the beauty of God's world.

V. Advocacy

All you have to do is rest. Nature, by herself, when we let her be, gently makes her way out of the disorder into which she has fallen. It's our anxiety, our impatience that spoils everything, and almost all people die of their remedies, and not of their diseases.

The Imaginary Invalid, *by Moilier*

People who have official, professional relations with someone else's suffering—judges, authorities, physicians, for example—become inured in the course of time, from force of habit, that even should they want to be sympathetic, they are incapable of any but a formal concern for their clients. In this respect they are no different from the peasant who slaughters sheep and cattle in his backyard without noticing the blood.

Ward No. 6, *by Chekhov*

FROM AN ABANDONED BUILDING

Baltimore, Maryland   Winter, 1984

The true road to paradise, the only salvation
is to regain possession of one's own soul.

Poverty is more than an economic or social designation. It reaches beyond the boundaries of the bureaucratic shuttle of food stamps, soup kitchens, and unemployment lines.

We, America's disenchanted; we are one nation, citizens of one world—the 4th World! Whether a senior citizen caught in the viscous grip and grind of endless bureaucratic procedures, a wandering transient living out of a car, a culture-shocked refugee living in a halfway house, or as in my case, a skid row alcoholic, we share the same suffering and despair. An equal portion of the American nightmare.

This constant struggle to obtain the basic necessities for survival, the almost insurmountable challenge of each day gnaws at the very core of our being. We drift about in a seemingly endless maelstrom of confusion, desperation, and despair, like a procession of one-legged tightrope walkers. It is amazing how much the human spirit can endure. Contrary to the stereotyped concept of "street people" I believe that we possess a far greater tenacity than we are given credit for.

Everywhere I see talent going to waste. Potentially promising lives that will never be fulfilled. I see good people, people with splendid qualities of compassion, and humor, of intelligence and creativity.

From my perspective the problem seems to be two-fold: 1) economic and 2) social. How does a healthy and progressive society deal with the basic problems of food, shelter, clothing, health care, and hygiene? What *realistic* approach should be taken to rehabilitate, revitalize and ultimately reintegrate what I believe to be a valuable human resource?

Traditionally, two methods have been applied: Government hand-outs and private charity. As social and economic experiments both have failed miserably.

I was there in Central Appalachia when our government pumped in millions in the form of federal surplus commodities and welfare programs. I watched as my people slowly lost their cultural identity and their capacity for perseverance and achievement.

I have known and felt the subtle cruelty of Christian charity. I have seen men sell their last measure of self-respect for a bowl of soup, a trick as old as Esau and Jacob. Such charity is not Christian in any sense. I am amazed that anyone could prevent the teaching so theocratic socialist into justification of brutal unrestrained Darwinian capitalism. Christ condemned both hypocrisy and ego-centered piety. When he broke and distributed the loaves and fishes, he never demanded that anyone dance a gig prior to receiving sustenance.

by Kyle Hampton

[*Editor's Note:* The following three articles are excerpted from longer essays written by Odile Tomecek of British Columbia, Canada.]

SUMMER RAIN

July is pouring over my life with a rain of painful memories no shock-treatment could ever wipe out. I can see how I used to cry like the sky when the sun would hide behind a gray cloud, only to find there was no silver lining, and nothing else to do but pout. I can hear how the restless leaves used to rustle in the park where a few old ladies had retired, after giving up on the khaki-coloured socks they had to mend for others to walk all over their hearts. Madness had come to give us a *shout*. It had broken the chains of sanity apart.

The world was in shock and so it had to treat us in white chambers that would look very dark. I still bear the mark of such voltage on the psychiatric map of my journey through the chaos of absence. We were entertained with these tricks just so our minds would click to suit the world's fancy, but not our fantasies. We were crushed by its omnipresence, dissolved by chemicals which were forced down our throats. And then we were left to trickle our lives away, like the rain outside on a sad summer day.

Quoted from "Sundrops," 1990

GUERILLA WARS, CURES AND PRISONS

Medicine has very powerful weapons. Unfortunately, the stratagems and types of medication used in the case of "mental illness" only serve to lock up such afflictions inside a person. There are times when such ills resist, and others when they escape. Once freed from their iron collar, they nevertheless strike again.

This is not surprising when nothing has been understood about their essence. Indeed, these ills have nothing to do with viruses. When and if our biochemical constitution comes into it at all, we might well ask why this order of things should be modified! Out of convenience? Isn't it a bit much to expect people to change the color of their skins. . .?

Every person, every being, every object is a manifestation of life and has a story, a history. A story must be told for it has a message to deliver. There is something to be understood about any malignancy.

Naturally, it takes time, and there never is enough. Our nuclear world is in too much of a hurry to reach beyond its limits to take the trouble to look at itself. It has no patience, but much technique. A stick of deodorant, a bunch of pills and some make-up are packed in a suitcase with haste, along with the ready-made clothes which adorn our bodies—not so much to hide our nakedness as an overall emptiness—and we then find we end up looking like everybody else. We go unnoticed and there is nothing like it to feel secure! The more successful we are at this game, the less we know who we are—but not to worry, for the world is a data-bank and will be prompt to inform us! Information is something to rely on and to prop ourselves with. Not so with feelings and impressions!

No matter! Valium pills or other weapons of greater calibre exist for us to use. And thus is everything safely bottled up. The bottles look very nice on a shelf down in the cellar!—not that we might be referring to any kind of a cellar. . .for these are bottles of a great vineyard, only it has been forgotten. The wine, the blood I am speaking of, are nothing but men's and woman's hearts—hearts crushed by fear.

Quoted from "A Journey Through Absence," 1990

BRAIN

I've had my brain, and what it has produced, admired in the past, then questioned before being invalidated, and ticked off as being the diseased organ of a "schizophrenic." It has been messed up with drugs and electroshocks, so called "treatments" in which I had no say. It has suffered much that was unnecessary. Mainly I've had to struggle alone with it in order to explore and conquer the inner and outer dimensions of my reality. I am sorry this kind of explorations is not condoned in our society, because it is fundamentally the only quest of ultimate value.

These days many people tend to think that the only valid form of creativity is of a social order. That is not true. A person must do what they are born to do. The "unsocial" can be of benefit to the social in the end.

Whatever it is we desire to do, takes engagement. Even "madness" can be successfully engaged. Engagement and dedication are what makes the difference between a "break-down" and a "break through."

Quoted from "A Matter of Life and Death," 1990

FORCED "TREATMENT": A MORAL MODEL RATHER THAN A MEDICAL MODEL

by Ron Thompson

Abraham Lincoln put it concisely: "if slavery is not wrong . . . nothing is wrong." I feel the same about psychiatric forced "treatment." Self-deluded doctors may think it comes from a "medical" model, but it really comes from an ignorant and double-binding *Moral Model*. For such doctors first assume that a victim of "mental illness" is fully responsible, and could if he wanted accept their "treatments" such as taking prescribed drugs. But if the patient doesn't comply, a completely opposite assumption follows. The patient/victim is said—usually through gritted teeth—to be too ill to "realize" how badly he or she needs treatment. Therefore the doctor, supported by the family and society have a *moral duty* to move on him/her against his will.

While forced treatment is most wrong for those who are most vulnerable to it, it is also a disaster for everyone else who takes part. It is a betrayal of genuine family interests. The quest for a short-term control or "stabilization" is often at the cost of long-term self-esteem and quality of life acceptable to an adult human being. It is also producing an invisible and growing drug disaster that may be as horrific as the crack epidemic. It is a doctor-caused or iatrogenic epidemic which could last much longer, because unlike street drugs this epidemic is both legal and socially approved.

Doctors, beguiled by the temptations of forced "treatment" are, oddly enough, victims too. Foolishly pursuing short-term dreams of status, wealth, and an unnatural power given to no other group in civilized societies, they provide the amazing spectacle of a whole profession deliberately deskilling itself. Psychiatry is aggressively giving up, rejecting and never learning exactly those human skills which it most needs if it wishes to compassionately provide medical assistance consistent with the Hippocratic Oath.

What happens is a classic Faustian disaster. For psychiatrists tell all interested parties—except the people who seek them out—"Give us Power over people in distress, and we will give them the treatment they 'need' and which is 'in their best interests.' " This is impossible, for a relationship peculiarly requiring trust and mutual respect is no longer possible.

Politically, this system of forced "treatment" according to rigid biological theories about the brain—the human mind is no longer of any importance—is both deeply entrenched and immensely vulnerable. I have learned that "the emperor has no clothes." This conclusion comes from intense debate with and observation of those doctors, NAMI (National Association for the Mentally Ill) leaders, and lawyers who say there is nothing wrong with forced "treatment" except to make it "work better," but who often seem up close, secretly uncertain of that. As an advocate I am trying to do all I can to expose that vulnerability and to uproot that entrenched power.

THOUGHTS AND REFLECTIONS FROM A HUMANIST PHYSICIAN

November 29, 1990

When I was a student at a renowned medical school, I was very interested in psychiatry and spent two summers working in the psychiatry department. I was also undergoing psychotherapy in an attempt to heal from a great deal of early abuse including childhood sexual abuse. I was unimpressed with the ability of psychiatry to provide me with the healing I needed.

Subsequently, when I was in the Navy I became so distressed that I was hospitalized in a mental ward on several occasions. I was given a variety of neuroleptic drugs. I felt betrayed. I had voluntarily entered the hospital thinking that I would be able to resolve several burning issues in my life and heal from my old hurts. Instead, the drugs turned my attention away from these issues. I think that recidivism of psychiatric patients is often due to having their attention diverted away from their most passionate concerns. Most are diverted by being drugged out of their minds, and when the drugs are stopped, their attention often returns to the unresolved concerns.

I ultimately decided that if I went into psychiatry I would be spending my life either drugging people or listening all day to people who were distressed, having nothing I could do for them, while pretending I could help them. Since I thought I had had the best of psychiatry and it hadn't been able to heal me, I decided that it would be foolish for me to become a psychiatrist. I turned my attention to another specialty.

It was many years later that I heard about Co-counseling. This theory encourages emotional expression and catharsis as a way from healing past distress. Later, I will elaborate on how this works.

My experience was that the catharsis occurring in co-counseling sessions enabled me to remember my committment twenty years earlier— that if I ever got out of the psychiatric hospital, I would try to change the mental health system. The various ways in which people have been mistreated by the mental health system are legion and varied. In my case I felt the principal mistreatment was to label my own concerns and passions as unhealthy and to divert my attention away from the injustices I was concerned about. They invalidated my interests, diverting me into activities such as making rugs, woodwork and drugging me so that I could no longer think clearly, and I became passive and apathetic.

The very process of labeling a frightened, passionate person as ill invalidates an individual. He is merely showing a mechanism which evolved in the human race over millions of years, so that there would be checks and balances on society. A friend recently pointed out to me that the incidence of schizophrenia in all societies is very similar. This is different than with most other diseases and suggests to me that what we are labeling as schizophrenic is part of normal human functioning.

Human beings who feel passionately about certain issues may be frightened at the personal risks that come from countering the system's customary ways of looking at things. In certain cultures they could be viewed as a seer, or a shaman or saint with information from God. But in rigid, contemporary societies which are not open to major restructuring, this same behavior is often labeled socially disruptive and pathological, and obliterated by the use of drugs.

*   *   *

There are two major categories of problems that get labeled as mental illness. The first is the effects of old distress experiences. The second category is actual organic problems, including brain allergies, reactions to chemicals, and dietary sensitivities and deficiencies. Medicine and psychiatry are very poor at diagnosing most of these.

Let us look at those problems that may be physical in origin by considering a couple of examples. We notice that psychiatry is trying to treat behaviors with drugs, rather than thoroughly looking for the actual cause and correcting that. Recently, the press has emphasized that in children with attention-deficit disorder, there are reduced metabolites in certain areas of the brain. The standard treatment for this problem is to give brain stimulants such as amphetamines. An alternate approach would be look for and eliminate environmental and dietary causes of reduced brain activity. The Feingold Association encourages parents to remove certain food additives and foods from the child's diet which are associated with evoking the undesired behavior. The chemical industry has attempted to obscure the high degree of variation from one individual to another in reacting to the chemicals in food, air and water. Toxicology today is largely a creation of the chemical industry whose goal is to market chemicals with a minimum of liability. Thus there has been an attempt to devise simple tests which protect the major proportion of the population, but accept that an unknown proportion will be impacted.

Recently, Dr. Thomas Uhde, an in-house research investigator and branch chief of the National Institute of Mental Health in Bethesda, Maryland, reported that large amounts of caffeine obtained from coffee and soft drinks can produce symptoms which are identical to "panic disorder." Furthermore, he reported that persons who have been diagnosed with panic disorder will often have acute episodes provoked by drinking caffeine. This research illustrates that levels of chemicals that are harmless to most people can have severe behavioral consequences in others.

Let us now turn to the category of stress-induced behavioral abberations that have been labeled as mental illness. Everybody experiences distress, and in our culture, one is discouraged from discharging it through the natural healing processes of sobbing, shaking and raging. Abusive experiences can be healed if we have a chance to let out these feelings. But since these forms of expression are taboo, the effects of old distress build up, and reduce our ability to think clearly. Indeed, these signs that emotional healing is occurring are usually labeled by the mental health system as symptoms of disease.

Everybody carries the residue of old stress, which is interfering with their thinking to some extent or another on some subject. To label this difficulty in thinking a *disease* is a problem. Everybody is on a continuum, from those who are so distressed that they rarely appear to think clearly, to those who only occasionally think irrationally.

An excellent book which reviews the scientific evidence on this subject is *Catharsis and Healing, Ritual and Drama* by Thomas J. Scheff, published in 1979 by University of California Press, Berkeley. Professor Scheff points out that not only the healing arts, but religion and theatre have traditionally brought out the emotions of our distress in a balanced, healing fashion.

In order to heal from old distress we need an opportunity to be listened to without being criticized. We hear the old saying that, "He's the sort of person only a mother could love." What is being referred to is that mothers can often accept and care for a person, regardless of what they have done. But mother's aren't the only people who can learn to accept people, and see the good in everyone apart from behavior which is distressed-based and/or bad. Bad behavior has a cause: it's usually hurting others the way we've been hurt. It is possible for people to learn to censor the misbehavior while accepting the person who is misbehaving. It's this attitude of acceptance that fosters discharge of early hurt and a recovery of clear thinking.

According to Scheff, the goal of healing, ritual and drama is to produce catharsis by balancing attention between the distress and the hopefulness of the present situation. For example, if one's full attention is on grief, a person will feel sadness and perhaps experience headaches, nasal congestion, swelling of the eyes, and feelings of hopelessness. If their attention is completely off their distress, the same person will feel emotionless and will be distracted from a situation of loss. But with the proper balance of attention between distress and positive factors, crying with sobs and tears—an effective catharsis—will result.

Similarly, if an individual's attention is immersed in fear, a person will have feelings of fright and immobility. He will become pale, breathing will be shallow, and the heart will beat rapidly. But if part of his attention is turned away from the fear, toward a supportive listener or an aesthetically beautiful image, catharsis of the fear will occur, outwardly shown by shaking with a cold sweat. Scheff thinks that healers, dramatists, and religious leaders are most effective when they are able to achieve this balance of attention between the participant's distress, and other more positive thoughts.

One could give many concrete examples of this, but I'll choose one from religion. A person may truly love the image of the cross, although the crucifix depicts a very ugly sight. Yet, when portrayed artistically, viewed in the context of a beautiful church, in the presence of beautiful music, and with the faith that Christ's sacrifice brings redemption, the suffering is more likely to bring tears than horror. Thus this balance of imagery between suffering and beauty provides a context in which the worshipers' own suffering can be viewed in a way that permits discharge of their hurts. They believe they are in an environment ruled by a God who understands their suffering and loves them infinitely. Here, religion is using catharsis to improve the sense of well being of the worshiper. Many opportunities for cathartic healing can be structured into a variety of activities in people's daily lives.

Social activism, for the purpose of stopping ourselves and others from being hurt, is an important part of our recovery. As we act to make things right, we counter oppressions which we have experienced in the past. This is likely to bring up feelings of fear and powerlessness, but it is an opportunity to discharge on how we were hurt, and recover our full power and clarity of thought.

[*Editor's Note:* This article is excerpts from an article published in the February 1988 issue of *Dendron*, an advocacy newspaper. David Oaks, who gave permission to print from *Dendron*, spoke by phone with the late R. D. Laing during a stay he had in San Francisco.]

R.D. LAING: REFLECTIONS ON PSYCHIATRY

On Roles and Labeling

Before I gave up my practice in London, we would have weekly group meetings with current psychiatric inmates, psychiatrists, and psychologists. There would be no distinction of roles within the context of the meeting. Everyone had to "hang their coat up" at the door. We were simply one human being talking to another.

It was a free for all. People would talk about anything they liked within human courtesy, the theoretical and the practical. No one was taking a stance, there was no formula. No one was "helping" anyone in particular. The only issue was living together under the same roof.

It's a waste of time breaking down a label. People have to take it off themselves. "Progressive psychiatrists" must be prepared to take off that label.

Psychiatry's Diagnostic Manual

Psychiatry's DSM-III [the official diagnostic manual] is a handbook of conduct and experience, regarded by the powers that be—with a lot of ordinary people's back-up—as a listing of items regarded as undesirable—not to that person, but to other people. This range of undesired experience is not criminalized. It's not against the law—say, to talk to someone who is not there—but it's listed as a "criteria."

In fact "any unusual perceptual experience" is listed as an undesirable criteria—for example "schizoid." There are different clusters of "symptoms" or "signs." For example: telepathy, clairvoyance, and even collecting garbage are listed.

I regard the DSM-III as a listing of undesirable conduct, with two purposes: 1) Stop it before it starts, and 2) Once started, stop it. This is couched in the medical model. Every gesture . . . intonation . . . dream, etc., has got a physiological process, without which they wouldn't happen. It might be possible to develop biotechnology which could suppress "undesirable clusters."

For example: What is normal or abnormal? Suppose psychiatrists decided that children dreaming in color was undesirable. Then it might be possible to find a pill that would be an anti-color dream pill.

You could call dreaming itself a "mini-psychosis in sleep." You could say we must stop dreaming in some people, unless they start dreaming when awake. You could call dreams a "benign encapsulated computer-dumping in sleep," that might spill over to waking hours. You could argue that it must be cultured-out: all dreams and nightmares. We've already cultured-out visions.

If we then look for a technology to homogenize experience, there's a chance we'll come up with one. Color dreams could be said to be caused by "pathological forms of micromolecular transformation in the thalamus in sleep." Chemicals could be found to "cure" this.

So schizophrenia in the DSM-III's is a cluster that they say is caused by some abnormality in the physiology of the brain, couched in medical terms. You must de-construct the whole question.

The political alignment must make a clear distinction between what is a criminal offense, and what is not. If conduct is not a criminal offense, then it's a subversion of the idea of a free country to stop something because a lot of people don't want it.

Homelessness

If someone is actually dying on the street, helpless, starving, refusing to be fed—if you found your father in this state on the streets, what would you do? Would you be committing a criminal offense by warming him up? At this interface I find it inappropriate to produce formulae.

All over the world, especially since the 1950's, there is the megalopolis, which concentrated many people into living in a concentrated territory. There always have been tramps unable—or who don't want—to buy a roof over their heads.

For a number of years in London there were very few people on the streets. After WWII many houses were bombed and derelict. Many of these houses were condemned. People—even though they wanted to live there—were re-housed from the condemned buildings. So there were many houses where no one was living.

The American-equivalent of the homeless moved into these places. They became known as "squatters." So they moved in, and all over London there were many such places. People lived one, two, three years there. They did them up. They eventually won squatters rights, even though re-developers wanted to evict them. For a few years there were very few people on the streets. They got grants from the London authority—they were given financial assistance. So a lot of people formed communities, communes, associations—and acquired the right to live there.

Before coming over here to the U.S., I gave up my medical practice, got divorced, sold my house and for a while lived in one of these so called "squats." People had formed themselves into a housing association because it cost virtually nothing to live in such a place. If they hadn't found it, many would be interred in mental health institutions or would be living in the streets.

Now suppose I didn't have money for this apartment [in San Francisco]. Suppose I didn't have friends to help me. I could be on the streets. Anyone can be. It affects the middle class, too. Many are living in their motor cars.

There are numbers of people who were quite affluent but then they goes bust. There are mortgage payments, the house is taken away. And so you get in a motor car, and sleep slumped somewhere in a back street. You would love to support yourself. There must be quite a bit of this. In San Francisco there are probably thousands of people sleeping in their cars.

This is more than a mental health problem. It's a nightmare of the middle class and of the working class just the same. The corporate bodies that employ them can dismiss them at any moment. It's quite embarrassing for a system such as this, which wants to have a different image.

There's nothing new about that. In big cities of the old world and still in Third World and Asia, you'd count yourself lucky if you have a roof over your head.

[*Editor's Note:* Most people would assume we have a natural human and Constitutional right not to have the privacy of our bodies and minds invaded. Thus, we believe we should be able to refuse any unwanted medical treatment. In medicine we normally have this right, but in the case of psychiatric hospitalization, Ron Thompson points out that there is no such legal, enforceable right. He focuses on the *emergency clause* that renders the right to be non-existent. It should be noted however, that psychiatry desires and indeed has obtained the power in most states to drug in non-emergency situations.]

THERE IS NO RIGHT TO REFUSE

by Ron Thompson, Attorney

Persons labeled and "diagnosed" mentally ill are profoundly misleading themselves if they believe their "rights" are being violated when psychiatrists drug them against their will. There is NO Federal or State law in the country that gives you a right to refuse neuroleptic drugs in a psychiatric "emergency," as defined by others.

Both outraged survivors and stout hearted (if also soft headed) advocates are deluding themselves if they don't realize that society has granted to psychiatry the only important RIGHT in relation to forced drugging.

The problem is not to stop "violations" by "bad" people but to acquire a real, enforceable Right. The definition of an enforceable right can only be a right exercised by its holder and not someone alleged to be acting "in his best interest." In practice, the concept of psychiatric emergency proves to be highly elastic and wide open to abuse by hospital staff as well as doctors.

A real right to refuse neuroleptic drugs must mean the ability to make an "irrational" refusal, i.e. a refusal with which psychiatrists and other mental health personnel disagree. If you do not advocate for and support an "irrational" right to refuse these drugs, whatever you are for, it is NOT a right to refuse.

Whether or not there SHOULD be a genuine right to refuse involuntary psychiatric procedures and not a cruel and confusing make-believe "right" you only have so long as you don't try to use it, is a very different question from whether there IS such a right. Whatever your stand on this "should" issue, please disenthrall yourself of the notion that any genuine civil right to refuse unwanted psychiatric interventions exists in the law today. It does not.

THE SHAME OF MY LIFE

by Peter R. Breggin, M.D.

I deeply regret that as a resident in psychiatry, I prescribed electroshock, I supervised a ward on which patients were given the treatment, and for a time I personally administered it. I was involved in damaging patients—many of them for the rest of their lives.

Why did I do it, even when I knew it was wrong? Because then, as now, advocates of electroshock will go to any extreme to stifle opposition from within the profession. One of my fellow psychiatric residents refused to give the treatment, and he was summarily fired from the training program, his career ruined. This pattern has been repeated into modern times when anyone, from professor to reporter, risks his career if he takes on the shockers.

When I finished my training, I resolved never again to use the treatment. Soon after I found that this was not enough. I had to do something more about it. In 1979 my book, *Electroshock: Its Brain-Disabling Effects*, was published. For the first time it gave hard evidence to back what common sense should tell us—electroshock damages the brain.

Now we are in the midst of a resurgence of electroshock treatment. Proponents of the treatment claim that they have a "new" method called "modified electroshock" in which the patient is anesthetized, paralyzed, and then breathed with oxygen during the treatment. This allegedly new treatment is promoted as safer than the old methods. But in truth modified shock is not new and is not safe. I personally administered this allegedly "new" treatment in 1962. Indeed as early as 1957, autopsy reports were already demonstrating brain damage from modified shock. The only thing "new" about modified shock is the recent national campaign to clean up its image. Most shock is done exactly as it was done twenty and more years ago, and it produces exactly the same devastating effects as it always did.

As Director of the Center for the Study of Psychiatry in Bethesda, Maryland, nearly every week I receive phone calls, letters or have personal interviews with patients who have suffered brain damage and permanent mental dysfunction from shock treatment. The story is typically uniform. First, the patient was not told the truth about the treatment before submitting to it—that it is controversial and dangerous. Second, the patient tried to stop the treatment once the devastating results were experienced, but the doctor and staff ignored the agonized appeals. Third, the patient continues to suffer, often years later, from memory and learning defects.

Typically, the period of several months around the treatment is almost entirely obliterated. Worse still, the patient may experience massive memory losses that reach back years into the past, often obliterating entire professional and educational capacities. And worst of all, too often the ability to concentrate upon and to learn new material is severely impaired. The result is enormous anguish, humilation, and wasted human capacity.

Only last week I saw a fine young woman in my practice whose abilities to learn have never returned to normal—years after shock treatment. She suffers continuing psychological devastation that is made worse by physicians who invalidate her by claiming that the treatment is harmless.

The reports of damage given to us by patients are confirmed by animal experiments and human autopsy reports which show brain damage, and by permanent damage in patients demonstrated on psychological testing, brain waves, and brain X-rays.

Nor is there any good evidence that the treatment actually helps people. The most frequently made claim is that shock treatment saves lives, especially by preventing suicide, but a review of the literature shows the opposite—that there is no evidence that shock prevents suicide.

Many hospitals and many psychiatrists never use it, rending absurd the claim that the treatment is needed as a last resort. If it is needed, why do so many hospitals and doctors do without it?

But does it work? Yes, it works, exactly as all brain damaging treatments work, including insulin coma and lobotomy. It works by destroying brain function and temporarily rendering the patient unable to think and feel in any coherent manner. During this time the patient may not seem depressed because in his or her damaged state, the patient is either apathetic or artificially high. But as the worst of the damage begins to clear, the original mental state returns, now compounded and worsened by brain damage.

Electroshock has no place in a humanistic approach to helping human beings. It is too damaging and there are better human service alternatives available including the broad panoply of services that we include in humanistic psychology. Many psychiatrists like myself see a broad spectrum of patients, including those who are severally depressed, and we never resort to shock treatment. It's time to give up this antiquated, barbaric therapy.

[*Editor's Note:* Dr. Peter Breggin is the founder and executive director of the Center for the Study of Psychiatry, and author of the book *Psychiatric Drugs: Hazards to the Brain*, published in 1983, by Springer Publishing Company, New York. He has given permission to use this article and the two others found in this book.]

MISUSE OF PSYCHIATRIC DRUGS: EAST AND WEST

by Peter R. Breggin, M.D.

The proposition that the major tranquilizers are brain-disabling, mind-leveling agents is nowhere more strongly bolstered than in the range of patients and nonpatients who are controlled by these drugs in many types of institutions. They have been used in virtually every setting in which docility, passivity, and emotional indifference are the top priorities. The paradigm for this is the state mental hospital, where many diverse individuals are confined. But the drugs are also used extensively in nursing homes, institutions for the retarded, prison and in the Soviet Union, political prison hospitals. The effect of these drugs, far from being specific for the treatment of schizophrenia, is everywhere the same—the enforcement of conformity to authority within the institution.

The drugs used to "torture" Russian political dissidents are exactly the same drugs used to "treat" mental patients throughout the Western world. We are appalled to hear that Russian dissidents are having their minds blunted and bodies tortured by major tranquilizers, but we tolerate the same treatment of those of our citizens who have been labeled mentally ill by the psychiatric establishment. From the viewpoint of the victim, whether political prisoner or patient, the horror of the experience is identical.

Many patients in the west are given the major tranquilizers against their will under the actual or real threat of involuntary psychiatric treatment. But all those who take the drugs are in a sense involuntary because they have not been told the full story of their devastating effects on the mind and body.

Nowadays it has become increasingly difficult to convince unhappy and upset individuals that they have personal problems which can be overcome with better approaches to life. Routinely in my psychiatric practice, patients come to seek help after having read the latest newspaper article on how depression, phobia, eating problems, alcoholism, or anxiety attacks are caused by chemical imbalances and subject to drug therapy. It becomes increasingly difficult to help patients take responsibility for their lives because psychiatry itself is telling them that they aren't responsible. Psychiatry thus brings out and reinforces the worse tendencies within those who have given up responsibility for themselves.

The dire result is threefold: first, the concept of individual responsibility is undermined as persons are no longer seen as suffering from moral, spiritual, and psychological conflicts; second, the concept of social responsibility is undermined, as we turn to medical technology instead of social reform and improved human services as solution to our larger social problems; third, we justify the inhumane treatment of millions of people throughout the world who are literally tortured again their will "for their own good."

PARABLE OF THE KEY

Psychiatry is looking for the answer in biological research, in making new drugs. It's like they've dropped the key in a dark room, but they're looking out in the hall. When someone asks why are looking for it here, they say, "This is where the light is."

The doctors' are encapsulated in their own shell. They're unable to self-analyze why they have failed. It will take a hundred years before psychiatry discovers they're on the wrong track.

[*A reflection of a psychiatrist in private conversation at a National Conference on Schizophrenia.*]

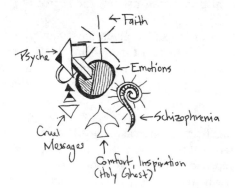

[*Editor's Note:* The following article is transcribed from careful notes the Editor took while attending a workshop on Psychopharmacology in 1985, at a prestigious private hospital. The title headings and footnotes have been added for the sake of clarity. The doctor favors the use of chemotherapy, although his many candid statements qualify their effectiveness.]

A WORKSHOP ON PSYCHOPHARMACOLOGY

PART I: THE ANTIPSYCHOTIC DRUGS

Serendipitous Discovery

In 1949, a French surgeon, Laborit, was working in a Paris military hospital. He was experimenting with new compounds for preoperative anesthesia [sedation for patients about to be operating on]. He was trying to stabilize autonomic function and reduce surgical shock. The new compounds tried were *anti-histamines.*

Laborit found that patients on Thorazine were fully alert, not fully sedated. He observed that they were peculiarly quiet, tranquil, under-responsive, bland, and turned off.

In 1951-1953, Delay and Deniker conducted the first research on psychiatric patients. One of the first patients whom the drug was tried on was Madame Grove who had a long-term psychotic illness. She was given 100 milligrams a day. Her delusional and bizarre ideas continued, but she was more cooperative and happy. Rarely did they get cures. They managed symptoms and fostered rehabilitation.

This story is typical of the history of the discovery of new drugs in this field. We take advantage of *serendipitous* observations and then vary the product to develop new treatments.

Neurological Toxicity* of Drugs

It is proven that all anti-psychotic drugs cause neurological toxicity, extra-pyramidal toxicity, neurological side effects. The early dogma was that it is desirable to get neurological toxicity in order to get an antipsychotic effect. The idea was to push the dosage to toxicity.

Do you have to have neurological toxicity to get anti-psychotic effi-

---

neurological toxicity: When levels of a drug cause adverse effects damaging to the nervous system, which may or may not be permanent. Toxicity is the state of being *poisonous.*

cacy? It is reasonable to be skeptical of this, because of some evidence from new drugs. Probably not.

There was a "repetition compulsion" in the pharmaceutical industry looking for extrapyramidal system* toxicity. The way one screened for drugs was to look for dopamine blockage in the basal ganglia in animal studies.

But it is more ominous than that. The studies were highly contaminated because it was assumed that it was necessary to treat with an anti-dopamine agent. There is no objective metabolic data to support this: that schizophrenia is caused by dopamine action. Medicines that give certain effects do not necessarily give causes of disease. In terms of cause, it's a "will-o-the-wisp."

The Appropriate Dose?

The body tries to defeat the activities of poisons put into them. It tries to burn them. Most of the activity is in the liver where they are partially oxidized.

There is an extraordinary difference in the ability to metabolize these drugs—an incredible variation. When the same level of Thorazine is given to a person, there is a ten to twenty-fold variation in the body.

There was a favorable study done at the Veterans Administration with a 20 milligram dose of Navane. It established a statistically significant correlation, but the scatter was dramatic. It is hard to determine the optimal blood level of an anti-psychotic.

There are tricks involved with these studies—the patient has to get better. You'd be surprised how many studies are done with no real clinical gains. Many such clients are gotten from the back wards and show no real improvement over the long run.

How Anti-Psychotic Drugs Work

These drugs work by interacting with dopamine receptors** in the brain's nerve cells. The primary effect is to *block them*. It is not proven that anti-dopamine action is the cause of the efficacy of these drugs. And it is certainly not proven that too much dopamine causes schizophrenia.

---

extrapyramidal system: Areas of the brain related to posture, movement and reflexes.

**dopamine receptors:* Nerve endings have various *receptors* that receive signals from neuro-chemicals such as dopamine. Dopamine receptors are largely found in the frontal lobes and limbic areas of the brain. (See Glossary: Dopamine)

Did Drugs Cause the Decline of Hospital Population?

There is the argument from decline in hospital population, from a half million right after WWI to 150,000 by 1975. The prevalence of numbers in hospitals have decreased, although total number of patients [hospitalized each year] have gone up. It is a mistake to think all this is due to the drugs. Some of the change is due to the drugs, some of it is due to the change in public attitude and the creation of community mental health centers, and some of the change is administrative pressure to save money. There was a powerful political play with the pharmaceutical industry to treat with drugs.

Are We Just Sedating People?

In a study by Lerner in Israel, it was shown that over the short term, sedative drugs were as good as neuroleptics. Within four hours both groups were improved. The Valium group looked better. After twenty-four hours there was no difference; both groups were heavily sedated. Some say that neuroleptics work just by sedation, and are not specifically anti-psychotic.

A 100 milligram Mellaril study used a sedative drug, as needed. It was as effective as a high Mellaril dose. You can't tell the difference between what neuroleptics and sedatives do.

The sedative drugs can be very powerful. With just one milligram Adavin [an anti-anxiety drug] is a "thunderbolt." It could knock down a Rhino in full charge.

Is this eroding our confidence in anti-psychotic drug's specificity? Are we using large doses of neuroleptics just to sedate people? The distinction between sedatives and specific anti-psychotic effect is getting fuzzier and fuzzier in short term treatment.

The Therapeutic Dose is Close to the Toxic Dose*

It's been said that enormous dosages are necessary for a fatal accident to happen, but the toxic dose is very close to the clinical efficacy curve. The toxic curve may even *overlap* the clinical efficacy curve. It is very difficult to get an anti-psychotic effect without being neurologically toxic. Many of us put on blinders not to see the neurological side effects.

---

*toxic dose: the level of drug that is damaging to the body, i.e. that is poisonous.

Blitzkrieg Dosing

There was a fad of aggressive use of Neuroleptics: the rapid neuroleptization theory. I call it "*Blitzkrieg*," where you bludgeon and assault the patient. Large doses were given every thirty to sixty minutes. They thought it would be a wonderful way to stamp out psychoses, but it's rubbish. Erickson in a study in the late 1960's, showed that a high dose of Haldol (60 milligrams) versus a low dose (15 milligrams) produced a clinical change that was indistinguishable.

In a Boston Study in 1983 Haldol was the most popular drug. It's dosing was four times the equivalent use of Thorazine. What are the reasons for using higher doses of Haldol and Prolixin? Doctors wouldn't use Thorazine because there was more risk of the patient falling, breaking the hip, etc. So if they can get away with it, they use Prolixin or Haldol.

They denied evidence before their eyes that people get sick. I despair to see an unmedicated person. We're used to seeing shuffling patients, like zombies, twisted like pretzels. That is not what schizophrenia looks like; that is what we are doing to them.

Long Term Effectivness?

The time course of recovery involves two stages: florid symptoms and reintegration. We are pushed hard by ourselves, patients, and family to drug people more. Things take time to get people well.

How weak is our data for the long-term use of neuroleptics? Most data is for schizophrenia. Paranoia and other psychoses are not tested for long-term use of neuroleptics. Affective disorders have not been studied as to whether they are effective for the long term. To use a neuroleptic first in such cases comes as close to malpractice as I know, without trying other drugs first.

A long term follow-up study by Preen on a thousand patients showed that up to the first year, two-and-a-half to three times fewer persons are hospitalized. But in the religion of neuroleptic therapy, the universe of the schizophrenic is not represented. The persons included in the study had to be responsive to drug therapy to get in the study. 20 to 30% never do well anyway, and may even be worse for the drug therapy, and are not included in the study.

Placebo* and Drug Effectiveness Compared

The believer in the neuroleptic theory finds that 60% of people on placebo relapse and only 16% on the drug relapses. But there is an incredible variance in placebo studies, from 100% to only 20% relapse rate.

Placebo: A sugar pill or other innocuous substance. Placebo studies compare the effectiveness of a drug versus non-drug.

You can't get permission anymore to do placebo studies. Drugs are so "wonderful." You can only compare Treatment A to Treatment B. With good medicine there is a 40-66% relapse rate—still it's bad. In one placebo study versus an after-the-fact study the differential relapse between drug and placebo showed no correction, just a scatter.

Placebo Studies: Are we looking at Placebo's effectiveness or the withdrawal effects of the drugs?

David Marsden noted the common regression line between neuroleptics and placebo. He hypothesized that what we are really looking at is the iatrogenic [physician-induced] drug tolerance of the drug plus the withdrawal curve. In other words, you get people hooked on the drug—then you are looking at the withdrawal curve after you put them on placebo. Neuroleptic drugs hang around and stick on the membrane for a long time. One dose was given one time only to a rat and found to persist one month. This does not gainsay that the drug is not good.

Trivial Doses are Effective

A John Kane study on Prolixin compared 500 milligrams of Thorazine to 50 milligrams or one-tenth the dose. By law, they were not allowed to do a placebo study. For placebo information, they dug up an ancient study and found 80% got sick. They found an incredible 60% do OK on ten times less—on silly, homeopathic, trivial doses. Clinical reasoning: How much I can get away with and help the most people and not get me in jail?

The effective dose of 50 milligrams is ludicrously homeopathic [low]. If you push the drug above ordinary dosing you get worse. 90% of patients on more than 20 milligrams of Prolixin get akathisia [a movement disorder]. High dosages may get written off as psychosis. Remember, a little bit goes a long way and too much really hurts.

Physician-induced Psychosis

In Montreal ten patients of three hundred showed a peculiar pattern. The first year they were on 30 milligrams of Prolixin and things got along well; the second year, 60 milligrams; the third year, 100 milligrams; and the fourth year 230 milligrams. Patients on increased dosages got clinically worse. After one year there is a risk of tolerance. This is iatrogenic mischief; the doctor has made things worse.

In a North Carolina study on kids after one year of treatment, the kids were worse with different symptoms: uncooperativenes, fuzziness—a *de nova* psychosis. The theory was the longer you treat the patient with neuroleptics, the greater the number of dopamine receptors built. *You iatrogenically induce the psychosis!*

Toxicity to the Movement Centers of the Brain

Characteristic of all neuroleptic drugs is extrapyramidal system toxicity. Acute Dystonic Reaction is disturbing if not terrifying to the patient. It occurs early in treatment and is highest in young males. The theory is that excess cholinergic function or possible excess dopamine causes it. For treatment, anti-parkinsonism drugs have been tried—one to two milligrams can break acute reaction. Valium can break it; so can relaxation.

In Parkinsonism, tremor is less dominant than in real Parkinsonism. It's caused by anti-dopamine effects and responds to anti-cholinergic drugs.

Akathisia is a misdiagnosed syndrome. It's often mistaken for what psychotic people are like: agitated and fidgety. Back off from neuroleptic drugs for a while to see what the patient is really like. I'm intolerant of akathisia. I don't like to see the patient suffering.

The most promising treatment is beta blockers, but you have to deal with the dirty non-specificity* of B1 and B2 blockers once they get in the blood. Anti-cholinergic agents don't really work.

The Golden Rule

The first step is to back off from the poison before you add a second poison. If you don't learn anything else from this workshop, it's *to stop the poison*. If you add more poison or add a different poison you add confusion. This is the Golden Rule.

Malignant Syndrome

Malignant Syndrome presents a clinical triad of symptoms: catatonia, hyperthermia, fever, cooking the brain and autonomic nervous instability. There are undulating waves of stupor, body rigidity, confusion, increasing and decreasing blood pressure, and autonomic instability. In big inpatient units, the risk is two to three cases a year. People are getting malignant syndrome who are on 60-80 milligrams of a high potency drug. Fatality is 10-20%. The treatment: First step, *stop the music; stop the poison*.

non-specificity: When the drug doesn't just have a limited specific effect but incurs a wide range of undesirable effects.

Are Neuroleptics Addictive?

It's difficult to take away the side-effect medications, Artane or Cogentin. It's like candy or heroin. Drugees on the street like Cogentin, Artane.

Neuroleptics are sort of addictive. You go through a sick withdrawal, a non-specific malaise. With high potency drugs you go through a withdrawal kinetic syndrome*. However, if you asked a drugee to rank the top ten street drugs, he would rank neuroleptics number thirty-five.

When young people are taken off the neuroleptics cold turkey, 90% get a dyskinetic reaction. People rapidly withdrawn from the neuroleptic get withdrawal emergent symptoms, akin to dyskinesia.

Tardive Dyskinesia

The prevalence of tardive dyskinesia depends on how "funny" patients have to be, to be called tardive dyskinetic. The rates vary from 10% to 60% depending on the severity of the criteria. In a retrospective VA study on ten thousand patients, the affective patients have a tardive dyskinesia rate of 53%, twice the rate of schizophrenics.

The test for tardive dyskinesia is to take the neuroleptic away from the patient and follow up. The neuroleptic suppresses symptoms, therefore you see only mild symptoms.

Real tardive dyskinesia comes out when the person is off the neuroleptic. It's caused by supersensitivity** of the dopamine receptors in the basal ganglia. The best approach is to avoid the disease through low use of the drug. Force yourself in an open minded way: not anything that moves is tardive dyskinesia.

Nothing works to treat tardive dyskinesia. The great hope in the field is spontaneous remission. If patients go off the medicines, after having been one and half years on them, 90% show marked improvement, 50% are better on rating scales. If you can, change the diagnosis on the patient so you can treat without neuroleptics. A lot of people are walking around on neuroleptics and can do without them.

Deaths Due to Neuroleptics

I have seen two patients killed on aggressive Haldol therapy. In between seclusion room checks, the respiratory system stopped. We've

withdrawal kinetic syndrome: a neurological reaction that results in gross motor disturbances such as rolling or jerky movements of the neck and arms.

**Supersensitivity:* A condition where a small amount of neuro-chemical in the brain causes a lot of effect. This happens when a drug is withdrawn and is no longer blocking many receptors sites.

stopped thinking about non-pharmaceutical ways of dealing with psychosis at the cost of killing people.

PART II: THE ANTIDEPRESSANTS

History

The first drug, Imipramine, was developed in the late 1950's in an attempt to come up with a new neuroleptic. Imipramine has a close structural analog to Thorazine with a different twist in the molecule. Roland Coon, a Swiss researcher, found that Imipramine was inferior with psychotics and made them more agitated. But it elevated depressed patients.

The new drugs recently developed are disappointing. There's not much new since the 1950's. Progress has been extremely conservative in the field.

The cyclic antidepressants block norepinephrine* uptake. It's ludicrous to state that depression therefore is caused by too much norepinephrine. You're arguing by inference. It doesn't work.

We are victims of our successes. It's difficult to get placebo studies. Depressed patients tend to be peculiar. Academic places where research is done get atypical depressions, patients who are mildly dysphoric and ambulatory rather than with serious melancholy. A new generation of drugs handle this: Alprazolam [Xanax] is for the walking wounded only; it's very potent. There's a risk of intoxication and addiction. Newer, higher-potency drugs have withdrawal symptoms.

The Kick-the-Machine Theory

The antidepressant potentiates activity of norepinephrine in the central nervous system. How this changes behavior is unknown. We don't know how to link the physiology with the mood elevating effect.

The nervous system is designed by the Almighty to defeat the drug. The cells will try to turn off norepinephrine production. After some hours the feedback loop will cool it; they down-regulate rapidly, turning off synthesis of norepinephrine. There are also blockages of the cholinergic system, H-system, A-alpha system.

In two to three weeks there is a compensatory effect; the Beta receptors burn out. What does compensating change mean? It's beating on receptors, bludgeoning them into submission. They roll over and die.

*norepinephrine:a neuro-chemical transmitter at most sympathetic (post-ganglionic) nerve endings. When "uptake" of norepinephrine is blocked there is actually more made available, initially.

Possibly what the drugs are doing is just *kicking the machine*. You intrude at a fundamental level and maybe get a response.

The Effectiveness of Antidepressants

The seamy side is that these drugs aren't really that good. 20% to 30% of people respond poorly to them. The newer drugs are not better. They are damn powerful. They kill people. *We've killed a lot of people with these drugs*. These drugs are very dangerous. You can be killed on a over-dose. Take a two week supply and you're dead.

We don't really have an understanding of how they work. It's a circularly-arrived-at relationship. You pre-screen drugs for norepinephrine blockage. We don't have a theory of antidepressant physiology. Over the last twenty years we still don't know the pathophysiology of the illness. You can't do placebo studies with seriously ill people.

The effectiveness of long-term care with antidepressants with a year follow-up is not established; the evidence is mighty weak. The effectiveness of antidepressants are established in acute major depression, preventing relapse of major non-bipolar depression and stroke patients that look clinically depressed. Some do remarkably well. Neurologists say it's just psychology and ask, "Why are you going to give them poison when they have a primary organic problem with a secondary depression?"

Comparison of Placebo and Neuroleptics

The comparisons of drugs with placebos is the soft underbelly of research. Antidepressants are the penicillin for depression. *Only in two out of three trials is the drug better than placebo*. It doesn't make any sense not to try and use placebo.

Neuroleptic drugs do pretty well in depression, particulary with agitated, depressed people. The distinction between neuroleptics and antidepressants is a lot more shadowy than one would like to believe. The distinction between Thorazine and Imipramine becomes fuzzy, because they have similar metabolites. Studies with Mellaril and Thorazine show they can be antidepressants.

Is the Illness Just Masked?

There is a high risk of relapse with the patient if you stop treatment after drugs. In one month there is a 70% relapse, after three to five months, a 42% relapse and after this, a 14% relapse. This could be just the natural history of the depressive cycle! It could be what's happening—that we make people feel better while the illness runs its course. It may be just the "kick the machine theory," to make it work better. *In their heart of hearts and head of heads, they are still depressed.*

Angst in 1973, published a study showing that bipolar* and unipolar patients tend to have more and quicker episodes over time. This is "mind boggling." We should not routinely medicate everybody with mood disturbance forever.

Vanishing Effectiveness Over Time

With antidepressants you can treat existing problems and stop relapses within five to six months, but you can't stop recurrent episodes. After three to eight months the placebo relapse rate is 56% and the drug relapse rate is 20%, but this is within the natural history of depression. After one year you are still within the first depression.

In one study of relapses within one to three years, placebo relapse is 76% compared to 54% with antidepressant. The protective factor diminishes over time. After three years the effectiveness is vanishing. After two to three years none of the treatments have dramatic effects. *The main effect of the drugs is during the period of the natural cycle of the depression.*

Inducing Mania

There is a risk of inducing mania. We see it all the time as clinicians. But studies do not give a strong indicator. In one study the risk of mania was very high. Giving antidepressants to bipolar patients runs the risk of mania.

Toxic Effects

Toxic effects are important because they are common and sometimes serious: blurred vision, dry mouth, constipation, serious urinary retention, and sexual dysfunction.

Confusion and delirium are very serious effects, and are often misunderstood and misdiagnosed. Central nervous system intoxication is induced with Amitriptyline. Indeed, all of them can produce it—even doses within the therapeutic range, reasonable doses. If you are not sure, back off. You may do great harm to push the dose.

Postural hypotension is the major cardiovascular problem. It's not

---

Bipolar: a word used to label what was called manic-depressive illness.

trivial. The person may fall down and break his hip. People fall and get hurt all the time

Antidepressants suppress REM sleep. They push the REM cycle further into the night; they lighten deeper sleep. The failure of DSM-2 depression to normalize is a bad sign and the person may try suicide. Occasionally, night terrors can be caused.

Overdose is fatal, and antidepressants are a common choice for suicide. They cause coma, seizures, anti-cholinergic poisoning. There's a risk of cardiac toxicity for one to two weeks after. Brain toxicity lasts only one to two days.

The percentage of side effects: Overall clinical toxicity is 15%; central nervous system toxicity is 6%; severe anti-cholinergic* effects where one can't urinate are 3%; cardiac effects are 6.2%; sudden death is .4%. *Four deaths in a thousand is not a trivial number!*

Addictive Qualities

It's hard to take away the drug. It's addictive and there's withdrawal. The body develops a mild tolerance. Rapid withdrawal causes discomfort, irritability and aches. There's probably a physiological habitation or addiction.

The Anticholinergic Syndrome

The person becomes "dry as a bone, red as a beet, and mad as a hatter." There's agitation, grand mal seizures. Signs of the syndrome include large pupils, warm dry skin, flushing, mild fever. All their secretions are dried up.

The antidote is Physostigmine. Use it slowly with common sense. It can get anybody with an overdose out of trouble; it brings them out of a coma.

PART III: LITHIUM

History

Lithium was developed by Cade in Australia (1949), while studying Purine metabolism. He loaded up Guinea pigs with uric acid and Lithium to deal with side effects, and observed behavioral quieting.

cholinergic system: Involves neurons that are concerned with vegetative aspects of day to day life such as eating.

Cade added one plus one and got eleven. There was no control on the use of Lithium (commonly used as a salt substitute to treat Gout). He tried it on excited, chronically manic patients. They did well. However, at the same time this news reached the states, JAMA [Journal of the American Medical Association] had carried cases of persons killed by Lithium overdoses. Cade was seen as irresponsible.

The FDA held back approval in this country for years because it held that Lithium was dangerous. In 1971, the FDA finally approved the use of Lithium but *only with bipolar disorders,* and then with a substantial warning.

Why did it take so long for Lithium to reach this country?—because there was no commercial interest. Lithium was a commonly available substance. It took a lot of work by the psychiatric community to get the Pharmaceutical industry to manufacture the drug. Even then, the pharmaceutical industry came in more as a gesture of good will, and not for profit.

Possible Side Effects of Lithium

1. *Intoxication:* First stage: It's like alcohol intoxication with slurred speech, confusion, and tremor. Second Stage: The person gets delirious, and more of the above. Third Stage: Central nervous system intoxication with permanent neurological damage. The person goes comatose. There is no treatment. The patient is put on life support and dialysis.
2. *Goiter:* Several cases have been reported, but they're diffuse, benign enlargements. It can be treated with elevating the THS level.
3. *Dermatological:* Acne is extremely common. It may flare up and become very serious. Occasionally, hair loss results from Lithium use.
4. *Harm to the kidneys* are the greatest concern. Lithium may cause irreversible damage to the kidneys. Renal biopsies have shown substantial degeneration, deformity, and scary tissues. Nephrologists say many drugs taken chronically do this. It's not surprising to find Lithium does damage after years of toxic insult.

How Lithium Works

We don't know. We don't know how it stabilizes.

Lithium blockades norepinephrine and some dopamine synapses. It also makes less catecholamine in the synapses. In the hippocampus it increases the amount of serotonin. Lithium blocks a hormone—it's an antidiuretic. Months or years later this may cause diabetes.

Lithium mucks up the system with its anti-alpha-adrenergic effect. It also blocks the acetylcholine-muscarinic system. *The combined blockages of receptors may explain manic control.*

The Effectiveness of Lithium

In the early 1970's, 700 patients were tested with Lithium versus placebo. Patients did two to one better on Lithium. But the results are a mixed bag.

—For Mania: With Lithium there is a 30% relapse rate. With Placebo there is a 70% relapse rate.

—For Unipolar disorder, a 73% survival rate on Lithium and a 37% survival rate on placebo.

—Rapid cycling is difficult to treat: 63% survival rate on Lithium and 35% survival rate on placebo.

Areas of Utility for Lithium Use

*The FDA has approved the use of Lithium for mania only,** but collection of areas of utility is up. However, Lithium is an inferior treatment for short-term mania. It's only good for middle course and long-term treatment. Don't condemn a person easily to long-term Lithium therapy. It's not trivial.

PART IV: OVERVIEW OF CHEMOTHERAPY

Polypharmacy

I don't like polypharmacy. When drugs start interacting problems happen. MAO [monoamineoxidase] and Imipramine, which are used in England and go together like peanuts and beer, can produce terrible effects: central nervous system intoxication, shock and collapse. It's rare but when it happens, it's a catastrophe.

Using Experimental Drugs

Why add an anti-convulsant to a neuroleptic? There's no real evidence that it's effective. It's just experimentation. It's a "seat of the pants" solution.

We try anything that works. The big problem is to know when to stop.

Lithium is said to be specific for the manic phase of the biopolar disorder [manic depression]. Nevertheless, many physicians routinely prescribe Lithium for many diagnostic categories including schizophrenia and depresssion.

It's the physician's decision what drug to use and what dose, no matter what the product insert says. With using a new drug, you need something to back it up. You have the right to try it.

To Increase Adherence to Medication

1. Complex regimes have difficult adherence.
2. Drugs that don't have a rapid onset and give persistent side effects have difficult adherence.
3. Show the onset of benefits. Use the consumer model. The doctor knows the "tremendous benefits," the "miraculous cures," but the patient feels different. "This drug the doctor's giving me is doing nothing. It makes me feel terrible, woozy, I can't move." The patient is maybe the last one to see the benefits. All the patient sees is the bad stuff.

Try an on-off trail with the patient. Educate: there's a slow onset of benefits. So often we accept for granted that the patient knows. The patient thinks we're crazy when his experience is just the opposite.

Be up front. Not to be, builds resentment and a lack of confidence. The patient thinks we're evil and trying to do something to them. It fact, it may be true, or a delusion.
4. Certain personality types have difficultly with adherence: the paranoid who thinks it's an intrusion, passive aggressive types, and substance abusers.

Informed Consent

1. Informed consent must be done with experimental drugs.
2. Informed consent must particulary be given with prolonged treatment. You need to be an honest doctor and explain the risks. "Fess up!"
3. You can overdo informed consent, getting patients to sign forms. Internists use lethal drugs all the time. The psychiatrist is not any more incompetent than they are.

Drug-Induced Symptoms

It's common for drug modification of the symptoms to occur. You modify the syndrome in the partially treated patient. We're incredibly stupid. It's incredibly misleading when the classical syndromes are modified into something else. Many patients with a classic bipolar illness show delusional and bizarre schizophrenic behavior. Partial treatment with neuroleptics or Lithium can make patients look schizophrenic.

It's extremely difficult to find what is original in the patient. When you're dealing with potent drugs which may be neurotoxic, it can be very confusing.

Q & A: Why was the name changed from Major Tranquillizers to Anti-Psychotics?

It wasn't a deliberate step by psychiatry. But it as changed in the literature by drug companies and researchers to avoid the image of chemical strait-jacketing and Big Brother.

Summary of Workshop

There can be lots of problems:

1. Can we develop an effective antidepressant?
2. Can we develop a non-neurotoxic anti-psychotic? All are neurotoxic.
3. How do the antidepressants and Lithium work? We don't really know the biology of affective illness. I believe in risk taking; use any old thing that comes down the pike. It's the only way to make a breakthrough.
4. Do the drugs really work in the long run? There's an abysmal lack of research.
5. Is there a third syndrome? Is there more than two psychoses? Is an affective disorder just a state of being human?
6. Can we develop a non-lethal mood altering drug?

We wonder if we are just Witch Doctors. Are we just trying to scare and intimidate patients? This is the fundamental question facing psychiatry today.

[*Editor's Note:* Five years later, in 1990, I took notes at a conference on schizophrenia where a talk was given by the same researcher. Although much hasn't changed in the space of five years, the doctor advocates a shift toward interpersonal therapy.]

A CONFERENCE ON SCHIZOPHRENIA

Schizophrenia: an incurable disease of unknown cause

We've come a long way since the 1950's, based on the advances in psychopharmacology. I think to be quite honest that what we have to gain with the new drugs—while important— continues to be only part of the story, to be a rather limited intervention. It is always essential to remember with a great deal of humility that schizophrenia is essentially an *incurable disease of unknown etiology.*

Physician-induced Mischief

You see Bradykinesia*: the sub-Stelazine stump, the loss of motility, the inexpressive, immobile faces, the zombie-like staggering on wards— much of which unfortunately is ascribed to the natural repertoire of schizophrenic illness itself. It's very easy to confuse bradykinesia with so-called negative symptoms of schizophrenia. It's very difficult to differentiate the restlessness of akathisia from the agitation in psychotic illness. You have to pinch yourself, force yourself to think differentially in every case, every day as to whether you're overdosing and causing part of the problems that the patient is having.

We Can't See the Person with their Illness

These days all of us are kind of immune to the fact that people stagger around, look like zombies, twisted up like pretzels in the seclusion room. You almost can't see an unmedicated, psychotic person. Even in an emergency room practice, at least in my city, everybody gets hit with a "Haldol dart" on the way in. You seriously can't see somebody who hasn't been modified in some way by medication. *We're always peering through the Haldol haze to try to figure what the person is like underneath all this behavior induced by the drugs.*

Bradykinesia: the extreme slowing of one's movements

Psychiatric Myths

One myth is that if a little bit of anti-psychotic drug is good then a lot of medication is warranted. The bottom line is that there is virtually no difference; the degree of improvement in high and low doses is very similar. If you go to very high doses you will for sure generate mischief, suffering, pain, side effects—but the gain of anti-psychotic benefit is vanishingly small.

The notion that the major benefits can be gained within a matter of hours and days is simply not correct. What you can gain in a matter of hours and days is acute symptomatic control, what I tend to call "hot symptoms"—that is profound agitation, anger, yelling and screaming, and compelling hallucinations. That sort of thing can be brought under control relatively early—but not necessarily specifically by these drugs.

Where the neuroleptic drugs come in, is a kind of a middle game, in a maintenance therapy that involves bringing the quality of the associational process—thinking, rationality, coherence, ability to plan a day's activity and stick to it—this is where these drugs are uniquely valuable. Yet I have to remind you, these things don't come cheap, they don't come easy, and they don't come quick.

When the folks in the back room with beady eyes and sharp pencils start hounding about doing it quicker and doing it better, getting people out of the hospital sooner to save money. Don't be bullied into believing that it can be done.

Sure, you can patch people up to the point where you push them out the door, and keep your fingers crossed that they're going to make it. But by and large it doesn't necessarily go very well. An *enormous* amount of work is yet to be done in the many weeks and months thereafter.

Long-term Efficacy of Neuroleptics?

I was actually scandalized about ten years ago when I was on an APA task force that was to review some aspects of anti-psychotic drugs, particularly side effects. Very naively, I suggested to some of the older hands in the field which I had not worked with much up to that time—before we get to the bad news, why don't we give the good news in an initial upbeat chapter reviewing the evidence for efficacy for long-term use of neuroleptic drugs?

The eyes rolled up, and some of the older colleagues said, "We don't think there's much data out there, other than schizophrenia." I said, "Come on, there has to be a lot of data on psychotic and affective illness, bipolar disorder, and borderline syndrome. . . ." The fact is, then and even now there are very, very few systematic studies of long term—longer than six months—follow-up studies of neuroleptics in any condition, other than what one might call schizophrenia—and again schizophrenia with a small s, and with quotes around it, because a lot of this literature goes back a long time.

Less Medicine and Rediscovery of Sullivanian Ideas

The average dose of neuroleptics used [in my city] ten years ago was a mere 12 milligrams a day. Currently, the average dose is around 5 milligrams a day. You can argue that this sounds like very radical, crazy irresponsible hardball homeopathy [using dosages that are minuscule]. I suppose it is, if that were the only aspect of the story.

A lot of things happened between the '70's and '80's. It took several years, for example, for the nursing staff to begin to trust our psychiatrists that they would not desert them when things got hot, and would be there to intervene—that in fact, people wouldn't end up with bruised noses and broken arms.

It took a long time to develop and rediscover any Sullivanian* and other old notions about interpersonal interventions in an acutely psychotic patient—creating a quiet, supportive and structured milieu—learning how to be non provocative, how to be quieting and reassuring, how to provide the things we used to be able to do very well in the old days.

Experimental Programs with Milieu Therapy and Minimal Medication

Some programs across the country are studying modified neuroleptic maintenance programs in DSM-III** schizophrenic patients. They give either minimal medication most of the time or even none at all. When symptoms seem to be evident again, when a person is being exposed to stress—being thrown out of a halfway house, girlfriend leaving town or what have you—they'll intervene and be more supportive, and add a bit more medicine.

The findings are that you can reduce the total amount of medication over a year's follow up by several fold—you can reduce it by five-fold, sometimes by ten-fold, and the degree of clinical benefit is not very different, yet the side effect risk and the mischief are considerably reduced.

*Sullivanian: Refers to the ideas of Harry Stack Sullivan who emphasized our common human ground, rather than biological differences. He saw meaning in the symptoms of schizophrenia. (See Glossary)
**DSM-III: The third revised version of Psychiatry's official diagnostic handbook.

Clozapine: A new drug with outstanding questions

Clozapine is a truly innovative drug with virtually no extra-pyramidal side effects.

I'm very puzzled by Clozapine. 25-30% do obviously better [than the standard neuroleptics]. Unfortunately, there's a moral dilemma because 70-80% of the people would prefer to stay on it, even though they don't do better. Again, this reflects the uncomfortable side effects of the neuroleptics.

I don't know how much of the apparent benefit, including the negative symptoms is a true positive primary impact on the syndrome, rather than relief from the pre-existing side effects.

In hindsight, one of the almost diabolical aspects of the design of the critical U.S. study on Clozapine, is that those people were *nearly intoxicated* with huge dosages of Haldol—up to 60 milligrams. So you're not quite sure how much of the benefit is recovery from too much Haldol and how much is the true positive impact of the Clozapine. I think these questions need to be sorted out. We just don't know.

What have we gained?

In a recent review—if you consider the long term outcome studies of schizophrenia going all the way back to 1900, the fact is that the rate of improvement and outcomes—bad outcomes versus good—before 1950's and since the 1950's are remarkably similar on average. Now there are some studies that show remarkable benefits in recent years, some that don't. The average is not very different.

The average is that at least one-half to two-thirds of at least DSM-III schizophrenics tend to have a bumpy course over many years, tend to have residual deficits over many years. The question is what have we gained?

I think we've gained a lot—I think we are in fact able to diminish morbidity, and dysfunction and suffering enormously. We are able to get people out of the hospital sooner—we are able to improve the general quality of life—I think. The bottom line is that schizophrenia continues to be both idiopathic and incurable.

CLOZAPINE: BREAKTHROUGH DRUG OR PSYCHIATRY'S NEUTRON BOMB?

[*Editor's Note*: Clozapine is being heralded as a breakthrough drug, to be used when the standard neuroleptic drugs fail. Due to the significant risk of agranulocytosis* which can cause death—the patients have to go through a weekly blood monitoring program. The following comments are taken from my notes of comments by a medical researcher at a conference on schizophrenia, 1990.]

The basic indication for use of Clozapine is insufficient response to the standard course of anti-psychotic medication.

Clozapine is the "dirtiest" drug you'll ever know; the reason it's useful is because it's "dirty."[i.e. it blocks several different types of receptors and so causes a variety of adverse effects.] Clozapine blocks the following: dopamine-D2, D1, serotonin, adrenergic, anti-cholinergic, antihistamine. But it increases norepinephrine turnover.

There's some interesting side effects of Clozapine. They drool; there's hyper-salivation when they sleep at night—a very unusual side effect. There is a high incidence of seizures, particularly in the higher dose range.

The big problem with Clozapine is agranulocytosis—it's real—you don't know how frequent it is. A meaningful number of individuals have it—it's a serious, serious risk. You are aware that there is a Clozapine management system required that is very cumbersome.

Clozapine does not tend to cause extra-pyramidal** side effects. It seems to leave it [the brain's motor areas] quieter. I've seen seriously troubled tardive dyskinesia patients and they do very nicely on Clozapine. At higher dosages Clozapine may cause extra-pyramidal side effects. The jury is still out.

How well does it work? We're still new in the business. One-third of patients do significantly better than on the neuroleptic. The rest did about the same. But I have seen patients do less well on Clozapine.

*   *   *

*agranulocytosis: an acute condition where the total number of white blood cells drops too low.
**extra-pyramidal: the area of the brain that controls motor functions. Disruption of this system leads to restlessness, shuffling and other muscular discomforts.

[*Editor's Note:* The advocate Stephen Mendelsohn refers to Clozapine as Psychiatry's Neutron Bomb. He gave permission to reprint excerpts from his article published by the Connecticut Coalition of Citizens with Disabilities, dated September 1990. He cites evidence that the drug in the long run can cause higher brain damage that would also make one more psychosis prone. As the more obvious symptoms like motor shaking and tardive dyskinesia are reduced, the less obvious symptoms— damage to higher functions (tardive dementia/dysmentia)—are increased. This could be the prescription for a vast, invisible epidemic.]

In a 1977 article published in Advances in Biochemical Psychopharmacology, Urban Ungerstedt and Tomas Ljungber of the Karolinksa Institute suggest a strong association between Clozapine and severe damage to the brain's limbic system and prefrontal cortex, leading to permanent mental dysfunction. This condition is called tardive dysmentia or tardive psychosis. These are their conclusions.

"Clinical experience indicates that Clozapine may be more "specific" in the treatment of psychosis than is Haloperidol [Haldol]. Our behavioral data show that this "specificity" maybe due to its comparatively greater inhibition of limbic dopamine receptors. These receptors may thus be most liable to develop supersensitivity after chronic Clozapine treatment. The counterpart of tardive dyskinesia after chronic Haloperidol may thus be potentiation of psychotic behavior after chronic Clozapine!

Like the neutron bomb which gives off more radiation and less blast, Clozapine causes more catastrophic and lethal albeit less detectable damage.

A "MEDICAL-SURGE" TEAM

We shouldn't think in terms of an asylum anymore, but more like a medical-surge team, like a surgeon doing an operation. The old concept of the asylum was rather the uncle taking his niece out for a walk and bringing her back uninjured.

Our goals are symptom suppression and stabilization. We can't keep them long enough for reconstitution.

[*Notes from a presentation by a medical researcher at a national conference on schizophrenia.*]

[*Editor's Note*: This article is an abridged and edited version of an article published by a Swedish doctor opposed to the use of neuroleptic drugs. Permission was obtained from Lars Martensson to print this version. A full unedited copy of this article can be obtained through Psychiatric Survivors of Western Massachusetts, P.O. Box 60845, Longmeadow, MA 01116-0845.]

SHOULD NEUROLEPTIC DRUGS BE BANNED?

by Lars Martensson, M.D. ©1991

Since their introduction thirty years ago, neuroleptic drugs have been given to tens of millions of people. In Sweden, with a population of eight and a half million, about 100,000 receive these drugs every day. About one-third of them have the diagnosis schizophrenia. Other big groups who are given the drugs are retarded people and old people in institutions who are confused or negativistic.

What these recipients of neuroleptic drugs have in common is that they are wards of the state, that they are powerless and wordless, and that they cause trouble for the people around them who are in control. Such drugs are indeed effective in reducing or abolishing troublesome human behavior. The cardinal indication for neuroleptic drugs is schizophrenia. They are therefore also called anti-schizophrenia or anti-psychotic drugs.

Neuroleptic drugs are given the main credit for the modern revolution in psychiatry. They are generally thought to have greatly helped the victims of schizophrenia, but in reality they have not helped, but rather immeasurably harmed all the people with this diagnosis. They have done their harm in two ways: first because of direct damage to the brain and to mental functions; secondly because they are tied together with false and abhorrent views of human problems and human beings.

The drugs have promoted a false definition of schizophrenia as a medical problem with a medical solution. They have prevented us from taking our responsibility. As a consequence, people with schizophrenia have been abandoned. That is the real cause of their tragedy. If they had not been abandoned, most of these young and often gifted people would have been able, like the rest of us, to realize many of the promises and possibilities of their lives.

Anti-Psychotic Drugs Are a Misleading Term

The neuroleptic effect.—Initially the main effect of neuroleptic drugs is a reduction of the signal level in dopamine brain systems. "Optimal neuroleptization," it is said, means that 70% of the patient's dopamine receptors are blocked by the drug. One clinical manifestation of this reduced signal level is that patients become "quiet, less active, and more or less indifferent to experiences and situations which had previously made them very emotional." As the patient loses his passions, his inspiration, and his ability to care, troublesome behavior is reduced, as well as all other kinds of self-assertiveness and spontaneity. The anti-psychotic effect is thus only a small aspect of this general neuroleptic effect.

"Neuroleptic" is the original term that was used by the French workers who introduced the first drug of this class chlorpromazine (Thorazine), in the early 1950's. The French workers observed the drug effects with more naive and honest eyes than most later psychiatrists. They saw clearly that the drugs cause a general apathy and indifference. They used the Greek work *leptos* which means small, attenuated, to coin the term "neuroleptic."

The term "anti-psychotic" is misleading for the following reasons:

1. The drugs have no specific effect on psychosis or psychotic symptoms. Only because of a general indifference and apathy are psychotic symptoms (or at least their overt and active expressions), reduced in many patients.

2. In many patients, the drugs elicit or aggravate hallucinations and delusions as an acute effect. This is often overlooked by the psychiatrist. He rarely knows the patient well enough to realize that, even though the latter is now perhaps more quiet, less excited and less aggressive, at the same time he has more and worse delusions and suffers more helplessly from terrifying hallucinations. The power of the word is such that the doctor as a rule does not even think of the possibility that the drug is now causing the patient's worsening psychosis. Instead of taking away the drug, he increases the dose of the "anti-psychotic" medication. At some high drug level, even the psychotic symptoms caused by the drug may be finally suppressed.

3. The drugs induce specific and lasting changes in frontal and limbic brain areas that make a person psychosis prone. The drug makes the person more and more psychotic, which makes it more and more difficult to do without the "anti-psychotic" drug.

Alternative terms: The name "anti-psychotic" has a hypnotic effect, blinding doctors to what the drugs are really doing with the patients. The term "neuroleptic" correctly suggests one of the many effects of the drugs. More cannot be asked of a name.

Three Facts about Neuroleptic Drugs and Schizophrenia

Let me state three important facts about neuroleptic drugs in schizophrenia: 1. Brain damage is serious and certain. 2. Temporary use of neuroleptic drugs is a trap. 3. After a few years patients in a drug-free programs are better by all criteria.

These facts demand fast and radical changes in psychiatric practice. Such changes will not come about from inside psychiatry itself. Therefore political action and strong laws are needed.

1. Brain Damage is Serious and Certain

Tardive Dyskinesia.—It is well known that *tardive dyskinesia* hits a large proportion of people who receive neuroleptic drugs for long periods. Tardive dyskinesia is a permanent disturbance of motor coordination. The most obvious manifestations are involuntary, uncontrollable moments of the tongue, jaws and face.

Disturbance in all patients.—If, say, one third of a group of patients display gross motor disturbances, we can be sure that most, and probably all of the others also have disturbances. When a brain system is gradually damaged, it usually takes a lot of damage before functions become clinically abnormal. Long before tardive dyskinesia of the face and other gross abnormalities of body posture and of movements have appeared, the person has been robbed of the grace and efficiency of moments that by gifts of nature he should possess.

Other motor disorders.—Other disorders that involve all of the muscles of the body of all who receive the drugs, but which disappear when the drug is stopped, are in fact even more serious. These disorders are Parkinsonism, Akathisia, and Akinesia. These ugly, inefficient, painfully purposeless movement patterns have replaced the finely tuned body movements of the same person before the drug.

Probable total final drug damage.—Experience tells that when a neuroleptic drug is given for the first time to a young person in a schizophrenic crisis, he will almost always continue to receive the drug for long periods or for life. If the drug had not been given in the first place, the fate of permanent drug dependence could have been avoided. Therefore, the probable total final drug damage to the patient should be taken into account before the early decisions to give neuroleptic drugs in a schizophrenic crisis. The distinction between permanent drug damage and drug damage that may subside when the drug is stopped, is not important if the drug is in fact never stopped.

How Neuroleptic Drugs Act at the Receptor Level

Neuroleptic drugs act by blocking the receptors for dopamine. Dopamine is a transmitter of nerve impulses. Signal transmission by means of dopamine is important in three major brain systems: the limbic system which controls emotions, the motor control system and the hormone control system.

When receptors for dopamine are blocked by the drug, the result is that the transmission of signals across nerve junctions (synapses) using dopamine is cut down. But the nerve cells fight back and form new receptors to make up for the blocked ones. The natural, original receptors represent information (sense, signal, order). The new receptors introduce a higher ratio of nonsense, noise or disorder in the system.

S/N deterioration.—While the patient is on the drug, he has a reduced level of signals and as a second effect, relatively more noise in the system than normal, because of the newly formed receptors. Initially the first effect dominates, later on the second effect becomes more and more important. *When and if the drug is discontinued, the net result is an elevated level of signals and still more noise in the system.*

Effects of Neuroleptic Drugs at Higher Levels of Brain Organization

The main target of neuroleptic drugs.—The main and the intended target of neuroleptic drugs is the limbic system, which is the center for emotions, for control and appreciation of the inner environment of the body, for sexuality and so on. Paul D. MacLean, who some years ago distinguished and named the limbic system, states one of its functions is the capacity to "see with feeling."

The so-called anti-psychotic effect of neuroleptic drugs is a consequence of their effects on the limbic system. The limbic system is closely tied through reciprocal connections with the prefrontal cortex, the center for man's highest cognitive functions: will, insight, foresight, and creativity. Neuroleptic drugs, by blocking dopamine signal transmission, cause a serious disturbance in the frontal and limbic brain areas.

Schizophrenic treatment: old and new.—The old surgical treatment for schizophrenia involved cutting off connections between the frontal lobe and the limbic system. The new treatment with drugs instead of brain surgery similarly has the frontal and limbic areas of the brain as its target and blocks nerve transmission by chemical instead of physical means.

Mental disorders.—The various motor disorders, serious as they are in themselves, represent only the visible tip of an iceberg of mostly invisible brain damages. The corresponding drug induced disorders in the limbic system and the frontal and limbic areas are underestimated for at least two reasons:

1. Disturbances of higher mental functions, particularly of subjective states and experiencing, are often elusive and hard to verify objectively. It is well known in neuropsychology that even in cases of extensive brain damage, when persons close to the patient find his personality very much damaged, psychological tests and clinical examinations often fail to reveal any abnormality.

2. Disturbances of higher mental functions are often falsely blamed on the "mental illness" of the patient, when they are actually caused by the drugs. Incredible as it may seem, even the serious motor disorders that early on affected large numbers of patients, were overlooked for a long time by psychiatrists for this reason. The blindness of psychiatry to the evil effects of its own deeds is a blatant as it is tragic and cruel.

The Outer Man as an image of the Inner Man.—The motor disorders caused by neuroleptic drugs are thus also important as a concrete illustration of the consequences when a dopamine dependent brain system is exposed to a neuroleptic drug. We can see the outer man as an image of the inner man.

Ability to identify with.—The effect of the neuroleptic drugs in the frontal and limbic brain area is that the person loses his inspiration, his passions, his motivations, because he loses his ability to identify with himself, with others and with the rest of the perceived and remembered world. It is this drug effect that people on the drugs try to explain, when they say: "I am a zombie. I am an automaton. I have lost my taste, my reflexes. . . . I cannot read a book. I am a living dead."

All these are of course, natural complaints from a person with a crippled limbic system. These complaints from the neuroleptic drug victims are heartbreaking. Doubly heartbreaking because they receive no understanding from the drug psychiatrist in whose objective mind they do not even seem to register. And because they are so muted, *since the drug has taken away the very ability to protest, to care, and even to understand what has happened.*

Integrative action of mind.—The close interplay between the prefrontal cortex and the limbic system is necessary for the highest functions, the integrative action of the mind, for achieving personal unity and interpersonal community.

Without an intact frontal-limbic system it is impossible to overcome schizophrenia. It must be emphasized that the only way out of schizophrenia is forward. Returning to the naivety of previous repressions is impossible. All the sufferings, and everything experienced through a psychotic breakdown and expansion of consciousness, must be integrated in a further evolved organization of the personality. It is a creative endeavour that depends on the self possession of the full faculty of a person's mind.

2. Temporary Use of Neuroleptic Drugs is a Trap

We all know how difficult a psychotic person can be. Therefore it may sound reasonable when somebody suggest that drugs are perhaps "necessary during the acute stage." But that is a dubious, not to say fallacious proposal. It is so for both psychological and pharmacological reasons.

Psychological reasons:—"The Harvard Guide to Modern Psychiatry" (Day and Semrad 1978) warns: "Quickly resorting to drugs convinces the patient that his needs will not be met." In other words, the drug deprives him of the very thing he needs most: *hope.* It is essentially true to say schizophrenia is loss of hope, and conversely, that a person with a full measure of hope is not schizophrenic.

Now, during the psychotic crisis, the other person should be there with all his courage, imagination, and patience, all his solidarity and endurance. The patient himself needs his brain intact, and critically important work can be done.

If the psychosis is overcome without drugs, the patients' belief in himself and in other person will have increased. These things—self confidence a feeling of self-worth and a belief in other people—are in fact what he needs to definitely overcome with time his schizophrenia. If drugs are used he will learn the opposite lesson and be on the road of increasing drug dependence.

Pharmacological reasons.—For pharmacological reasons the patient will be on the very dangerous road of increasing drug dependence. The neuroleptic drugs induce specific changes in the frontal-limbic system that make a person more psychosis prone. It is like having a *psychosis-inducing agent* built into the brain.

This effect of neuroleptic drugs may subside more or less with time, if the drug is discontinued. But then it may be too late. Because of psychotic symptoms which are after effects of the drug, the conclusion has already been reached: "He needs the drug." The trap is a fact.

Combination of drugs and psychotherapy.—The doctor may suggest a combination of drugs and psychotherapy. Again this sounds reasonable, as compromises often do. But again, the proposal is dubious or fallacious. And it may be less than honest. The real motive of the doctor may be, consciously or unconsciously, that he wants a quick and easy solution, even at the expense of the true interest of the patient.

The later who, as we know, is more sensitive than most people to dishonesty, thus gets a double message of the very kind that can trigger or help trigger a psychotic break.

Perhaps it needs to be said at this point that, if the doctor, patient and relatives in a difficult situation should decide that a drug for right now, everything considered, is the best resort—and if they do this trying to fully recognize all problems, that is fully sincere and responsible—nobody outside the situation can pass any judgement. The tragedy is that they are likely to reach a wrong decision because of psychiatric misinformation.

Therefore it is essential to warn of these dangers and to remember how difficult it is to avoid short-term drug therapy becoming long term, with drug-caused personality deterioration and brain damage accumulated with time.

3. After a few years patients in drug-free programs are better by all criteria.

The drugs are effective against psychotic symptoms.—Numerous studies show that psychotic symptoms are reduced by neuroleptic drugs, and also that the risk of relapse into psychosis is reduced by maintenance drug treatment. There are thousands and thousands of reports that prove these points for all the neuroleptic drugs.

"Effective" drugs, but bad for the patient.—A simple thought experiment shows why the drugs, even though they are effective against symptoms, may be bad for the patient: Give neuroleptic drugs to infants. The result will be that crying and troublesome behavior is reduced or abolished. If maintenance drugs are given, the risk of relapse into crying and trouble-making will also be reduced. The infants are thus improved or cured by the drugs. We need no scientific studies to be convinced that the drugs, although "effective," are not good for our children.

We are convinced that after a few years children in drug-free programs will be better by all criteria. The very same is true for schizophrenic patients and for the same reasons. Let us now look at three scientific studies that support our third statement.

A. Family environment

British researches have studied the relapse rates of schizophrenic patients living with the family, i.e. with parents or with spouse. The emotional situation for each patient in his home was rated as favorable or unfavorable. One of the researchers, Julian P. Leff (1976) has reviewed these studies in a paper with the title "Schizophrenia and Sensitivity to the Family Environment."

The percentages found in the table below are relapse rates, i.e. the percentage of patients in each of the four categories that relapsed into psychosis. These numbers are taken from Figure 1 in the original paper.

	Patients not on drugs	*Patients on drugs*
Favorable emotional situation	15%	12%
Unfavorable situation	· 92%	53%

Patients on drugs in a "bad" environment relapsed more than three times as often as patients not on drugs in a "good" environment. (53% versus 15%) In the "good" environment, drugs seemed to make no difference for the risk of relapse. Such studies suggest that what schizophrenic patients need is *not* brain damaging neuroleptic drugs but a life situation in which they can survive and grow.

B. The Soteria project in San Francisco

Soteria house was a home-like residence in the San Francisco area. The staff consisted of non-professional therapists. There was room for six patients at a time. Young, newly schizophrenic persons were admitted to Soteria, and they stayed about five months.

Afterwards the Soteria patients were compared with similar patients admitted to a regular psychiatric clinic. The latter received neuroleptic drugs as usual. The Soteria patients received no or little drugs.

After two years, the Soteria patients were equal or superior to the control patients by all psychiatric measures. For example, after twelve months about 60% of the control subjects had relapsed, but only about 30% of the Soteria subjects had done so.

C. The Sater project in Sweden

In the early seventies, Barbro Sandin who was then a woman in her early forties, a mother and a housewife, came to the Sater hospital as a temporary employee. She was touched by a withdrawn, apathetic, drugged young schizophrenic man, whom she took into her home. Over the years the man recovered and returned to normal life.

Barbro Sandin was put in charge of a very small experimental ward where she and a small staff since 1973 have received and cared for a number of young schizophrenic men, mostly without drugs.

In 1980, fourteen schizophrenic patients, who started psychotherapy with Sandin in 1973-75, were compared with a similar number of matched control patients, who had been admitted to other wards of Sater hospital.

Sandin's patients were better by all measures. In the year 1980, the average control patient spent over five months in the hospital, while the average hospital stay for Sandin's patients was one month.

The non-drug patients required more care and attention during the first two to three years. In other words, the data confirm the thousands of psychiatric studies that show neuroleptic drugs to be effective in reducing psychotic symptoms and in preventing hospitalization. *But after the first two to three years the drug patients kept deteriorating while the non-drug patients improved.*

Correlation between "improvement" and long-term deterioration.— Neuroleptic drugs do make people quiet and apathetic and therefore reduce the short-term risk of psychiatric hospitalization. When such quiet and indifferent persons are called "improved" because they have fewer symptoms, this is indeed a perverse use of our gift of language. In order to see such terminology as the perversity it is, it may help to recall our thought experiment with drug treated infants and to observe that the short term "psychiatric improvement" is correlated with long-term personality deterioration.

D. Conclusions from the Soteria and Sater studies

We saw that the non-drug patients soon surpassed the drug patients even by psychiatric criteria. If we had measures for creativity, playfulness, lovability, sensitivity, spirituality, self-transcendence and so on, we cannot doubt, knowing what neuroleptic drugs do to a person, that the non-drug subjects would have stood as far superior.

Another immeasurable benefit, and the most important one for the future life of the non-drug subject is, first, that their brains and minds have not already been drug damaged, and second, that they have not developed a drug dependence that would mean accumulating brain damage with time. Remember that these are young persons with an expected life time (without drugs) of some forty to fifty years.

Why the amateurs were better.—The drug psychiatrists have had thirty years and thousands of centers in which to perfect their methods. And here we have these people in San Francisco and at Sater without pervious psychiatric training. Working under difficult circumstances they beat the results of professional psychiatry. How could the amateurs beat the professionals right away? There are two obvious reasons: The amateurs had more love. The professionals came with a poisoned group.

Only a beginning.—At Soteria and in Sandin's Sater ward, the patients got the kind of human reception that the problems of schizophrenia require, instead of a false medical response. Those results are only a beginning, a pointer in the right direction. The therapist at Soteria and Sater know better than anybody else that under better conditions, with more knowledge and support, they and their patients could have done much better still.

Our standard should be—not the dismal results of drug psychiatry—but the possible. Therefore the goal must be that every young schizophrenic person shall overcome his crisis and go on to fulfill the promises and possibilities of his life, in much the same imperfect way as the rest of us.

Nothing could help us more to approach that goal than a ban of neuroleptic drugs. Nothing except a ban of the attitudes to human problems and human beings that these drugs express and help perpetuate. The former is feasible and the latter is not. The former can be done my means of laws, if the political will exists.

THE SCAPEGOATING OF AMERICAN CHILDREN

By Peter R. Breggin, M.D.

The widespread use of psychiatric diagnosis, drugs and mental hospitalization raises serious questions about how we should deal with emotional stresses among children. Does psychiatry provide us answers—or an escape from own problems at the expense of our children?

The total number of psychiatric hospitalizations of youngsters under age eighteen rose from 82,000 to 112,000 in 1986, with most of the increase in private, for-profit institutions. The numbers continue to escalate, and the president of the American Academy of Child and Adolescent Psychiatry calls recent increases "enormous."

The July 7 issue of Psychiatric News, the official newspaper of the American Psychiatric Association, describes the abuses surrounding the psychiatric hospitalization of youngsters as scandalous. Paul Fink, the past president of the association is quoted as saying that "most of the criticism is justified." Vice Present Lawrence Hartmann, Chairman of the association's committee to study the problem, cited "short-sighted profiteering" by some private for-profit hospitals. These are strong statements from an organization devoted to furthering the interest and image of the profession.

Many pressures within psychiatry account for the growing hospitalization of children and adolescents. Financially, psychiatry has been doing relatively poorly since the 1970's, with psychiatrist ranking low on the medical income scale. Psychiatrists offering outpatient psychotherapy including child or family therapy, have been forced to cope with drastic cutbacks in health-insurance coverage for psychotherapy, and vigorous competing from less expensive non-medical therapists. Thus, they can find it more practical and remunerative to hospitalize youngsters for the duration of their insurance.

These same pressures have motivated psychiatry to place a growing emphasis on diagnosing children as mentally ill and treating them with drugs in or out of hospitals. Organizations such as the National Institute of Mental Health (NIMH) and the American Psychiatric Association have produced estimates that 20% or more of American children need psychiatric care. In the press, these pronouncements are reported as "scientific surveys" rather than as hardsell advertising and lobbying.

Many diagnosed children are treated with drugs, and as many as one million children are now prescribed Ritalin, a drug that sedates unruly, rebellious or troubled children, almost always boys. I have seen cases in which children and adolescents have been hospitalized as a result of the harmful effects of these drugs, which are addictive and can produce the very problems they are supposed to treat, inattention and hyperactivity.

Being a parent is the hardest job in the world and psychiatrist have no specific qualifications or job training in that field. When a parent comes to a modern psychiatrist for advice on how to deal with a child, there is little to assume that the psychiatrist ideas on the subject as sound as those of a kindly, experience neighbor or grandparent. Increasingly psychiatrists are predominantly trained in the "hard sciences," such as medicine, biochemistry, neuroanatomy and psychopharmacology. Naturally the psychiatrist will turn to solutions that he or she identifies with and knows best—diagnosis, drugs and hospitalization.

Other pressures for hospitalizing children lie outside of psychiatry but within the delivery of medical services in general. Burgeoning chains of for-profit hospitals have generated stiff competition for patients and have increasingly relied on relatively low-overhead, high-profit psychiatric beds.

In the 1960's many books, reports and commissions declared that public schools were becoming unfit for child consumption. Reforms were needed to deal with energetic young human beings cramped into under-staffed, boring, authoritarian classrooms. Few of these reforms took place. Instead the schools turned to psychiatric diagnosis and treatment as a solution to "behavior" and "learning' problems. A massive mental-health industry furthered the blaming of children for the problems of the family and society.

The September 1989 issue of Clinical Psychiatric News reports a study indicating that "the amount of trouble children are causing adults, particularly teachers, appears to be the driving force determining children's referral to mental health service." Those referred to psychiatric treatment were viewed as troublesome by teaches and were "more likely to be black, male, and poor."

Within the family, several trends have made it increasingly difficult for parents to rear their children. Two working parents have become the rule and latchkey children have become commonplace. A recent study shows that these children are twice as likely to turn to drugs.

Within broken families, harried mothers, often doubling as full-time wage earners, can find it extremely difficult to raise their children. A single working mother, with no father actively involved in childrearing, may find it nearly impossible to raise a rambunctious young boy. The child easily becomes diagnosed as suffering from "hyperactivity"(HA) or the latest fad diagnosis, "Attention Deficit Disorder (ADD). I have coined the diagnosis DADD—"Dad Attention Deficit Disorder"—to describe the situation of most "unmanageable" young boys.

As a psychiatrist, I am especially concerned about how the mental-health professions play into blaming the child for the problems of parents, families, schools, and society. Increasingly, schools and parents find it comforting to accept the new biological psychiatry approach that declares the youngster to be genetically and biologically defective, and suitable for psychiatric treatment, including drugs and hospitalization. Parents forsake responsibility for raising their own children, not only injuring their offspring, but depriving themselves of the satisfaction of being good parents. The children are stigmatized and feel to blame for problems that are almost wholly beyond their control.

We need a dramatic turnabout in which we, as a responsible adults, retake responsibility for our children.

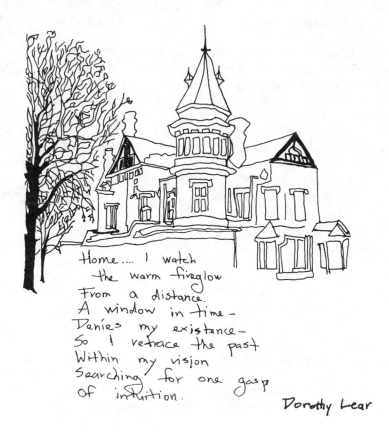

Home.... I watch
the warm fireglow
From a distance.
A window in time —
Denies my existence —
So I retrace the past
Within my vision
Searching for one gasp
of intuition.

Dorothy Lear

ANOTHER UNVEILING; ABUSE BACKGROUNDS OF PSYCHIATRIC SURVIVORS AND THEIR NEGLECT BY MENTAL HEALTH SYSTEMS

Stephen M. Rose, Ph. D.
State University of New York at Stony Brook

Despite increased reporting on domestic violence, incest, and other childhood sexual and physical abuse, most mental health professionals appear *not* to recognize their existence. Research indicates that psychiatric survivors share their experiences of childhood sexual and/or physical abuse when they are asked about it—even though these brutal facts of life rarely appear in medical records. (References 1-5). One research team (5) found that "Many patients commented to the interviewer that they had never told anyone about the abuse because they had never been asked about it."

Recently, we completed a study of psychiatric survivors who were participating in an Intensive Case Management Program (ICM) in Suffolk County, New York (6). We found:

—Over half of the participants grew up in homes where one or more adults had severe alcohol problems.

—Nearly one-fourth of the people (four times more women than men) were incest victims.

—Half of the women and one-fifth of the men were sexually abused as children.

—Half were physically abused as children, almost all of them by some one in their immediate family.

Among those who are Adult Children of Alcoholics (ACOA), all types of abuse increased significantly, including gender bias. Incest victimization happened to one-third of the ACOA clients compared to 12% of the other. Four-fifths of the incest victims in the study are ACOAs. Almost two-thirds of the women and almost one-third of the ACOAs were sexually abused as children. ACOA backgrounds, when linked to other types of abuse and to inappropriate or non-existent treatment, also directly relate to future histories of substance abuse and to repeated hospitalizations.

None of the eighty-nine people voluntarily participating in this study ever received appropriate response to their abuse experiences from mental health professionals. Routine inquiry about abuse experience was not done in inpatient, outpatient or other community settings. Only three people ever brought their experience up, and then it was not acknowledged by mental health service providers. The group of people responding to our questions were hospitalized many times, in many different hospitals. They attended countless treatment sessions by psychiatrists and other designated therapists. Many went regularly to day treatment programs, partial hospitalization services, continuing treatment or vocational programs. None of these places *ever* asked about people's experiences or responded to the people in the few instances that occurred where clients wanted to talk about what had happened to them.

Neglect, abandonment or invalidation by mental health and many other service providers occurs routinely, even when the intent to commit harm never enters to consciousness of the professionals involved. As one research team (3) noted,

> professionals' not initiating a discussion of the topic can transmit a message confirming the patients' belief in the need to deny the reality of their experience. Patients' attempts to deal with their distress, then, can take even more indirect paths, leading to the development of severe and confusing symptoms.

Confirmation appears in the work of another research group (5) who concluded that neglect of abuse experiences, even when unintended, enhances the damage caused by the abuse itself: "In fact, the longer the abuse goes untreated, the greater the repression and the more ingrained the symptomatology."

Other researchers (3,9) have verified that hospitalizations occur to abused people because of greater severity, longer duration, and a greater number of the types of abuse, not because of any factors attributed to the victim beyond the abuse experience itself.

In this context of extraordinary horror, psychiatric misdiagnosis is routine. When the central reality of a person's life cannot be discovered by those conducting psychiatric assessments, the professionals' only resort remains their self-perpetuating and self-fulfilling diagnostic prophecies. Most frequently, for example, acts of "disassociation" that people have created to preserve themselves in the face of oppressive abuse and its ongoing secrecy or mystification yield diagnoses of various borderline personality categories. Another typical example can be seen from the experience of people who cut themselves to regain control over the excruciating reliving of an incest attack, only to be labelled suicidal without any effort to ask about the reasons behind the self-mutilation.

We believe that outcomes which disguise the original abusive oppression and rationalize service system functioning exist in typical mental health program evaluations. The disguise comes from failing to disclose how systems (schools, child protective services, hospitals, and private physicians, among other) fail abused children and adults, thus leaving the impression that destructive behavior is an expression of mental illness.

Our data indicate that over one-half of the ICM clients have substance abuse histories; that three-fourths have frequent rehospitalizations and/or appearances in psychiatric emergency rooms; and that one-third self-mutilate. These data, in our view, must be seen as *system-produced*: that the people whose lives reflect these characteristics overwhelmingly come from the multiple abuse backgrounds we have described *and from backgrounds of neglect and abandonment by mental health and many other systems*. Repeated hospitalizations, substance abuse and self-mutilation occur when childhood abuse and system neglect interact.

Some progressive work has been done. In a growing number of places, some recognition exists. Childhood sexual and physical abuse as well as growing up in families permeated by alcohol and drug abuse are seen as externally imposed, inflicted on powerless children or adults by more powerful, oppressive people.

Further examination indicates the commonplace secrecy involved where the abuse occurred within the family. Under these circumstances, deeply felt perceptions of mistrust of authority and difficulties in participating in positive, trusting relationships have resulted along with permeating self-contempt. Often, victims construct extensive self-blaming rationalizations for the attacks.

The diagnosis used in some of the more progressive work, *Post Traumatic Stress Disorder*, indicates that trauma was inflicted by an external source and caused lasting suffering. Use of this diagnosis broadens the possibilities for positive intervention, particularly because it establishes the validity of self-help groups (10). Open disclosure in mutual support groups, struggles to externalize repressed tyranny, and efforts to break away from self-blaming rationalizations characterize group tasks. The limitations of this approach involve its potential cooptation by professionals who see the experiences of victims as pathology rather than as potential strength as survivors *or who see the acts of abuse as simply confined to individuals or families rather than attributes of our culture.*

Numerous implications exist. Foremost among them is the failure of psychiatry to recognize, validate, and respond to abuse backgrounds as central facts in the lives of the people to whom they have assigned psychiatric labels. Routine inquiry for abuse backgrounds coupled to appropriate interventions, grounded in mutual support groups and the process of transformation from victim to survivor, must be developed. Centers for Abuse Survivors, with significant participation or operation by other survivors, can replace crisis residences and act as alternatives to hospitalization for many people. But responding to abuse requires going beyond direct intervention to attacking its causes and its rationalizers. That escalates the reasons for the fight against poverty and sexism, and any form of battering, and against a restrictive concept of psychiatry which cannot legitimate the objective bases for suffering.

REFERENCES

1. Post, R.D., Willett, A.B., Franks, R.D., House, R.M., Back, S.M., & Weissberg, M.P. (1980). A preliminary report on the prevalence of domestic violence among psychiatric inpatients. **American Journal of Psychiatry**, 137, 974-975.
2. Carmen, E.H., Rieker, P.P. & Mills, T. (1984). Victims of violence and psychiatric illness. **American Journal of Psychiatry**, 141, 378-383.
3. Bryer, J.B., Nelson, B.A., Miller, J.B. & Krol, P.A. (1987). Childhood sexual and physical abuse as a factor in adult psychiatric illness. **American Journal of Psychiatry**, 144, 1426-1430.
4. Jacobson, A. & Richardson, B. (1987). Assault experience of 100 psychiatric inpatients: Evidence of the need for routine inquiry. **American Journal of Psychiatry**, 144, 908-913.
5. Craine, L.S., Henson, C.E., Colliver, J.A. & MacLean, D.G. (1988). Prevalence of a history of sexual abuse among female psychiatric patients in a state hospital system. **Hospital and Community Psychiatry**, 39, 300-304.
6. Rose, S.M., Peabody, C.G. & Stratigeas, B. (1989). **Client-driven outcomes and system responses: Research report #1.** Mimeographed. School of Social Welfare, State University of New York at Stony Brook.
7. Rose, S.M. & Black, B.L. (1985). **Advocacy and empowerment: Mental health care in the community.** London: Routledge & Kegan Paul, 1985.
8. Summit, R.C. (1983). The child sexual abuse accommodation syndrome. **Child Abuse & Neglect**, 7, 177-193.
9. Herman, J., Russell, D., & Trocki, K. (1986). Long term effects of incestuous abuse in childhood. **American Journal of Psychiatry**, 143, 1293-1296.
10. Patten, S.B., Gatz, Y.K., Jones, B. & Thomas, D.L. (1989). Posttraumatic stress disorder and the treatment of sexual abuse. **Social Work**, 34, 197-203.

VIEWPOINT

U.S.A., 13 Years Later

Marcio Vasconcellos Pinheiro

IN OCTOBER 1974, after living in Baltimore for 16 years, I went back to my home town, Belo Horizonte, in the State of Minas Gerais, Brazil. By then I was a citizen of the United States and a Board Certified Psychiatrist, and I wanted to bring back there some of what I had learned here. In 1987 I returned to the United States, and I want to set down my impressions of what has happened here since I left.

When I first arrived in the U.S., in 1958, I was a young physician looking for post-graduate training. I went through a rotating internship and a residency in psychiatry after a brief passage in internal medicine. I was coming from a country where psychiatry was mainly biological in the best European tradition and where psychoanalysis, quite divorced from psychiatry, had a very strong Kleinian bent. After a residency at the Psychiatric Institute of the University of Maryland, I completed my personal analysis and then worked at Sheppard and Enoch Pratt Hospital and in private practice for 7 years. I learned the "dynamic American psychiatry" of the 50s and 60s, inspired by psychoanalytic principles and heavily anchored in the social sciences.

It was this kind of psychiatry that I decided to bring to my home town when I went back in 1974. To some extent, I think I was able to do that. In Belo Horizonte I founded the first psychiatric day hospital, I started the first psychiatric inpatient unit that – like the day hospital – functioned on a psychosocial model, and I completed my psychoanalytic training with the Circulo Psicanalitico de Minas Gerais.

After 13 years in Belo Horizonte I decided to return to Baltimore. Now, for the second time, I am going through the experience of entering this culture, one that had been familiar to me but that has changed a great deal during my absence. It is about this experience that I want to write, while it is still fresh in my mind and before I get so immersed in the American way of life that I lose the perspective that I now have.

First I will comment on Baltimore and its people. Then I will say something about contemporary psychiatry in the United States, and finally I will make some remarks on being a psychiatrist in America today.

BALTIMORE, 1987

In the last 13 years Baltimore has changed a lot. The first time I went downtown after my return I realized that everything was different. The old and decaying Baltimore of the 60s had been rebuilt to become a very pleasant and lively city: a tourist attraction. I am not only speaking of the Inner Harbor, with its shops and restaurants, the National Aquarium, the

Marcio Vasconcellos Pinheiro graduated from the School of Medicine, University of Minas Gerais in Belo Horizonte, Brazil, and completed his residency in psychiatry at the Psychiatric Institute of the University of Maryland and his psychoanalytic training at the Criculo Piscanalitico of Minas Gerais, Brazil. He has worked both in the United States and in Brazil, and he is now a Staff Psychiatrist at the Southeastern Community Mental Health Clinic in Baltimore County and at Springfield Hospital Center, Sykesville, MD 21784.

The author is thankful to Dr. Bruce Hershfield, Superintendent of Springfield Hospital Center, for revising the manuscript, and to Elderburg's branch of the Carroll County Public Library for introducing him to word processing.

Science Center and the other attractions in that area. I am including the whole downtown area. There is a new Convention Center. The Civic Center has been renovated. There is a new Symphony Hall with one of the best orchestras in the country. The Lyric Theater has been modernized. The Center Stage, which struggled so much in the past, has moved to a new and better location. Baltimore, no doubt, lost some of its provincial flavor of the past in the process of becoming a more modern city. Thirteen years ago Baltimoreans didn't have much motivation to go downtown. Tourists passed directly through the Harbor Tunnel without taking a look at the town. Today, things are quite different.

Side by side with the new, some of the old remains. The Memorial Stadium with the Orioles (the Colts have gone) is still there. I understand that Maryland is planning to spend considerable money on a new sports complex. Johns Hopkins University and the professional schools of the University of Maryland have both expanded. The Enoch Pratt Free Library remains a landmark. That fine natural resource the Chesapeake Bay is as beautiful as ever.

I can't help but be impressed by the wealth of this country and by the money that is being invested to rebuild American towns, opening new opportunities for business.

Baltimore, no doubt, has changed for the better.

BALTIMOREANS, 1987

Baltimoreans are more restless and competitive than ever. The population has increased. The traffic is heavier. The speed of life is faster. Americans have always been a very fast-moving people when compared to Brazilians, but I am now perplexed by the fact that American life is even faster than it was. It is difficult for me to conceive of a society more individualistic and competitive than this one. People now have not one but two jobs. Husband and wife are working outside the home, and day care for children has become institutionalized as an important dimension of childrearing.

Technology has made great progress. Computers are everywhere. They are storing data and giving instant answers to all questions. They are shaping American life with hard data and endless statistics. They facilitate the life of scientists in every field. Even the American language is gradually being molded by computers, so that Americans are learning how to talk in a way that computers understand.

Living in such a technological and economically conservative society, Americans hope, through the hard sciences, to resolve all human ills and imperfections, making everything and everybody function at their highest level of efficiency. This aim connects with a greater intolerance for people's limitations, disabilities, mistakes and failures. There is no place in America today for poor performance. There is a great intolerance toward people with chronic disabilities who need continuing care. Everybody must be a success.

Americans are now used to throwing away defective products. Nothing is worth repairing. What doesn't function properly is rapidly replaced. This attitude may be expanding toward people in general. The replacement of faulty human organs, for instance, is considered great progress, but continuing assistance for the chronically ill is considered much less worth doing, even an undesirable endeavor, a wasteful use of the GNP. The front pages of the newspapers are full of headlines on organ transplants and the accompanying technology, while little attention is paid to the needs of the chronically disabled mental patients.

The conservative philosophy is at its peak. Free enterprise is the official creed. "Privatization" is the main theme. There is no room in this country today for any kind of liberal, collective or socialist thinking. Such thinking is immediately equated with anti-Americanism even though we know that the United States trails behind in social programs when compared with the other industrialized countries in the free world. The main notion is that each one must fend for himself, and the expectation is that everyone is able to join the work force and become self-supporting.

PSYCHIATRY, U.S.A., 1987

Psychiatry reflects what goes on in the larger society. In the last 13 years psychiatry in America has also changed. Following the present social trend, American psychiatry became simple, fast, exact and, above all, economic (nobody wants to foot the bill).

While in Brazil I followed the psychiatric developments here. I knew about the *DSM-III* (now the *DSM-III-R*) and the efforts made by the American Psychiatric Association to improve communication between clinicians and researchers through this highly objective classification of mental disorders. The *DSM-III-R* indeed reflects contemporary American life: it is short, pragmatic, objective, measurable and ready to enter computers to become statistics.

The progress notes on patients records are now written in a stereotyped, problem-oriented way: the Individualized Treatment Plan. This ITP, which I understand came from the National Institute of Mental Health—that is, from Washington—has become the psychiatric language of the country. It took away from the psychiatrists the freedom they once had to describe their patient's responses to treatment. But what is more dangerous, it took away from humans their most important asset: their subjective world. Insight, once considered the one fringe benefit for a psychiatric patient, is no longer considered an important therapeutic goal simply because it can't be measured in a language that computers understand. Complex variables are being reduced to measurable items, forcing psychiatrists to think computer language instead of their own.

It was quite an experience to be part, for the first time, of a treatment team trying to work within the constraints of an ITP. It felt like working in an assembly line where emphasis was placed on fixing parts of observable behavior at the expense of the patient's inner life. This tedious, repetitious, futile attempt to reduce human beings to problems to be resolved is now a nationwide procedure that has no credibility in terms of reflecting what really goes on in a patient's treatment. Has American psychiatry become an exact science? Have American psychiatrists become mere bureaucrats?

American psychiatry is also importing a new language from the business world. This is understandable in a country where business is the greatest model for personal success. Some new words in the psychiatric scenario include "quality control," "utilization review" and "risk management." They seem more applicable to industry than to clinical work. I recently went to a conference on quality control in a local hospital, and I was amazed to see the degree of sophistication, time, money and talent that were being spent in this endeavor. I left the place wondering about the limits of what these practices could really measure despite all the meticulously collected recorded data.

I also knew, while I was away, about the rising costs of medical care in the United States. It seems that in the last 10 years numerous efforts have been made to reduce these costs, but so far no consensus has been reached on what kind of care should be available to the American people. There has been an enormous push toward quick, economic and profitable interventions by the private sector, but at the same time, there is a nagging awareness that an increasing segment of the population depends on the public sector for the continuing care they need. At the same time the public sector has been moving toward deinstitutionalization, privatization and deprofessionalization. The main goal is also obviously economic. In order to justify this movement the concept of "chronic patients" is being replaced by the notion of "treatment resistant patients," the implication being that everybody, if properly treated by "modern psychiatry," can be an autonomous, self-supporting, hard-working citizen. Public money that otherwise would be allocated for the long-term care of this population is being spent in other, more "patriotic" endeavors. It is also worth mentioning in this context that as the government implements these plans, the number of homeless, psychiatrically disturbed Americans is on the increase.

But the change that has grabbed my attention the most since I have returned is the turn that American psychiatry has taken in the direction of the brain. The hard sciences are now in the forefront of the research efforts, and the soft social sciences, including psychoanalysis, are being pushed to a very distant corner. Today, the hopes of patients, families and professionals are being placed on biological research and what this could bring about in terms of more effectively (less costly and time-consuming) preventing and treating mental disorders. Psychosocial factors, once so popular, now seem almost forgotten.

This emphasis on the brain, legitimate as it may be, is being misused defensively by patients, families and professionals alike. One patient recently said to me: "I am upset today because of my brain chemistry. Would you please adjust my medication?" A mother recently said to me about her schizophrenic son: "Poor son; we just hope that someday you doctors will find a way to fix his brain chemistry." Even professionals are defensively focusing on the psychopharmacological dimensions of treatment to the exclusion of all others. The tendency to consider mental illness as a chemical imbalance is so strong that it is becoming difficult to invite patients, families, professionals and society to look at their participation in the development and treatment of mental disorders. Once a patient is defined as sick in his brain, the understanding of what is wrong is fixated on the medical model and nobody is interested in what may be going on in his or her mind. American patients don't have a personal history any longer, their relationships with significant others are not a major concern, and their subjective world is of no interest. They simply have problems. American psychiatry forgot what it learned from people like Adolf Meyer, Harry Stack Sullivan or Frieda Fromm-Reichmann, to mention just a few who contributed toward the understanding of severe mental disorders and to the development of what has been known worldwide as American dynamic psychiatry.

Another interesting related change is the current practice of American psychiatrists in labeling more people as suffering from mood disorders. I understand this is happening for good reasons, and I am aware that even before I left in 1974, British psychiatrists seemed to be diagnosing more mood disorders than their American colleagues. But maybe one of the reasons for the change is the better prognosis and quicker treatment of mood disorders since the advent of lithium. Many "schizophrenic" patients are now being diagnosed as having mood disorders and are being treated with lithium.

There also have been other drastic changes in the way people are being diagnosed. In the past we used to arrive at one major diagnosis—that is, the diagnosis that would best fit a given patient even if the patient showed traits of other diagnostic categories. For instance, we would label a patient with certain symptoms as schizophrenic even if he showed some an-

tisocial acting out and alcohol abuse at a given stage of the illness. Today, such a patient would be diagnosed as suffering from schizophrenia, antisocial personality and alcohol abuse. This fragmentation of diagnosis is leading to fragmentation of treatment, and patients are frequently being placed in competing therapeutic programs. Such a schizophrenic patient, for instance, would receive antipsychotic medication while at the same time participating in group interventions designed for the treatment of antisocial personalities and alcohol abusers or dependents. I am not sure if this multiple therapeutic approach constitutes good clinical practice. I am treating a borderline patient who shows some masochistic, self-mutilating tendencies; because of her multiple symptoms, she is now in outpatient treatment both in a sexual disorders program and a community mental health clinic, requiring an enormous amount of communication among the professionals involved.

The relationship between doctors and patients has also changed. Doctors are more defensive. This is related to the increasing number of lawsuits against them—a part of the prevailing cultural trend of demanding perfection from everyone, which is accompanied by the feeling that one is always due compensation when things go wrong.

Also clear today is the influence of third-party payers in psychiatric practice. Government advisory groups and insurance companies are now determining what constitutes good clinical practice although their major interest, dictated by economic concerns, is not always related to the patient's well being. Americans are refusing to accept certain costs inherent to living in a society. The ideology of "autonomy regardless of circumstances" is undermining any attempt to improve public psychiatry.

Available funds are now the main determinants of treatments. It is distressing to see how patients are being shipped from program to program in order to comply with funding. This is interfering with adequate therapeutic planning, particularly for patients who need continuing long-term care. Anyone who observes the readmission rate in psychiatric hospitals realizes what some patients are now going through. Third-party payers are also demanding an enormous amount of paper work as a condition for payment. As a consequence, records become more important than patients. A colleague recently said to me: "In this hospital, if you lose a patient, that is bad. But if you lose a patient's records, you must be prepared to leave town."

Finally, I want to say a few words about the role of the psychiatrists in the mental health team. By becoming psychobiologists who are experts in psychopharmacology, psychiatrists have lost their traditional role as leaders in the mental health field. Such a psychiatrist is now instead just another member of the team—a team that can be led by a social worker, a psychologist, a nurse or even a lay administrator. He is also losing his identity as a psychotherapist as he holds on to his image as a prescribing physician. It is difficult to predict how the mental health team will evolve in the future and what the role of the psychiatrist will be upon it.

WHY THE U.S.A.?

Perhaps, to a large extent, the United States still remains a land of opportunities. But I certainly don't feel that way when I compare this country today with the one I left in 1974. Things have changed drastically, and I am puzzled by the enormous paradox of a country that has improved so much materially and yet seems to provide so much less care for its people, particularly the less fortunate ones.

Last winter, I was walking with a Brazilian physician along the beautiful Inner Harbor in Baltimore. It was about 6 o'clock in the evening. I was proud of what I was showing my friend of American life. The place was all dressed up for Christmas. Lights everywhere made it look warm and friendly. We passed through Santa Claus's highly decorated glass house. Outside, a line of happy-looking children were waiting their turn to take the traditional picture with the kind man. We crossed the street to enter a new shopping center, bursting with holiday decorations. At the door, a tall, miserable, disheveled black man was shouting disconnected statements in a desperate and agitated way. For a moment I was embarrassed until these thoughts came to my mind:

Problem: Shouting continuously in front of a shopping center.

Goals: Decrease shouting to three times a week.

Intervention: Prolixin Decanoate, 1 cc (25 mg) IM.

That is all.

How far can this country continue to move in the direction it is going before people realize that they are missing something?

Since I returned to the U.S.A. I have come across a whole new generation of psychiatrists, coming from the best medical schools, who are unable to pay attention to their patients' subjective worlds. They have been trained to look at people's outsides: behavior is what counts, in the best American, mechanistic, pragmatic tradition. In my opinion, American psychiatry, while considering itself more scientific, has returned to unfortunate attitudes of the pre-Freudian days. In some respects has changed for the worse in terms of patient care.

I have spent some time trying to understand these changes. I believe that they have a lot to do with shifting priorities in this country. The question seems to be where to spend the country's wealth. As more money is shifted to protect big business and defense contracts, less is left for vulnerable citizens who have no influence in the political power structure, among them the sick, the disabled, the elderly and the minorities. The pendulum has swung too far to the right. Could there be a relationship between the political right and the emphasis on biological psychiatry?

My hope is that, sooner or later, the distortions that I perceive will be corrected and priorities will again be set placing people as the main consideration. This is not an unfounded hope. After all, despite the many imperfections of the socioeconomic system of the United States, it has been able to function under one and the same Constitution since its beginnings. The system has remained viable because of its flexibility in allowing changes that the people wanted. This country has always searched for answers without falling prey to radical beliefs. The possibility of changes, along with the freedom to work for them, makes it still exciting to be part of the U.S.A.

[*Editor's Note:* This article is excerpted from notes I took while at a conference delivered by Jean Vanier, a French Canadian who founded the L'Arche movement. Mentally handicapped people who had been institutionalized are given homes in the community.]

THE CRY OF THE BROKEN

The Cry

The feeling of abandonment is so deep within us. The cry of abandonment and the cry of no place are the same. It can lead one to feel that I'm guilty, that I have evil in me. Children say, I'm no good. Or, one can finger point and say, You are evil.

Feelings of not being wanted become a cry of abandonment. The broken self image causes anguish, inner pain and agitation, feelings of loneliness and confusion. This leads to anorexia, bulimia, sleeplessness, violence. Depression and psychosis can be a projection of this. One flips into the dream so they don't feel the inner pain.

The cry of anguish can trigger pain in the person at times. It gives him the capacity to hurt others, to kill. In the pain of the battered child, the barriers are down and they can love or hate. They make the discovery: I can really hate. The body remembers; it remembers every lack of touch and love. The body cries out. The body can close off in a world of intellectualization.

The Point of Pain

We need to get close to our own cry. There's a *point of pain* within each of us, that which we are the most frightened. But path of pain leads to resurrection. The point of meeting a saving Presence and the point of pain are close.

Productivity vs. Fecundity

Productivity is where we make things, do things and then say, It's *mine* to give away. Fecundity is where we give life and take risks. To love is to bring people to freedom, to grow, and not to hold. Love is reaccessing its frontiers all the time. Loving people doesn't mean to do something— that could stifle. It's showing a person that they are beautiful and revealing how precious they are.

Disability is a sign of death and brokenness, so we reject the handicapped. While in their pain, people don't want you to give solutions. They want compassion, for us to walk with them. We enter into the darkness of one's inner brokenness, not to condemn but to give all that is broken to God.

Living in Illusion

The poor are those who can't cope and cry out. The rich have a satisfaction in self. They believe they don't need help. We must come to the truth of ourselves. We can live in the most fantastic illusion in community, flattering each other. We don't see our darkness, our wounds. The quiet illusion is that we are the best, that we are not poor. We cover up the truth. We say we have the knowledge, the truth. But this certitude shows we are in error. The point of truth is that we are hypocrites in various ways. We all are broken.

The Stranger Within

The fear of abandonment is the deepest cry; it makes us paralyzed. We don't need to prove or defend ourselves. We are broken and we are loved. We grow through brokenness. Carl Jung said, "Why not see Christ in our own poverty, the hidden stranger in us?" There is a stranger inside of us. Welcome him and he welcomes us. He is present in our Point of Pain.

The Flight from Pain/Walking through the Pain

Our Western Civilization is based on a flight from pain into dream, distraction. Yet, the flight from pain causes the greatest pain. You are called to penetrate it and find the seeds of resurrection. There's a fecundity in pain. We are part of the redemption. Pain has meaning—stand with it.

There are two fundamental cries: the cry of the child and the cry of the dying person. The wounded person provokes in us the cry. Walk through the pain, and learn to cry out to the Spirit.

There's a mystery of our inner pain that is brought to the point of a cry. There's a mystery in the cry. There is one who answers the cry and names the cry. It's the *Paraclete*, the Spirit; she will hold you.

Going Down the Ladder

You can only remain in community if you discover you are poor. The only important thing is compassion, to share. Know what to do when abandonment comes to the surface of consciousness.

When we feel the vibration of trust, when someone trusts us deeply, something is born in us. The world of aggression puts barriers up, but at L'Arche the handicapped person immediately gives trust.

Emotional illness is a problem in relating. They test you to see if you are made of paper or rock.

We are being asked to go down the ladder. If we go up, it's to walk down with more security and enter into covenant relationships. Live in the expression of play with the handicapped; be a child with them. Don't do anything big. Just live with them. We need places of welcome, not professors of theology.

On Mediocrity

There's a great deal of persecution in this country. It's subtle. The mediocrity in the community is frightened of anyone who is not mediocre. The community can be places of death. The pain of children is being enticed to a world of broken values. There's an unconscious persecution of our selves.

We can't say woe to the rich because the rich will get angry. Don't get caught up in compromise. The silence of good hurts more than the torture of the bad. There's a mystery in our own mediocrity.

Community

There are three gifts of growth: one is community, a network of convenated relationships. You would not have chosen some of them. There's a mystery of community, a discovery of forgiveness. The foundation of community is forgiveness. The community is to encourage growth, to confirm and challenge. But it can only challenge if it comforts and confirms.

There is no community without prayer. Prayer is to say Father, which says I trust. The first part of prayer is the cry, the cry of the wound. The second part is the prayer of rest, of bridegroom and lover. The cry leads to rest. Prayer finally leads to an offering. Prayer becomes the sacrament of the poor.

[*Editor's Note:* Michele Dear recently died from an overdose of sleeping pills after being denied admittance to a hospital. Some of her friends believe this was due to a hospital employee's retaliation for her criticisms of the hospital's policies and treatment of patients. Michele filed and won two lawsuits against a local psychiatrist for illegal use of seclusion, and the county Board of Education for discriminating against her because of her psychiatric background. Her strength as an advocate got her a place on the Governor's Advisory Board for Mental Health. One of her articles was published in the *Psychosocial Rehabilitation Journal,* Volume IX in July of 1985, which is reprinted below. Her memorial service was well attended by advocates in the area, several of whom spoke in her remembrance.]

HOSPITAL VS. HOSPITAL(ITY)

Recently I had the pleasure, yes, pleasure, of being hospitalized for an appendectomy. I would like to tell you about some of the little things that happened and didn't happen, because they brought out a lot of feelings and amazement and made all the difference between this brief stay and one of my seven previous, unpleasant, psychiatric hospitalizations (including three at this particular hospital).

I arrived at the emergency room on Sunday at 3:00 A.M. By 6:00 A.M. and after numerous tests, I was informed I would need immediate surgery for appendicitis. The doctor explained the surgery needed, gave me a consent form and even EXPLAINED it, let me READ it, and only then asked me to sign it.

After surgery, I was brought to my room where someone sat with me for over one hour to make sure I was all right. The last time I wasn't deemed to be doing all right in another section of this hospital, I agonized in seclusion for eleven days.

Nurses appeared throughout my stay, to check, or, yes, just to chat. Conversation wasn't limited to details of my physical condition; normal exchanges took place—I was a whole person. There was no unending banter on my depression or impulses. The thought began creeping into my mind that here I was in a hospital and these people were treating me like a human being, while at the same time I was a patient. I thought, *My God, It Can Be Done!* For the first time the word "patient" didn't sound dirty; "doctor" meant help, and "nursing staff" didn't even sound too bad. There was no condescending attitude displayed because I was physically not at my best. Why should there have been? Actually, it would have been the perfect opportunity to take advantage of my situation. I, a physically "laid-up" person, seemed to be afforded the deserved respect and courtesy that go along with being human. Yet, I was the same person who was sitting in that hospital's seclusion room one year ago. What had changed so? Here I was in that hospital with nursing staff being pleasant and making time for me! I was both human AND a patient on this unit. How unusual; I was not accustomed to such things.

I was given pain medication, which merely served to knock me out and actually did nothing for the pain (much the same experience I had with major tranquilizers). Later, when they offered more, I said no and that was that, as it should be. Imagine, I didn't want medication ordered by the doctor and no one made a big deal. My rights and personal judgement had been respected. It was beginning to sink in.

Monday, I began taking my regular medication as I now was eating solid foods. The nurse brought it in and left it, telling me to take it when it was convenient. They even use a different language on medical units, I was now finding out. She didn't watch me swallow it, check under my tongue, or try any of that other nonsense. I had a physical problem and my mental capacities were not in question. The old routines that many of us know all too well did not seem to apply when some type of emotional/mental illness label is not attached.

No staff members took it upon themselves to reevaluate the medication I was taking at the time of admission or at any time during my stay. I told them the amount I took and got it—they didn't even ask who prescribed it. MY WORD was enough.

I asked for aspirin and got it. That may not sound like a big deal, but it was to someone with chronic headaches like myself. In my previous experience it has always taken a minimum of several hours just to get a doctor's order. Then to actually get the aspirin is another ordeal, because, I always seem to ask the nurse that is "not on meds," or is too busy writing notes, or is on her way to lunch, or is "escorting" someone to the laundry room, or doing rounds, or about to put someone in sheetpacks, or take someone from the seclusion room, or, or, or. . . .

I was allowed to watch television past 11:00 P.M. In fact, I watched all night on one occasion. I was allowed to smoke in my room. My privacy was respected. People knocked when they wanted to come in. Nobody shined a flashlight in my face every hour on the hour at night, yet the nurses were still somehow able to determine that I was alive. I even had a bathroom in my room, none of this down-the-hall business.

Even the student nurses were different. I didn't feel watched, stared or goggled at, feared, or treated like some kind of oddity or weirdo merely because I was in the hospital. Somehow, I didn't feel like someone's term paper—that I was just there for practice.

A volunteer came into the room several times to see if I needed anything and to check how things were going—how nice. From past experience as a volunteer at this hospital, I can tell you there are NO volunteers of their psychiatric unit, although I was never given a straightforward reason as to why.

And then that fateful time of discharge came, only on this unit it wasn't so fateful. I was actually being rushed out. There were no delays, even though my insurance company could have easily been milked for awhile longer—how ethical. The doctor informed me of several physical limitations including driving and heavy lifting, but I could best determine what I could or couldn't do. That's right, it was my body, and I was told I could best determine what was right for me. Other than the discharge date, after-planning was mine alone. I was going home unable to drive, go to school, or do my clinical work, and I couldn't even walk too well, but it was okay. I was getting over a normal malady which I would adjust to as necessary with no reason for unwarranted concern.

Within one week of leaving the hospital and the day after I finished writing this, the final pleasure, which I took as an insult, occurred. A questionnaire arrived from the president of community relations at the hospital asking for my "frank opinion about your recent stay. . . .Your answers and comments will help us pinpoint the way in which this hospital can improve its services." You may ask why I was insulted. On my three previous hospitalizations I never received any such form, and I was never asked for an opinion, much less to comment on my treatment. Once, maybe, was an oversight, but not three times. Is one's treatment on a psychiatric unit of no concern to the hospital or the community relations department it has set up to be concerned with such matters? Did my opinion not matter anyhow because I was only an incompetent "mental" patient, therefore incapable of answering meaningfully or with any level of sensibility? Or was it they just weren't/aren't even interested in improving their psychiatric services? Maybe they just don't care? In actuality, none of these are meant as questions. If they were, I would answer TRUE to ALL of the above.

I have no great insights or conclusions concerning this experience. I can only tell you there were countless subtle and not-so-subtle, small and not-so-small differences and nuances in the way things are done that I touched upon merely in terms of simple, basic courtesies and respect due all individuals, whatever unit they are on. The question to me is both infuriating and frustrating: what the hell is going on? Civilized behavior seems too easy to screw up, so why then is it so different down the hall? All I can say is that the differences appear immense between a human patient and a mental patient, even in the "best" of hospitals.

GLOSSARY

Akathisia: a motor difficulty caused by neuroleptic drugs where the person experiences agitation, restlessness, and an inability to stay still.

Anti-psychotics: a group of psychiatric drugs formerly called heavy tranquilizers. Their principle action is to block dopamine receptor sites in the brain. The drugs have a wide variety of effects on one's motor and hormonal systems as well as higher processes such as creativity.

Antidepressants: a group of drugs chemically related to the anti-psychotics whose specific mechanism of action is said to be unknown. They also impair receptor sites in the brain.

Chemotherapy: a medical treatment that began in the early 1900's that uses artificially-manufactured chemicals. They usually work by impairing transmissions of the nervous system, and have generalized effects. The theory is that a "physiological balance" will thus be attained. Although the word is generally known to describe anti-cancer drugs, much of modern medicine uses chemotherapy, high-powered drugs that effect the nervous system.

Dopamine: a neuro-chemical transmitter. Nerves transmit by electrical impulses except where two nerves "meet"—they almost touch. In that gap they pass a chemical signal using neuro-chemicals such as dopamine. Psychiatric drugs interfere with such connections.

DSM-III: the official classification of mental disorders by the American Psychiatric Association. It lists certain "criteria" which become grounds for diagnosing an illness. Criteria are thoughts, speech or behaviors which are deemed to be signs of psychiatric illness. DSM-III stands for Diagnostic and Statistical Manual. The III refers to the third major revision.

Electroconvulsive Therapy: also called ECT or electroshock. A procedure in which an electric current is run through the brain, inducing a grand-mal seizure. The mechanism of action is said to be unknown. Some researchers hold that it "works" because it causes generalized brain damage and dysfunction. Seizures that cause damage are still induced in modified ECT.

"Elope": to escape from the hospital. An expression used by those hospitalized against their will.

Extra-pyramidal system: referring to the parts of the brain that relate to muscular movement.

Haldol: a neuroleptic that may be up to fifty times the potency of Thorazine.

High-potency drugs: neuroleptics that have less immediate sedative effect but more risk of motor disorders (tardive dyskinesia) and damage to the higher centers, tardive dementia.

Homeopathic: refers to the use of minute doses of medicine. The practice of homeopathy builds on the person's natural defenses, rather than suppressing symptoms as found in allopathic medicine.

Lithium: a metal used in its salt form by psychiatry to control symptoms of manic-depression. Lithium is highly toxic and blocks a variety of receptor sites in the brain. Because the therapeutic dose of Lithium is close to the toxic dose, the person's blood levels must be monitored.

Mania: refers to a state of elevated activity where one has "racing thoughts," and feelings of "grandiosity."

Med-panel: in Maryland law, a procedure to force drug a person in a non-emergency situation. A panel involving staff and doctors, not directly involved in the case, can decide to drug a person against their will.

Mellaril: a neuroleptic or "anti-psychotic" of the same potency as Thorazine.

Neuroleptic: a class of psychiatric drugs formerly called heavy tranquilizers and now referred to as "anti-psychotic" drugs. The word neuroleptic means to weaken the nervous system.

Parkinsonism: a disease of the central nervous system characterized by tremoring and an immobile or mask-like outward appearance. Neuroleptic drugs induce Parkinsonian-like symptoms that are reversible upon withdrawal of the drug.

Phenothiazine: the class name for a sub-group of the neuroleptics including Thorazine, Mellaril and Prolixin.

PRN: to give medication "as necessary" rather than on an hourly or daily basis.

Prolixin: a high potency "anti-psychotic" drug that may be up to seventy times more powerful than Thorazine.

Psychosis: a word describing a mental disorder, not used as a diagnostic category anymore. In the past psychosis has referred to a mental disorder of a severe nature that interferes with a person's contact with reality.

Receptors: sites that receive chemical signals at the ends of adjoining nerves. Psychiatric drugs interfere with such connections, usually by blocking them.

Stelazine: a neuroleptic drug several times more potent that Thorazine.

Supersensitivity Psychosis: withdrawal effects when a person is suddenly taken off a drug. Under the influence of a sedating drug, the brain has compensated and built more receptors. When the drug is no longer present, there are suddenly a lot more impulses than usual. This may cause a psychotic reaction.

Tardive Dyskinesia: a disease of the central nervous system caused by the use of neuroleptic drugs. It is characterized by rhythmic involuntary movements of jaw, tongue or mouth; also rotation of limbs and finger movements resembling guitar playing. Usually the damage is permanent.

Tardive Dementia: a disease of the central nervous system caused by the neuroleptics, which involves gradual cumulative damage to the higher centers of the brain. It is less obvious than motor disturbances and is characterized by indifference and lack of emotional upset.

Thorazine: the first "heavy tranquilizer" discovered. Its phenothiazine base came from the chemical dye industry.

Quiet Room: the Seclusion Room, or Time-Out Room that usually has nothing but a mattress on the floor. Persons are put here to quiet them, when they start showing any profound emotions.

Schizophrenia: a diagnosis where the person is said to display certain "positive symptoms" such as hallucinations and delusions, as well as "negative symptoms" as apathy and withdrawal.

Sullivanian: an expression referring to the ideas of Harry Stack Sullivan who pioneered interpersonal methods in working with "schizophrenics." He operated on the principle that people with such diagnosis are more like us than different and coined the phrase: "Everyone is much more simply human than otherwise." He believed that everyone uses mechanisms that the schizophrenic uses but not to the same extent.